Interconnections of

Asian Diaspora

Asian Diaspora Christianity Series—2

Interconnections of Asian Diaspora

Mapping the Linkages and Discontinuities

Edited by Sam George

FORTRESS PRESS
MINNEAPOLIS

INTERCONNECTIONS OF ASIAN DIASPORA
Mapping the Linkages and Discontinuities

Cover image: Grungy Wall texture by jessicahyde and Background of passport stamps by ugurhan
Cover design: Kristin Miller

Print ISBN: 978-1-5064-7828-9
eBook ISBN: 978-1-5064-7829-6

Dedicated to

Dr. Sadiri "Joy" Tira

Mentor, encourager, and friend

An amazing champion for diaspora peoples everywhere

Contents

Acknowledgments

A book of this kind is truly a labor of love and the fruit of global friendship cultivated over more than a decade. Sustained interaction over emails, phone calls, Zoom meetings, and the like to collaborate on this edited volume have only strengthened those bonds. I had the good fortune of visiting some of their countries, eating with them, staying with their families, learning from them, preaching at their churches or teaching their seminary classes, and simply hanging out with them. So first of all, kudos to an exceptional bunch of scholars and friends who have contributed to this series. Thank you for sharing your insights on your community, what God is doing in your part of the country through your community, and your passion for the mission to and through people on the move.

I am also grateful for my association with the Lausanne Movement, which permits me to travel widely to serve the global church. It has provided connections with exceptional global leaders and many opportunities to learn and see what God is doing in different parts of the world. Being on the front lines all across the globe in the last five years has offered some incredibly rich perspective and comprehension of the critical nature of diaspora peoples in reshaping and advancing the Christian faith in the early decades of the twenty-first century.

I express my sincere gratitude to the endorsers of the second volume of this book series on Asian diaspora Christianity: Dr. Paul Bendor-Samuel of the Oxford Centre for Mission Studies (OCMS; Oxford, UK), Dr. Mary Lederleitner of Wheaton College (Illinois), and Dr. Prabhu Singh of the South Asia Institute of Advanced Christian Studies (SAIACS; Bangalore, India). I appreciate the kind words, valuable feedback, and many encouragements you have given over the last many years. Your passion to learn and teach for the cause of Christ around the world is contagious. I am thankful for an outstanding team of leaders of the Global Diaspora Institute at Wheaton College Billy Graham Center, like Ed Stetzer, Andrew Lee, Joel Wright, Yoman Mann, and Zaki L. Zaki. I am grateful to an amazing executive team of the Global Diaspora Network of the Lausanne Movement, especially to Bulus Galadima, my co-catalyst for diasporas, as well as T. V. Thomas, Paul Sydnor, Barnabas Moon, Art Medina, Mauricio Sanchez, Saji Oommen, and Elizabeth Mburu, all of whom embody an unmatched passion for diaspora peoples all over the globe and are deeply committed to the person of Jesus Christ.

I am much obliged to Jesudas Athyal of Fortress Press for his invaluable guidance in developing this entire series. I am grateful to Fortress Press for their partnership in producing and marketing this three-volume book series and their interest in writings on diaspora and global Christianity. Thanks to all who ardently worked behind the scenes in copyediting the manuscripts and creating the layout, design, and cover of the book.

I dedicate this book to Dr. Sadiri "Joy" Tira, who was my predecessor as catalyst for diasporas of the Lausanne Movement. A Filipino Canadian who makes his home in

Edmonton, Canada, but is at home with anyone anywhere and is popularly known as Kuya Joy or PJ to many, Joy has an indomitable evangelistic passion and a special love for diaspora peoples everywhere. I have known him for over a decade and was a former colleague. I consider him as one of my mentors and am grateful for his constant encouragement. I have traveled with him around the globe, and we have roomed together, eaten at his favorite places (often Starbucks), prayed, and ministered together at many churches, seminaries, and conferences. He has been shaped by his diasporic wanderings, and this makes him an exceptional spokesperson for the message of the diaspora mission. His clever, friendly, and funny demeanor is an essential asset that makes Joy the amazing person that he is. I am so grateful to God to pick up the baton that he had run with for over a decade so faithfully and for the privilege to shadow him for a couple of years on different projects.

Not least of all, I express my sincere gratitude to my wife, Dr. Mary M. George, who, with much wisdom, patience, and prayers, has supported all my ministry undertakings, including this book series. Also, I have much appreciation for our boys, Daniel and Joshua, who now stand taller than both of us. I thank God for the many meals and the time we have gotten to spend together as a family during the global pandemic lockdown that drew us closer to each other and allowed us to experience divine protection and providence.

Sam George
Summer 2021

Series Introduction

Asian Diaspora Christianity

Sam George

Migration, diaspora, and displacement have become defining issues of our time. They appear daily on the front pages of newspapers, in breaking news reports on television and Twitter feeds, and in academic discourses and political debates. Though human migration is as ancient as our history, the scale, volume, urge, speed, and direction of human displacement have reached unprecedented levels in recent decades. It is perceived to be at the crux of many of the dramatic transformations happening in our societies, economies, and nations. Since the prevailing frameworks of cultural, legal, financial, political, and religious orders are found inadequate to deal with contemporary migration, serious deliberations are occurring about this new reality in many circles and disciplinary domains. At the same time, innovative technologies, mass communication, and affordable transportation are creating new conflicts and crises owing to increased human mobility and connectivity.

The movement of people is of the utmost consequence to Christianity, as migrant and diaspora communities have shaped and reshaped the contours of its growth and expansion throughout history. At its core, Christianity is a faith that must move from place to place because Christianity is a quintessentially missionary and translatable faith. It is not bound to any particular land, geography, culture, or people. Since the beginning, it has continually diffused across cultural and geographical borders, and many different people in many different places have been chief representatives of the Christian faith. Christianity cannot be held captive to any geographical location or domesticated by any people because its nature is to break free of the prisons we enshrine it in.

Being the largest continent, Asia comprises forty-eight nations and has the most diverse population in the world, with nearly 4.7 billion people as of 2020 (about 60 percent of the world population)—and that figure is expected to swell to 5.3 billion by 2050. Among the top ten most populous countries of the world, five are in Asia (China, India, Indonesia, Pakistan, and Bangladesh), and Asia will continue to scatter multitudes globally year after year. Asia remains the largest source and destination of international migrants, with over 40 percent (110 million in 2019) of the world's migrants and more than half of them (66 million) residing in other Asian countries. There have been substantial surges into and out of Asia in the last decade, with many immigrating to Europe and North America (nearly 45 million).[1]

Asians are a widely dispersed populace and can be found all over the globe. Asia is a site marked by multivalent histories, people, cultures, economies, and religions, and their dispersion worldwide resulting from globalization, neoliberalism, ethnic conflicts and wars, and political and ecological crises has led to tectonic transformations in our understanding of ecclesiology, missiology, and theology. The existential ontology of diasporic living necessitates new ways of perceiving and interpreting reality concerning oneself, others, the cosmos, and ultimately, God. In this volume, we use *Asia* to mean the whole continent—from the edge of the Pacific Ocean to the Mediterranean states at the borders of Europe and Africa. Yet due to the confines of space and scholarship, this work does not include all immigrant groups of the continent or their divergent expressions of their Christian faith.

This series brings together scholars of Asian background and a few others (who have served in Asian contexts or among Asians for decades) who are situated in diverse locations all over the world to provide insights into Christian ministry from a diasporic-insider perspective. These volumes articulate the voices of Asian migrants and their progenies to weave together a kaleidoscopic intercultural theological tapestry. These manifold expressions of displacement, encounters, struggles, and complexities compel us to reimagine faith from our distinctive vantage points in order to develop new theological reflections and explore the missiological implications of Asian wanderings.

Migration and Mission: The Movement of People Transforming Christianity

Migration is fundamentally a disruptive phenomenon. The globalized diasporas seek social and economic upward mobility to break out of the bondage of geography and assimilate into other cultures while experiencing rejection and marginalization in host societies. They seek emancipation by migrating to nearby cities and faraway nations to live in relative anonymity, free from obligation bound up in a locality, and defying sociocultural and religious restraints while also comparing and exploring new ideas and worldviews. Some explore business ventures and partnerships abroad, while others invest in the land of their forefathers and send remittances to dear ones back in their native lands. Some pursue studies, jobs, and marital alliances overseas to escape coercion into antiquated traditions and the limited options available to their ancestors. A record number of people are forced to flee their homelands to seek refuge abroad. Many are victimized by native strangers in foreign lands who are threatened by their arrival and legislations that are quick to discriminate against and exploit the newcomers. These migrant journeys involve unexpected turns and misfortunes, even as the travelers grieve over many inevitable losses that come alongside their gains.

Just as the Jewish diaspora shaped the trajectory of Christianity in the first century, today's diaspora is shaping the frontiers of the faith and has become a global missionary force. This series explores the contours of Asian diaspora (the largest contemporary diaspora group in the world) and Christian mission to, by, among, through, and beyond these dispersed communities from a global perspective. These writings have benefited from the recent proliferation of diaspora missiology and theology and hope to contribute further to the conversations about these topics. The authors cover diaspora communities of Chinese, Indian, Korean, Japanese, Filipino, Vietnamese, Indonesian, Singaporean, Hmong, Nepalese, Iranian, Israeli, Lebanese, Thai, Malay, Pakistani, and Middle Eastern people while spanning intersecting angles of Buddhism, Hinduism, Islam, and Judaism. These chapters come from different continents of the world, with divergent sociocultural, economic, and geopolitical realities, and distill insights from multiple disciplinary domains, such as history, anthropology, sociology, economics, psychology, literature, theology, and missiology. These chapters are written by missionaries, professors, entrepreneurs, scientists, pastors, counselors, lay leaders, and doctoral students.

Taking diaspora as its primary lens and focusing on the continent of Asia, this project invited a select group of Christian scholars of Asian origin to reflect on and address issues related to their respective communities from the distinctive vantage points of their geographical and historical location. They come from wide-ranging backgrounds, institutions, and theological positions, though most come under the canopy of the Reformed, Protestant, Evangelical, and Pentecostal traditions, with diverse experiences and advanced scholarship in various fields. They encompass the ongoing and contested processes involving identity, belonging, meaning, affiliation, and allegiance while being embedded within varied social, cultural, and political webs of relations that are sustained concurrently.

Asian Christianity: Now Global

Christianity began in Asia and has now become the most global and diverse religion in the world.[2] At the turn of the third millennium, Christianity is returning to Asia and Asians around the world in some noteworthy manner. Many scholars have argued about the rise of Christianity in the Global South, which includes Asia, and how some Asian countries are playing an increasingly vital role in missionary undertakings and mission activities worldwide. The recent economic rise, the substantial growth of Christianity in some parts of Asia, religious persecution, and a host of other factors have resulted in the large-scale dispersion of Asian people. They have taken their distinctive spirituality, practices, hermeneutics, and institutions along with them to all parts of the world, and these communities have the potential to renew and revitalize Christianity in the coming centuries. On any Sunday morning, Christian worship services are conducted in Asian languages like Mandarin, Korean, Tagalog, and Malayalam in many time zones. The churches in Asia receive remittances in all major currencies of the world, and Asian pastors, evangelists, and leaders make frequent visits to their scattered sheep. As a result, churches in Asia are constructing a more global vision of Christianity and of their role in the mission of Jesus Christ.

Because Christians are a minority-faith group in much of Asia, they necessarily made immediate connections with Christians elsewhere. Coming from pluralistic societies with multireligious orientations, the Asian diasporas are transforming the religious landscape globally. Christian faith surpasses the geographical barriers that are present in many traditional Asian religions and cultures and provides many with the opportunity to explore lands far beyond their place of birth. The educational prospects, language skills, economic progress, and positive outlook of Asians have scattered millions within and without their country and continent, with many migrants embracing the Christian faith. Asian Christianity is not monolithic in any fashion, and its dispersion is making Asian ecclesial bodies more global and producing a great diversity within the larger body of Christ worldwide.

One central thesis of these three volumes is that the large-scale dispersion of Asians to far-flung corners of the globe over the last couple of centuries is transforming Christianity itself—just as migration has done with other peoples in the past. Subsequent to the Protestant Reformation in Europe in the sixteenth century, many Europeans relocated across the continent and around the world. This phenomenon came to be known as the Great European Migration, and it is estimated that around forty million people relocated over three centuries until the middle of the twentieth century. An unexpected consequence of this widespread out-migration was that it made Christianity look European all over the world. Upon moving abroad, Europeans established their distinctive religious orders and engaged in mission practices. In effect, Christianity took on their cultural garb. Likewise, the growth of Christianity in Asia and Asians' large-scale emigration is exporting Asian Christianity globally, and diasporic connections and resources are helping Asian Christians become a more global and missionary force.

Christians are at the forefront of migratory tendencies, as they are more likely to be mobile than others and are better connected with Christians elsewhere. Some say, "If you are a Christian, you will travel, and if you travel, you will become a Christian." Their bend toward education, their motivation to work hard and succeed, and their expectations of a more hopeful future take them across borders and oceans. Christian faith and practices have been translated, and Asian migrants and their offspring are actively engaged in adapting and renewing Christianity within their host cultures and nations. Just as missionaries with intercultural sensibilities and acquired linguistic competencies engaged in translating the gospel into diverse languages and cultures, today's migrants—whether their migration be volitional or involuntary—serve as mission agents and perform a missionary function. They translate the truths of the gospel into their new cultures. The experiences of marginality and powerlessness that migrants face force them to harmonize their state of in-between-ness, in-both and in-beyond, making them adept at interpreting the world of their ancestors to the new world of their neighbors and vice versa using theological terms—infusing new meaning while reinterpreting prevailing cultural norms and predicaments.

The diasporic culture is about being here (hostland) and there (homeland) simultaneously. People do not fully belong to either place yet feel incomplete without both, and their diasporic existence calls for continual interaction between and dynamic attachment to both worlds.[3] Culture and religion provide a strong link between homeland and hostland. The cultural flows between both places as people grieve the loss of the old world while also re-creating it in the new world and integrating into the host society. As James Clifford puts it, "Diaspora cultures mediate, in a lived tension, the experiences of separation and entanglement, of living there and remembering/desiring another place."[4] The remittances act as currencies of care and are used to negotiate and consolidate the soft power of the diasporas. The dispersed people become two-way conduits for religious traditions, ideas, and practices, which together result in remarkable religious changes. The transformational power of diasporas lies in their heightened awareness of both the perils and rewards of multiple belonging and in their exemplary grappling with the paradoxes of identity. In short, the diaspora communities remain a transformative force to both sending as well as receiving places because of their transnational orientation and mission. No wonder uprooted and transplanted people make exceptional missionaries, even without knowing it.

As they pitch their tents in the far corners of the globe, many uprooted Asians are becoming Christians in their new homelands. They are exposed to and come closer to the claims of Jesus in foreign lands, whereas Asian Christians are reinvigorated in their faith in overseas locations. They are drawn to the life and teachings of Jesus Christ, which cleanse their souls after their polluting voyages. In the process of liberating themselves from the bonds of the past, migrants come face-to-face with new ideas that set the inherited beliefs and worldviews of their native lands against those of their adopted homelands. They seek deliverance from cultural trappings and religious encumbrances while pursuing deeper spiritual realities. They are quick to abandon some identity markers, whereas others are reinforced, and subsequent generations assimilate into host cultures and become estranged from their ancestral homelands. They find a new freedom in Christianity, which is more suited for navigating the peripatetic ambiguities and contemporary meanderings. They have established distinctively Asian churches by worshipping in their own languages and cultures while also interfacing with local Christians and others from different regions of the world. Many members of Asian diasporas are joining local evangelical and charismatic churches in their host nations and now play an increasingly visible role in the leadership of many churches and institutions globally.

Global Christianity: Asian Version

The phenomenal growth of Christianity in the Global South is dramatically transforming the face of Christianity worldwide.[5] Although the percentage of Christians worldwide has remained constant since 1900, where those Christians live has moved southward and eastward. In 1900, only 18 percent of Christians lived in the Global South, but by 2020, that figure surged to 67 percent, which translates to 667 million Christians in Africa, 612 million in Latin America, and 407 million in Asia and Oceania (see appendix in volume 1: *Journeys of Asian Diaspora*). Andrew F. Walls had the foresight to note the shifting of the center of gravity of Christianity from its Euro-American center to Africa, Asia, and Latin America.[6] The continental shift of the locus of World Christianity coincided with the surge in global migration and the new missionary movement. Lamin Sanneh claims that the teaching of Jesus and his apostles is not confined to any particular location—"territoriality [has] ceased to be a requirement of faith"[7]—and when it takes root in a new place, the faith itself takes on something from there.

Though Christianity began in West Asia in the first century, it soon moved east, then south to Africa, and finally northwest to Europe, and in the process, the "new" places became home to Christianity. Throughout its history, the chief representatives of Christianity have changed. The surge of Christianity in Africa, Asia, and Latin America—and the massive migration from those regions to its former heartlands in the Global North—is remaking the portrait of Christianity to feature the people, cultures, and theologies of the Global South.

Contemporary examples abound. The current head of the Catholic Church is Pope Francis, who was born and raised in Argentina and is the first pope from the southern hemisphere. As a result, Latin American ethos and influence are clearly evident in the Vatican now. Likewise, among the Protestants, many presidents of the World Council of

Churches have come from Asia, Africa, and Latin America. Many leaders of the Anglican Church are from Nigeria, and there are more Anglicans in sub-Saharan Africa than in the United Kingdom, United States, Canada, and Australia combined. The same could be said of European denominations such as Presbyterians, Lutherans, and Methodists. The largest churches in major European cities are now headed by Africans, and the common public perception of Christianity is undergoing a dramatic makeover. The organization that I serve, the Lausanne Movement—which was started by Billy Graham and John Stott, two major voices in the latter half of the twentieth century from the United States and the United Kingdom, respectively—is now being headed by a Korean American who was a missionary in Japan. Christians from the Global South are rising to the topmost ranks in many ecclesial traditions and global Christian organizations. Another illustration in my context is that the new leader of the National Association of Evangelicals (NAE), a large and influential body of Christians in the United States, is again a Korean American. Many Asians are among the senior leaders of churches and ministries in North America, Europe, and elsewhere around the world.

This growing trend is evident in other spheres as well, such as missionary sending and funding as well as mission resources, scholarship, and theologies. Peter C. Phan makes a case for the emerging Asian face of Christianity by presenting theologies rooted in the Asian American experience, with a christological portrayal of Jesus with a Chinese face—as an eldest son, an ancestor, and a poor monk—using liberation and enculturation lenses.[8] Likewise, others have noted the changing face of Christianity in recent years, arguing that "cultural variety and plurality . . . were inscribed into the original character of Christianity."[9] Missiologists have been quick to note the seismic changes on the global Christian landscape and have cited the impact of migration and changing demographics on world missions.[10] Others have explored Asian migration from biblical and theological perspectives by comparing contemporary immigrant generations to the Jewish exile.[11] Non-Western churches are surging ahead in missions, with sizable numbers from China, India, South Korea, and the Philippines who are involved worldwide. It could be argued that mission itself is decentering Christianity from its former heartlands. Pentecostalism has been a decisive factor in the transformation of World Christianity as it took root in remarkable ways in the Global South.[12] The Asian diaspora people are reviving Christianity in their places of settlement, and they also provide strategic linkages to churches in their ancestral homelands to engage globally and partner with their Western counterparts, leveraging each other's resources and strengths to reach everyone everywhere. Along with other dispersed Christians of the world, Asian diasporas are helping the global church transition into a new era of mission.

Series Outline

This series comprises three volumes: (1) *Journeys of Asian Diaspora: Mapping Originations and Destinations*, (2) *Interconnections of Asian Diaspora: Mapping Linkages and Discontinuities*, and (3) *Reflections of Asian Diaspora: Mapping Theologies and Ministries*. The first volume traces select major Asian diaspora communities from discrete locations, while the second volume sketches the wide array of connections and disconnections arising out of migratory displacements of Asians through various disciplinary lenses. The final volume showcases an assortment of theological and missiological deliberations on migration, refugees, displacement, movement, and diaspora from biblical and evangelical perspectives and showcases select cases of ministry by and among Asian diasporas worldwide.

This series is pan-Asian in scope and attempts to cover all major regions of the continent, ranging from the Pacific Ocean to the Mediterranean Sea, comprising diverse socio-religious contexts, migratory history, and ecclesial traditions. It is not, however, comprehensive or meant to have the final say on this matter. It argues that the widespread dispersion of Asians over the past few centuries has firmly established a distinctively Asian form of Christianity all over the world. Asian Christians have flourished abroad and have added diversity to Christian expressions in their host nations. Their presence and faith practices are bringing fresh vitality and renewal to Christianity in many parts of the world. Altogether, this series paints a compelling portrait of global Christianity with a distinctive Asian face and flavor.

The first volume, subtitled "Mapping Originations and Destinations," focuses on journeys of Asian diaspora Christians and comprises twelve chapters that provide diasporic narratives of select Asians from wide-ranging geographical locations, such as Chinese in the United Kingdom, Japanese in Brazil and the United States, South Koreans in Central and Latin America, Vietnamese and Hmongs worldwide, Indonesians in Australia, Nepalese in the United States, Iranians in Europe, various immigrant Christians in the Persian Gulf, and ministry among dispersed people of Israel. All authors provide an insider perspective on their respective communities. An appendix at the end provides select charts and infographics related to Asian diaspora communities collated from various reports of the United Nations, World Bank, and other agencies, particularly the *World Migration Report 2020*.

The second volume in the series, subtitled "Mapping Linkages and Discontinuities," contains another twelve chapters that survey various connections of Asian diaspora Christians from different parts of the world. This work explores a wide range of topics including religious faith in diaspora with a particular focus on Buddhism and Hinduism, family life in transnational contexts, women and migration, cultural assimilation and hybridization, hyphenated identity, the future of ministry for foreign-born and foreign-raised Asians, diaspora writings in English, the globalizing of Indian denominations, bridging the digital divide as a mission strategy, mental health, and leadership styles of Asian diasporas. The chapters are written by scholars and practitioners situated in places as broad as Thailand, India, the Philippines, the United Kingdom, the United States, South Korea, Laos, Singapore, China, and Lebanon. The contributors come from divergent backgrounds such as religious studies, missiology, migration studies, literary criticism, anthropology, psychology, economics, and technology. By drawing insights from diverse disciplinary fields, this volume showcases the vital need for interdisciplinary work in diasporic studies and missions.

The third volume in the series, subtitled "Mapping Theologies and Ministries," contains another dozen chapters that attempt to trace divergent ministries and theologies developed in the context of Asian diasporas worldwide. It sketches a biblical trajectory for a theology of migration and develops a theology of nations and citizenship in the context of transnationalism, written by a Korean Australian and Filipino American, respectively. I develop a new theology of mission for the age of migration using the concept of *motus Dei* (God on the Move). An Indian doctoral student explores exilic theology for the dispersed, and a Korean American critiques diaspora using Asian American theology. A Filipino Canadian compares the concepts of reverse missions and diaspora missions, while a Korean missionary based in Japan assesses the global engagement of Korean missionaries and the challenges they are facing. Then a Korean missionary in East Africa investigates cross cultural training and mobilization for rural sub-Saharan African context. Subsequently, we have two chapters from non-Asians, one British and another Australian, stationed in Malaysia and China, respectively, who explore the discipleship of Asian migrants and international students studying in China. Finally, a Pakistani linguist and theologian presents the history of translation of Psalms into Punjabi in British India and the role of the contextualized worship in diasporic contexts. These diverse accounts make it abundantly clear that Asian diaspora Christians are globalizing Asian Christianity and Asianizing global Christianity.

Like Asia itself, Asian Christianity and its global manifestations are extremely complex, and it is preposterous to claim this series represents a definitive account of it. Instead, at the risk of being accused of distortion and colossal generalization, the authors of these volumes present a few broad brushstrokes on the multifaceted canvas of Asian Christianity from the distinctive vantage points of their global locations—without asserting them as comprehensive or conclusive on this matter. This Asian migratory rendering of World Christianity defies a simple explanation or any particular cultural formulation, as is evident by the voluminous themes and perspectives covered herein. They are featured here as illustrative cases that must constitute a much larger whole. It is our hope that this will generate further interest and spark nuanced conversations about the nature of Christianity and the role diasporas play in reshaping World Christianity in the twenty-first century.

Notes

1 See the appendix in volume 1 titled *Journeys of Asian Diaspora* for details. All numbers are based on International Organization for Migration (IOM), *World Migration Report 2020* (Geneva: IOM, 2019), https://www.iom.int/wmr/.

2 Todd Johnson and Gina Zurlo, *World Christian Encyclopedia*, 3rd ed. (Edinburgh: Edinburgh University Press, 2020).

3 Robin Cohen, *Global Diasporas: An Introduction* (Seattle: University of Washington Press, 1997). See also Patrick Johnstone, *The Future of the Global Church: History, Trends and Possibilities* (Downers Grove, IL: IVP, 2011).

4 James Clifford, "Diasporas," *Cultural Anthropology* 9, no. 3 (1994): 311.

5 The Global South and North are defined in geopolitical terms according to the United Nations. The Global South includes Asia, Africa, Latin America, and Oceania, while the Global North includes Western Europe, Canada, and the United States. See Philip Jenkins, *The Next Christendom: The Coming of Global Christianity* (New York: Oxford University Press, 2002); and Mark Noll, *The New Shape of World Christianity* (Downers Grove, IL: IVP Academic, 2009).

6 Andrew F. Walls, *The Cross-Cultural Process in Christian History* (Maryknoll, NY: Orbis, 2007), 64.

7 Lamin Sanneh, *Disciples of All Nations: Pillars of World Christianity* (New York: Oxford University Press, 2008), 7.

8 Peter C. Phan, *Christianity with an Asian Face: Asian American Theology in the Making* (Maryknoll, NY: Orbis, 2003).

9 Lamin Sanneh and Joel Carpenter, *The Changing Face of Christianity: Africa, the West and the World* (New York: Oxford University Press, 2005), 214. See also Philip Jenkins, *The New Faces of Christianity: Believing the Bible in the Global South* (New York: Oxford University Press, 2006).

10 Michael Pocock, Gailyn Van Rheenen, and Douglas McConnell, *The Changing Face of World Missions: Engaging Contemporary Issues and Trends* (Grand Rapids, MI: Baker Academic, 2005).

11 See, for example, Fabbio Baggio and Agnes M. Brazal, eds., *Faith on the Move: Toward a Theology of Migration in Asia* (Honolulu: University of Hawai'i Press, 2009); and John J. Ahn, *Exile and Forced Migration* (Berlin: Walter de Gruyter, 2011).

12 See Allan Anderson, *To the Ends of the Earth: Pentecostalism and the Transformation of World Christianity* (Oxford: Oxford University Press, 2013); and Amos Yong, *The Missiological Spirit: Christian Mission Theology in the Third Millennium Global Context* (Eugene, OR: Cascade, 2014).

Bibliography

Ahn, John J. *Exile and Forced Migration.* Berlin: Walter de Gruyter, 2011.

Anderson, Allan. *To the Ends of the Earth: Pentecostalism and the Transformation of World Christianity.* Oxford: Oxford University Press, 2013.

Baggio, Fabbio, and Agnes M. Brazal, eds. *Faith on the Move: Toward a Theology of Migration in Asia.* Honolulu: University of Hawai'i Press, 2009.

Clifford, James. "Diasporas." *Cultural Anthropology* 9, no. 3 (1994): 302–338.

Cohen, Robin. *Global Diasporas: An Introduction*. Seattle: University of Washington Press, 1997.

International Organization for Migration (IOM). *World Migration Report 2020*. Geneva: IOM, 2019. https://publications.iom.int/system/files/pdf/wmr_2020.pdf.

Jenkins, Philip. *The New Faces of Christianity: Believing the Bible in the Global South*. New York: Oxford University Press, 2006.

———. *The Next Christendom: The Coming of Global Christianity*. New York: Oxford University Press, 2002.

Johnson, Todd, and Gina Zurlo. *World Christian Encyclopedia*. 3rd ed. Edinburgh: Edinburgh University Press, 2020.

Johnstone, Patrick. *The Future of the Global Church: History, Trends and Possibilities*. Downers Grove, IL: IVP, 2011.

Noll, Mark. *The New Shape of World Christianity*. Downers Grove, IL: IVP Academic, 2009.

Phan, Peter C. *Christianity with an Asian Face: Asian American Theology in the Making*. Maryknoll, NY: Orbis, 2003.

Pocock, Michael, Gailyn Van Rheenen, and Douglas McConnell. *The Changing Face of World Missions: Engaging Contemporary Issues and Trends*. Grand Rapids, MI: Baker Academic, 2005.

Sanneh, Lamin. *Disciples of All Nations: Pillars of World Christianity*. New York: Oxford University Press, 2008.

Sanneh, Lamin, and Joel Carpenter. *The Changing Face of Christianity: Africa, the West and the World*. New York: Oxford University Press, 2005.

Walls, Andrew F. *The Cross-Cultural Process in Christian History*. Maryknoll, NY: Orbis, 2007.

Yong, Amos. *The Missiological Spirit: Christian Mission Theology in the Third Millennium Global Context*. Eugene, OR: Cascade, 2014.

Introduction

Sam George

This book is the second in this three-volume series on Asian diaspora Christianity titled *Interconnections of Asian Diaspora* and explicates the many linkages between the places of ancestry and the current habitations of emigrants from Asia and their descendants. In the first volume of the series, we traced the *Journeys of Asian Diaspora*, the diverse places of origin and destinations of global Asian Christians. The third volume in the series, titled *Reflections of Asian Diaspora*, will offer various theologies and ministries of and among Asian diaspora Christians in diverse contexts and locations.

A dozen chapters in this volume focus on various connecting and disconnecting elements commonly prevalent among all migrants, and the particular focus here is on Asian diasporas across multiple locales. Asian diasporas connect to maintain some form of familiarity and predictability while their disengagement brings a new sense of disentanglement and estrangement. Migration causes them to ask new questions that never crossed their minds before while constantly comparing and contrasting their assumptions about mundane as well as profound issues of life. It affords the required distance to critique and the safety to do so without geo-cultural subservience. For some, existential liminality offers objectivity, while for others it adds to the growing confusion, both of which provide an uncanny advantage to thrive in a globalized world. They acquire a new pair of eyes and ears even as they develop a new heart and mind about their moving experience. No wonder the ancient philosopher Seneca avers, "Travel and change of place impart new vigor to the mind."

In migration literature, the geographies and cultures of origin and arrival tend to dwarf the ethereal dimensions of transnational consciousness, yet transnational connections are central to diasporic imaginations and the remaking of the world by challenging the orders of homogeneous nation-states on both ends of migration. Diasporic living entails selective forgetting and remembering, abandoning and upholding, individual choices and collective communal ties that are both liberative and oppressive. Amid this transcultural wandering, the experiences of uprooting and transplantation to a different soil in distant lands intensify the yearning of migrants as they hold on to multiple strands of their existence even while cautiously exploring new realities. Their objectification by their host society, with all of its idiosyncrasies, forces the migrants to cling to their past even more tightly as their progeny naturally assimilate into the dominant host cultures. The diasporic intersubjectivity makes the rigid borders of yesteryear porous and helps reconceive Christian identity, belonging, and mission in new ways for themselves and their respective nations. Hence there is a pressing need to examine the emerging phenomenon of transnational spaces and the missional implications of the resulting networks and interconnections.

Diasporic Connections and Disconnections

This collection of essays closely examines the assorted connections and disconnections experienced by Asian diaspora Christians—the lived experience of the locales they left behind and their adopted homelands, between which they sense a continual tugging as well as distancing. Their migratory displacement to foreign lands creates a detachment while deepening their longing for native attachments. Though far, they feel closer than ever before to their ancestral homelands while being near to their new neighbors yet feeling strangely distant from them. Though contemporary migrants pitch their tents in distant corners of the globe, they never really leave home, as by using the latest technological gadgets and the internet, they are now able to sustain regular contact with those whom they left behind. They can take advantage of affordable transportation to return to their ancestral homes whenever needed and remit their earnings to support people in distant places. Their ethnic enclaves, mother-tongue media, communal festivities, and traditional food keep them from cutting their sociocultural umbilical cords. Migrants always carry pieces of the old world with them into their new worlds and try to make the most of both, though at times they experience the worst of both realities by not entirely belonging to either place.

Some of the themes featured in this volume on diasporic interconnectivity include religion, history, gender, family, identity, language, literature, remittance, use of technology, transnationals, mental health, cultural hybridity, and missionary engagement of Asian migrants from varied sites such as Thailand, India, the Philippines, the United Kingdom, Singapore, the United States, Qatar, the United Arab

Emirates, China, Lebanon, South Korea, and an unnamed North African nation. This is neither an exhaustive treatment of the subject nor inclusive of every facet of transnational dynamics, but it is a humble attempt to include diverse themes and narratives of Asian diasporas. In following the critical perspective in the study of migration and diaspora communities, these essays trace the importance of migrant interconnections by presenting a set of case studies of the dispersion of people of Asian origin that feature assorted linkages among people, places, and cultures. They explore these connections alongside the discontinuities experienced by global Asians from an insider perspective and the vantage point of the Christian mission of diaspora peoples.

These chapters feature nuances related to transnational linkages, as not all connections are necessarily positive, nor are all discontinuities essentially negative. The connections create the angst of identity confusion and multiple belonging among migrants and their descendants. They, however, are also manipulated to transfer the yoke of ancestral cultures. The disjunction suffered over a prolonged duration results in a new tussle over representation and infuses new meaning into the gospel and mission. The numerous simultaneous gains and losses in these migratory narratives affect people in complex ways, and the impact of some of them may only be perceived after several generations. Some chapters evocatively argue about issues associated with Asian transnationalism from their communal, locational, and situational frame of reference, and while more could be said on other issues, and much more on other themes, we could not include every-thing here regarding Asian transnationalism.

This volume delineates some contours of Asian migra-tory trajectories by presenting varied snapshots from diverse disciplinary lenses. It covers religious historical narratives as well as an in-depth sociological analysis of migration. It presents the challenges of transnational families who are separated for vocational reasons and what churches in the sending countries can do in this regard. It looks into gender issues for a women-led migratory wave of Indian nurses and identity struggles common among migrants, and it provides a literary analysis of Anglophone fictional depictions of religious fervor seen in immigrants. It includes an exploration of the economics of remittances and some of the socioreligious implications, as well as the use of modern technology to bridge the digital divide to empower the urban poor in an example of a reverse mission project. This book contains an evaluation of a national denominational structure that transcends geographical boundaries and the psychological issues and coping mechanisms to survive migratory displacements. It also features social and anthropological dimensions of hybridization prevalent among migrants and missional engagement of diasporic people in a third culture that is different from their ancestral and adopted homelands.

Diasporic Consciousness and Dilemmas

The scale of contemporary human mobility and connectivity holds tremendous potential to transform economies, societies, and nations as immigrants forge and sustain ethnic communities and gradually integrate into a new world. They innovate new tools of travel and interactions result in the reframing of policies for the common good in the face of unprecedented global geopolitical reconfigurations.

Large-scale, long-distance mobility and increased connectivity create a new breed of people who are rooted more in ideas than places or memories and who flourish with connections more than in land or material things. Hybridity resulting from increased human mobility and connectivity is an invaluable asset in the arsenal of migrant wanderers and their offspring, but it turns out to be a liability and a curse for some of them. Their diasporic identity is no longer singular, static, rigid, or permanent but multiple, complex, and continually evolving. It is fabricated through the perpetual interplay between heritage, otherness, and in-between-ness. It is fashioned in the roots of hearth and home as well as over routes of migratory displacements and linkages. They belong everywhere and nowhere at the same time while their hearts ache for another world entirely.

All chapters in this volume, while analyzing a particular Asian diasporic community through a given disciplinary lens, showcase what these diaspora peoples have in common with those in other regions as well as other diaspora groups. These communities exhibit prevailing tensions, dilemmas, problems, and impediments and show the development of coping skills, customs, and rituals to sustain their communities while reforming and transforming their religious beliefs and practices. There is an intensification of consciousness by virtue of displacement, and creative engagement in new contexts that requires continual adaptation and alteration generates renewed momentum for mission globally. The promises and perils of diasporic liminality bring forth new, imaginative vitality through creative creolization along the cultural borderlands, which is a catalyst to alter master codes, prevailing norms, and dominant ideologies. These halfway transitional spaces, where power structures are decentered and sequences are reordered, create new strategic inflection points to interrogate narratives, reaccentuate traditions, infuse new meaning, and develop new levels of devotion to the ultimate questions of life and eternity.

This intermediary book of a three-book series presents some strands of contemporary Asian diasporic transnational sensibility not as a monolithic rendition but as a complex, subversive, and multilayered portrayal of sundry characters, settings, and plots that defy simplistic sketches. The arguments range from religious reproduction and adaptation in foreign lands to cross-cultural diffusion on account of dispersion and mission through dispersed Christians. The traversing of multiple disciplinary domains makes this volume essentially an interdisciplinary investigation. Together they weave a narrative that moves away from presenting the diaspora community as successful and unproblematic and burrows deep enough to expose the vulnerability of dislocated subjects and the missional opportunities afforded by their peripatetic wanderings and the cultural diffusion of the gospel resulting from expansive Asian migration worldwide.

The scope of God's mission in the Bible is truly global, and Asian diaspora peoples, just as other diaspora peoples in the past and the present, are playing a vital role at the forefront of missional upheaval; simply through their obedience to go to the ends of the earth, they are unleashing a new era of mission from everywhere to everyone everywhere. Herein lies a glimpse of that global polycentric Christianity of the twenty-first century, where people on the move are playing a vital role in remaking it.

Book Outline

This volume explores the diasporic ties of Asian diaspora peoples between their nations of origin and places of settlements using a select lens, such as religion (Buddhism and Hinduism, as well as diaspora Christians in the Islamic Middle East), family life (transnational relational dynamics, women-led migration, and the second generation), church (ethnic-cultural churches at foreign locations and links they maintain to ancestral homelands), literature (diasporic writings about religiosity), economics (remittance and its social repercussions), and technology (efforts to bridge the digital divide to alleviate poverty). In exploring these transnational connections and the severing of ties that occur over prolonged diasporic living in foreign lands, one can discern both the reinforcing and dissipating influences of migratory dislocations.

After this brief introduction, Alex G. Smith—who served as a missionary among Buddhists in Southeast Asia, including two decades in Thailand—introduces us to dispersed Asian Buddhists. He surveys Asian Buddhists in different countries and various Christian ministries among them, particularly noting the high receptivity to the gospel among newly arrived Buddhists in foreign lands. Subsequently, John Arun Kumar, a religion professor at a seminary in Bengaluru (India), encapsulates the global Hindu diaspora and explores the growing influence of right-wing Hindutva ideology among some diaspora Hindus in the West and the role of caste and language among dispersed Hindus.

The next three chapters address issues related to migrant households from divergent perspectives—namely, family, gender, and identity. Each of these dimensions undergoes a profound transformation as diasporic people try to preserve norms of the old world while at the same time adapting to new realities after dislocation. Gerardo B. Lisbe Jr., a mission professor in Cebu (Philippines), explores the transnational family relations ubiquitous to Overseas Filipino Workers and explores the challenges they face to maintain "familyhood" across national borders and time zones. He analyzes the effect of role reversal, altered family structures, emotional and intimacy issues, and parenting from afar. He pleads to local churches in the sending countries to be more proactive in addressing issues facing transnational families and to consider the potential for mission through their dispersed members in faraway places and even in many countries that are closed for gospel work.

Next, sociologist Christy John Jacob examines the women-led migration of nurses from the southwestern state of Kerala in India to the United Kingdom and its repercussions for family and the immigrant church. She juxtaposes the tension between the professional skills in the Western health care system and the traditional gender-based roles ascribed to women in patriarchal Indian society. She recounts the solace these nurses feel at their ethnic church in the face of racism at work and in their host society while leaning on the religious institution for the construction of ethnic identity, a support system, and transmission of values to the next generation.

The next three chapters venture outside the traditional box of missiology and theology and into the disciplines of literature, economics, and technology to explore the transnational connections of various Asian immigrants. These authors are based in Singapore; Washington, DC; and Hong

Kong. Robbie B H Goh, an English professor at the National University of Singapore, investigates the Anglophone writings of the Indian diaspora for their spiritual longings and diasporic sensibilities by exploring the religiocultural negotiations prevalent among them. He analyzes the weakening and the rejection of inherited religious traditions in diasporic locations beside a succinct appraisal of the transformation of religious beliefs and practices after relocation to distant lands. Afterward, a developmental economist who worked with the World Bank for a couple of decades, Cherian Samuel, provides a historical and macro perspective of migration from and within Asia and closely examines the recent trends in remittance sent by migrants to families and communities back in their ancestral homelands and evaluates its social and national implications. Later, Bill Tsang, a social entrepreneur-cum-educator, showcases a missional technology project to bridge the digital divide among underprivileged youth in China, a mission that has now grown to several Asian urban centers.

The next four chapters chart the connections of the Asian diaspora in diverse contexts, such as the Persian Gulf, Lebanon, North Africa, and the United States. These chapters employ the lenses of history, anthropology, psychology, and missiology. I investigate the transnational ecclesial linkage of an Indian denominational church located in Doha and Dubai in the Persian Gulf. Later, Naji Abi-Hashem, a pastoral counselor and psychologist, presents the case of the widely dispersed Lebanese diaspora, the many challenges associated with their adjustments, and the coping mechanism common to all migrants. In the next chapter, Prasad D R J Phillips, a mission strategist and educator, illustrates the struggles of British Asians navigating the hyphenated identities using an interdisciplinary perspective and presents the contextual, constructed, and contested nature of identities for diasporic people. He discusses the missiological significance of diasporic Christians to host nations and the ethnic community itself. Subsequently, Byoung Ok Koo, a cultural anthropologist who teaches at a seminary in South Korea, outlines a brief history of Japanese, Chinese, and Korean migration to the United States and presents the implications of their resulting cultural hybridity for mission work globally, besides providing practical advice to East Asian American churches and ministry leaders. The final chapter of the volume comes from Peter T. Lee, a Korean American missionary who serves with an international mission organization in a predominantly Muslim North African country and interrogates diasporic life as a critique of and mediation for transcultural missionary engagements.

1

Global Buddhist Diaspora

Alex G. Smith

From ancient times, the mobility of people of all religious persuasions has played a consequential role in reshaping societies, cultures, nations, and religion itself. This chapter focuses on two aspects—the massive migrations of Buddhists worldwide and the urgent need for biblical witness and ministry to scattered Buddhists. Though statistical details of the Buddhist diaspora are difficult to estimate accurately, the trends of global dispersion of Buddhists are quite evident, and ministry among the diaspora Buddhists remains unaddressed and very challenging.

Wherever you find Chinese, Japanese, or Koreans dispersed across the world, there you will find Buddhists. One only needs to look at the expanding presence of East Asian restaurants in any city across the world. Chinese, Thai, Vietnamese, Japanese, Korean, Mongolian, and Malaysian cuisines are often just around the corner and seem to have become a staple diet of people everywhere. A flood of Buddhist refugees from Southeast Asia augments their numbers, and many international students and business executives from the Buddhist world are now spread globally.

Buddhist Diaspora History

Buddhism was founded by Siddhartha Gautama (born 563 BCE), who later came to be known as Buddha. Its origin can be traced back to Bodh Gaya, Bihar (India), where Gautama attained enlightenment while meditating under a Bodhi tree. Since most of the Buddhists now live somewhere other than the place of its origin, this makes Buddhism a totally diasporic religion. With over five hundred million[1] followers around the globe, Buddhism is the fourth-largest religion in the world and represents about 7 percent of the world population. A vast majority of Buddhists are in the Asia-Pacific region (99 percent) and are concentrated mostly in East, Southeast, or South Asia. Buddhism is the state religion of four nations in Asia, the majority religion in three other nations, and a significant minority in yet another seven countries (Cambodia, Thailand, Myanmar, Bhutan, Sri Lanka, Laos, and Mongolia). According to the Pew Research Center, about half of the world's Buddhists live in one country, China, and the others live in places such as Thailand (13 percent), Japan (9 percent), Burma (Myanmar; 8 percent), Sri Lanka (3 percent), Vietnam (3 percent), Cambodia (3 percent), South Korea, India (2 percent each), and Malaysia (1 percent).[2] There are also more than a million Buddhists in the United States and the United Kingdom.

From the beginning, Buddha himself went to different places to preach his message and later sent monks to scatter the dharma across north India and Nepal initially. After the death of Gautama in around 483 BCE, his followers began to organize a religious movement based on Buddha's teachings. A formalized version of Buddhism was gradually exported to other nations, and Buddhism became a widespread religion.

In the third century BCE, Mauryan emperor Ashoka made Buddhism the official state religion of India. He built many monasteries and encouraged missionary work. According to Bouvert Regulas, Emperor Ashoka made three major contributions to Buddhism: applying Buddhism to government and foreign policies, sending and supporting missionaries to spread Buddhism across his kingdom and beyond, and maintaining Buddhism as a major religion through positive interfaith dialogue.[3]

There are many forms of Buddhism in different regions of the world, and they are closely linked to the migration of Buddhists. Theravada Buddhism is found mostly in Thailand, Sri Lanka, Cambodia, Laos, and Myanmar, while Mahayana Buddhism is prevalent in China, Japan, Taiwan, Korea, Singapore, and Vietnam. Tibetan Buddhism is mostly found in Tibet, Nepal, Mongolia, Bhutan, and parts of Russia and northern India. Each of these groups reveres different texts and has different interpretations of Buddha's teachings. There are also other sects, such as Zen Buddhism and Nirvana Buddhism.

Causes of Buddhist Dispersion

Since the expulsion of Adam and Eve from Eden (Gen 3) and the global scattering from the Tower of Babel (Gen 11), the peoples of the world have been transient nomads. In the ancient times and Middle Ages, powerful nations captured regions beyond themselves and transported people as slaves. Famine, drought, and other environmental conditions forced many to find solace in foreign lands. Invading rulers of the Huns and Islamic Mughals attacked Buddhists in India and caused a widespread scattering of Buddhist people. In recent decades, a record number of Buddhist people have voluntarily migrated to distant lands for greener pastures and better living conditions.

Three centuries before Jesus Christ, Ashoka dispersed tens of thousands of Buddhist missionaries in all directions, as far as Cyrene (Libya), North Africa, Greece, and Macedonia.[4] Missionary monks traveled on the Silk Route to take the Buddhist message to mainland China and even Japan. Much of the early dispersion was deliberate, and centuries later, the Buddhist Dai people in China fled to remain free of the Han who encroached on their territory, and the Dai spread to Vietnam, Yunnan, Laos, Thailand, Burma, and into India's northeastern state of Assam.

For centuries, Buddhist rulers fought against neighboring kingdoms in greater India and Southeast Asia. For instance, frequent invasions arose between the Burmese and Thai; both were predominantly Buddhist nations. During the 1500s–1700s, the Burmese captured whole towns in Thailand and took them back as slaves. Today over 80 percent of Burmese and over 85 percent of Thai are Buddhists. Anne, the wife of famed American missionary to Burma Adoniram Judson, led the first Thai to Christ in Rangoon, Burma, in 1816. The first Thai Buddhist convert was part of that Thai Buddhist diaspora.[5]

The primary causes driving the dispersion of the Buddhists are war, poverty, famine, persecution, and political instability. Recent instances include Cambodia, Vietnam, Laos, and Korea. The fight for survival and the hope for a better life and freedom to worship, work, and seek education caused many people to scatter across the globe. Skilled and unskilled workers, as well as international students, constitute a major section of the diaspora communities. While some of the forces of dispersion have been involuntary, trade and international commerce also have added to the growing human dispersion of the Buddhist people. Buddhist migrants include both legal and illegal immigrants, war refugees, business travelers, and tourists. Many migrants from East and Southeast Asia and some from South Asia are Buddhists. A major surge in migration out of this region occurred in the 1970s, primarily for two main reasons—people who were forcibly displaced on account of conflicts in the region and those who voluntarily moved to foreign lands for economic opportunities. The United Nations (UN) designated 1980 as "the year of the refugee," and Asian Buddhists were a significant part of it. Furthermore, out-migration from Southeast Asia swelled dramatically because of the migration of skilled and semiskilled laborers to perform contract work in the new industrial nations of the Middle East and East Asia.

According to the UN Population Division, the total number of international migrants in 2019 worldwide was 272 million, up from 221 million in 2010 and 174 million in 2000.[6] This annual report provides details of international migrants from every country but does not provide their religious affiliation. However, it is fair to assume that a large number of migrants from countries such as Vietnam, Cambodia, Laos, Thailand, China, Tibet, Myanmar, Sri Lanka, Nepal, and so on are Buddhists or hail from a Buddhist background. There is an extensive intermingling of Buddhism with Chinese religions such as Daoism, Confucianism, and Shintoism. There are new offshoots of Buddhism in the form of Cao Dai in Vietnam, Falun Gong in China, and Soka Gakkai in Japan. Since the post-Communist era in Southeast Asia, Buddhism has experienced a new level of resurgence, and over the last sixty years, the geopolitical crisis in the Tibetan region, most of whose residents are adherents of Tibetan Buddhism, has caught the attention of much of the world. Buddhism became widely popular in the West on account of the Dalai Lama's worldwide travels, teachings, and books. Many international students and business professionals from China and Southeast Asia are another sector of the Buddhist population that is moving to nearby Asian countries and across the globe. The ease and affordability of travel and communication are further causing widespread dispersion while allowing people to remain in close contact with the rest of their family in their ancestral homelands.

Selective Sketch of Contemporary Buddhist Diaspora

Due to limited space in this chapter, I would like to provide a brief portrait of some key countries or areas of the Buddhist diaspora. Since the 1980s, the twenty-five-year civil war in *Sri Lanka* has pushed millions to Asia, Europe, North America, and Australia.[7] By 2004, upward of two million people of Sri Lankan origin lived outside this island nation. Between 1979 and 2011, the annual exodus of migrants increased tenfold, from 25,785 to 260,000. The bulk of these migrants came from the Buddhist Sinhala majority regions of the country. Most Sri Lankan migrants are contract workers in the Middle East, primarily in Bahrain, Kuwait, Oman, Qatar, Saudi Arabia, and the United Arab Emirates (UAE). Around 2010, these combined nations had a population of approximately 45 million, which comprised 52 percent nationals and 48 percent expatriate nonnationals. In some of the Gulf nations, such as Qatar and UAE, expatriate foreign workers account for nearly 90 percent of the population.

Vietnam is another Buddhist case in point. Between 1975 and 1981, an estimated 565,757 Indo-Chinese refugees arrived in the United States,[8] and between 1980 and 1994, the number of Vietnamese admitted into the United States reached 882,862.[9] I interviewed a Vietnamese leader who is actively involved in planting churches and training leaders among Vietnamese people in Malaysia, Vietnam, Canada, and the United States.[10] According to him, ten years ago, over 100,000 Vietnamese worked as contract laborers in Malaysia, including those who became wives of Chinese Malaysians. Usually, formal contracts are for four years, and then the workers must return to Vietnam. In recent years, the numbers have decreased to about 30,000 Vietnamese in Malaysia. One reason is the prospect of lucrative jobs for Vietnamese workers in China, South Korea, Japan, Taiwan, and in the last five years, the Middle East. South Korean men taking Vietnamese wives is another common practice. The first year Korean law allowed this, more than 13 percent of all weddings there were with Vietnamese women. An estimated 10 percent of the Vietnamese diaspora are wives in Korea. In 2016, intercultural weddings of Korean men with Vietnamese women amounted to 27.9 percent of 21,709 marriages, and nearly 27 percent of Korean men married Chinese women.[11] Asian tourist agencies provide tours for Vietnamese and other men to meet Asian brides. These figures are augmented by tourists who illegally over-stay their visas and are not counted in statistics. In Canada and the United States, the Vietnamese have set up Buddhist temples and monasteries. Many international students from

Buddhist countries go to Western countries for higher education and professional training. Though many churches have been established among the Vietnamese immigrants in North America, a vision for missions in their ancestral homelands is generally missing.

Taiwan has 630,000 foreign Southeast Asians working there, mostly from Vietnam and Thailand. In 2014, Vietnamese brides married to Chinese men in Taiwan totaled 120,000, and many others get married in China or America.[12] The brides come mostly from South Vietnam, while contract workers are largely from the North. Nearly three-tenths of Taiwanese are Buddhists, amounting to about seven million people, and most of them follow a blend of Buddhism, Daoism, and Chinese folk religion. During my visit in 2018 to *South Korea*, I learned that the foreign population in the country had doubled in the ten years between 2006 and 2016. More than two million foreigners legally live in South Korea, and over one million of them are Chinese and 151,000 are from the United States. Others include 144,000 Vietnamese; 93,000 Thai; 54,000 Filipino; and 54,000 Uzbeks. Other nations with 30,000 or more each are Cambodia, Indonesia, Japan, Mongolia, Nepal, Taiwan, and Russia.[13] The majority of foreigners in South Korea are from Buddhist-influenced countries. But these statistics do not include many illegal aliens living there, which may increase these numbers by 75 percent to approximately 3.5 million. Some churches have been started among Thai and Vietnamese diasporas in South Korea.

The *Chinese* diaspora is colossal, and there is a long history of migration from China to faraway lands. Zhu Guohong suggests that early international migration from China began some two millennia ago and constitutes the largest diaspora population in the world. The initial migrants went to Japan and the Philippines and later, during the Yuan dynasty (1279–1368), to Java, North Borneo, Siam (Thailand), Sumatra, and Cambodia.[14] In the last thirty years, they have been dispersed to almost every part of the world. There are also massive internal migrations from rural villages to urban centers in China and other nearby Asian cities. For example, in a couple of generations, hundreds of millions of rural dwellers have relocated to new cities, as they offer three to four times more earning power, and some estimate that nearly 80 percent of Chinese now reside in sprawling urban centers. The economic rise of China and growing investments overseas have taken millions of Chinese to Africa, Latin America, Europe, and elsewhere. Many Buddhists in the Chinese diaspora have converted to Christianity and joined Chinese churches.

Latin America has a considerable number of members of the Asian Buddhist diaspora, mostly from immigration. The Japanese began to enter Brazil in 1908, with the largest number of arrivals between 1925 and 1934.[15] In 2014, Brazil had 1.5 million Japanese migrants (the largest outside of Japan) plus 200,000 Chinese; Peru had 710,000 Chinese and 74,000 Japanese; Panama had 300,000 Chinese Hakka-speaking illegal immigrants; Argentina had 285,000 Chinese residents; Paraguay had 140,000 Chinese and Japanese; and Nicaragua had thousands of mainland Chinese workers, as they are projected to build a canal connecting the Atlantic and Pacific Oceans, though progress is slow.

Africa has received members of the Asian diaspora in recent decades, including Chinese, Japanese, and other Asian Buddhists. One researcher gathered data on the Chinese located in only eighteen of Africa's fifty-four countries.[16] In

2016, this totaled 816,845 Chinese across Africa, but because of illegal Chinese residents, three of those nations had double the stated figures. This adds up to an additional 350,000 and increases the number of Chinese in Africa to 1.17 million in only one-third of its countries without counting the other thirty-six countries. South Africa has the highest number—nearly half a million. Congo was next with 100,000 in 2015. No figures for Japanese or Koreans in Africa were recorded. China has now become the largest trading partner with the continent of Africa, and growing investment in the region for tapping into its oil, precious metals, and other resources will draw millions of Chinese to Africa in the coming decades.

Diaspora and God's Purposeful Witness

Historically, the Jews were diasporic wanderers: starting with Abram leaving Ur of the Chaldeans, migrating to Egypt, entering the Promised Land, and later being forced into captivity back in Babylon. Famine drove them to Egypt, and persecution sent them out of it. They wandered for forty years around Sinai before settling in Israel. In all these diasporic movements, God's purpose was for them to be a light to the gentiles "so that [God's] salvation may reach to the end of the earth" (Isa 49:6). When they failed to witness truly, the Lord exiled both Israel and Judah. Through their diaspora, they incidentally became witnesses for God to multiple foreign peoples in Assyria and Babylon, respectively. The Jews started synagogues wherever they went, and the exilic Pharisees began a missionary movement to other nations, including China.[17] The remnants of the Jewish diaspora, possibly from Solomon's time, are currently found in the Tamil Thattar[18] and Sephardi Jews of Sri Lanka and the Paradesi Jews of Cochin in South India.[19] In the twelfth century, Benjamin of Tudela (a Sephardi Jew of Spanish and Portuguese descent) declared there were three thousand Jews in Sri Lanka.[20] Since 1948, many have migrated back to modern Israel.

Sixty years after the fall of Jerusalem (587 BCE), Buddha claimed enlightenment hundreds of years before Christ. Some contact of Jews with Buddhism is possible, and contact of early Christians with Buddhism is probable through Jewish trade links to India. Following the Great Commission charge, the early Jewish Christians under persecution became diaspora witnesses across the Middle East and nearby regions.[21] Similarly, in modern times, Buddhist-background Christian believers in diaspora spread their faith both in their dispersed locations and to their natal lands.

The Asian Buddhist diaspora also propagated Buddhism wherever they migrated globally. They built Buddhist centers, temples, and monasteries and even established house temples, particularly in the Western nations. In some cases, Christian churches in the West were purchased and converted into Buddhist temples. Many in the West are attracted to the tenets of Buddhism, and even some celebrities have converted and become active proponents of the Buddhist faith. A new wave of renewal is sweeping across the planet among the followers of Buddhism.

Buddhist Diaspora and Christianity

The Christian church in Asian Buddhist nations is generally quite small (Japan 0.5 percent; Thailand 1 percent).

Exceptions are South Korea (25 percent) and Mongolia (10 percent). There are very few Buddhist-background Christians among the global Buddhist diasporas. Some diaspora believers start ethnic churches wherever they migrate, but like in their homelands, church planting is difficult and slow in diasporic settings. Some ethnic churches have been established in the West among Thai, Lao, Burmese, and Japanese, and larger churches have been established among Chinese and Korean diasporas. Some converts return to their native lands as witnesses to extended family networks or as missionaries.

The attitude of Christians toward Buddhists is important in ministry to Buddhist diasporas. The apostle Paul gave us a good example of how to relate to alien religions. He did not disparage their gods or rob their temples (Acts 19:37). He used the altar to the unknown god in Athens as a contact point to preach the gospel (Acts 17:23). Attacking another's beliefs is certainly not the best way to win a person to the Lord. Nor should we destroy someone's idols or spiritual objects. That robs them of the value of doing so in personal power encounters, which also provide a testimony to faith in God's power and protection. As only one supreme God is Creator of all, so only one gospel of Christ uniquely offers salvation to all. Biblical revelation is remarkable in its exclusivity. God is to be feared above all gods (1 Chr 16:25–26) and is greater than all other gods (Exod 18:11; Pss 96:3–5; 97:9). God commanded Israel not to make any idols or worship them (Exod 20:23). Jesus declared, "This is eternal life, that they may know you [Father], the only true God, and Jesus Christ whom you have sent" (John 17:3).

God gave clear commands related to dispersed people. The Israelites were responsible to care for strangers in their midst and to teach the Torah to sojourners. They were not to wrong or oppress them (Exod 22:21; 23:9). They had to exercise justice toward them, show love, and provide food and clothing for them (Deut 10:18–19). Nor were Jews to detest aliens in their land (Deut 23:7). King Solomon asked Jehovah to bless foreigners who came to the temple and requested that God answer their prayers offered at the temple (1 Kgs 8:41–43).

Aliens responded to God, as faithful Jews were lights to the gentiles. Examples were Solomon to the Queen of Sheba and Jonah to the Ninevites. Diaspora instances include Joseph under his Egyptian masters, the Israelite slave girl in Naaman's household in Assyria, Daniel to the Babylonians, and Esther's influence on Persian kings. They were firm in faith and witness. Jesus also reached out to foreigners like the Roman centurion, the Syro-Phoenician woman, and the Samaritan woman of Sychar. All were aliens amid God's people, and they encountered the Savior's redeeming love. Likewise, many churches and believers across the world are ministering to Asian Buddhists, and many are meeting Jesus in their sojourns.

Responsiveness to the Gospel in Diaspora

Peoples on the move are usually more receptive to the gospel, at least for a while. Their receptivity is often limited to two to three years after arrival in their new domiciles. Away from their traditional village control, familial pressures, and cultural constraints, the Buddhist diaspora experiences fresh contexts around them. Their openness to expanding horizons and experiencing new things provides churches with significant opportunities for social services, evangelistic outreach, and church planting. Generally, newly arrived people have a higher level of receptivity than those in their homelands because of their uprooting, mobility, and consequent disruption and are exceptionally receptive to the gospel of Jesus Christ.

In the 1970s, hundreds of thousands of Buddhists from Southeast Asia fled into Thailand. During that decade, over 100,000 displaced aliens in Thailand became Christians. Alien mobility is an essential dynamic for diaspora workers to observe and act upon strategically. Iu-Mien refugees provide a veritable example. Tin Nguyen affirms that most Mien practice ancestral rites and consequently were easily influenced by Buddhism, especially in Vietnam, where frequent ancestor worship dominates Vietnam's Mahayana majority. The fear of the spirit world also opens doors for the gospel. C. W. Callaway, a veteran missionary to the Mien, released a summary of the last two decades of global response among Mien.[22] In 2019, the Mien population was two million. The 80 percent majority in China have a minuscule 1,500 believers. Mien in Vietnam, Thailand, and Laos have a combined total population of 358,000, and 22,300 (or 6 percent) of them are now Christians. Also, a total of 42,200 diaspora Mien in America and France experienced a significant increase of 5,890 believers, or 14 percent of that population, over the last twenty years.

This potential for diaspora responsiveness calls for urgent attention and prompt action. However, local churches are usually slow to take the initiative to reach out to Buddhist diaspora newcomers. Some rise to the occasion, like one American church that has a vital ministry to waves of Chinese pilot trainees sent to the US Northwest. A few become believers before they return to China. There they often face tough challenges and new opposition from family members and the community. Assisting international students who have become Christians overseas to maintain their faith upon return to their homeland is crucial. One report found that nearly 80 percent who profess faith overseas do not attend a church after returning to Asia.[23]

Ministering to Buddhist Diasporas Locally

I will never forget the trauma of an aging Laotian refugee grandmother I once saw. She had never gone beyond her tiny rural village. Snatched from her tribal environs, she was put on a jet plane and flown overnight to San Francisco. She felt lost and was scared to death. She was checked into a large downtown hotel. At midnight, several fire engines roared down the street in front of her hotel, blaring loud sirens. She believed that demon spirits were attacking her and was numb with fright. No one could console her, so her family took her to a spirit doctor to get traditional assistance. I helped another Asian refugee family in the United States whose young daughter had been kidnapped, raped, and murdered in Oregon. How does one help such hurting migrants living in our midst? Elsewhere I have provided many practical approaches to understanding diasporas and how best to help them adjust to their new foreign place.[24]

One elderly American Christian couple was the best model I know for working with aliens. They met them on arrival, helped them settle in, and showed them where the post office, banks, and shops were. They introduced them to the public transportation system and helped with driving lessons. The wife was in a wheelchair, but that did not stop her. They related well to strangers and shared the gospel openly with all. They prayed for aliens' challenges and needs, stood by them amid their concerns for safety, and helped with language and cultural adjustments, sustenance, work opportunities, and discouragements. When evil spirits attacked them or fear of demons overwhelmed them, this aging couple prayed with them in the name of Jesus for protection. That spiritual strategy is one of the most vital tools for all diaspora workers.

This is an era when every Christian can truly be a missionary in their own land, reaching out to thousands of diaspora Buddhists nearby. Every local church worldwide can become a cross-cultural agent of the gospel to Buddhists residing in their local community. Today's urgent opportunities call for practical service to diaspora people. So what to do? Live like Christ among them. Build relationships with them. Demonstrate Jesus's love to them. Recognize the possibilities around you. Research diaspora Buddhists in your community and city. Open your eyes to see and befriend them. Many Asian immigrants, refugees, scholars, and international students follow their own folk Buddhist traditions. Their temples sprout like mushrooms, and they live right next door in your neighborhood. Catch a vision to reach out to them.

It is critical to build personal relationships with aliens in your midst. Take time to make genuine friends with them and their families. Open your ears to listen to them. Love and relate to them. Relationships are crucial to Asians. Take time and effort to make it a top priority. Pray for diaspora families and organize a plan to reach out to them. What frustrations do they have? What are the challenges you can face with them? Learn to understand them and learn to share the gospel. Pray with them about their personal concerns.

Reflect on the needs of diaspora Buddhists. How can you help practically? Find out where they are hurting and listen to their complaints. Be empathetic to their burdens, pains, and spiritual hunger. Serve them wisely and wholeheartedly. Stand by them in their struggles. Another step is to encourage your friends and the local church to join you in outreach to the Buddhist diaspora in your community. God has brought the mission field to our back door. The diaspora peoples from around the world are already in our localities and live together in clusters. Frequently they feel neglected, forgotten, and abandoned. Mobilize others to help you reach and serve diaspora peoples. God has sent them to us so that we may bless them with the gospel.

Also, find former missionaries in your area who understand these diasporic peoples and cultures. Years ago, a missionary to Japan had medical problems and was forced to return to the United States. The returned missionary family noticed several foreign students at nearby local universities, many of whom were from Japan. They began to befriend them, gather them together, and serve them. They witnessed to them and began to disciple them with the help of local churches. They began a Japanese Christian fellowship and were led by a Japanese Christian. They followed up with students after they went back to Japan and recognized a great need for effective nurture and connection of these returning students to churches in Japan. The Japanese leader moved back to Japan to set up an indigenous network to assist Japanese churches in integrating new returnee believers.

Conclusion

The global Buddhist diaspora poses a massive challenge to churches in their midst. Their great needs loom like immovable mountains. Prayer and service with faith and love can overcome all difficulties. Commitment and action through sacrificial service will accomplish much for God's glory among the diaspora. Though Christ followers among them may be sparse, that handful—supplemented by surrounding Christians—can accomplish much for extending God's kingdom.

The climax of God's missionary program indicates a host of converted aliens. They populate the kingdom of heaven from every tribe, nation, language, and people. They are a multitude that no man can number, not even with computers. This is not universal salvation of everyone on earth, but only those who are washed in the blood of the Lamb. With palm branches in their hands, they glorify Jesus as King. They shout Hosanna in praise of their Redeemer. They are a persecuted host also, having experienced the venom of Satan and the fury of his evil hordes (Rev 5:9; 7:9; 11:15, 17). This gives us a mission of hope among the Buddhist diaspora and much hope in our mission of reaching and serving aliens in our midst and around the globe.

Notes

1 As of 2010, there were 488 million Buddhists according to the global religious landscape of Pew Research. See Pew Research Center, "Buddhists," 2012, accessed November 1, 2019, https://www.pewforum .org/2012/12/18/global-religious-landscape-buddhist/. Also see the

Lausanne Movement, "Buddhism: An Infographic," accessed September 20, 2021, https://lausanne.org/content/buddhism-an-infographic.

2 Pew Research Center, "Buddhists."

3 Bouvert Regulas, "Lessons from the Buddhist Mission History of King Asoka" (unpublished paper presented at SEANET Forum XVII, Thailand, January 7–11, 2019), 127.

4 Kanai Lal Hazra, *History of Theravada Buddhism in South East Asia* (New Delhi: Munshiram Manchandal, 1982), 37–39.

5 Alex G. Smith, *Siamese Gold: The Church in Thailand* (Bangkok: Kanok Bannasan, 1999), 13.

6 UN Department of Economic and Social Affairs, *International Migration 2019*, accessed November 15, 2019, https://www.un.org/en/development/desa/population/migration/publications/wallchart/docs/MigrationStock2019_Wallchart.pdf.

7 Enoch Wan and Ted Rubesh, *Wandering Jews and Scattered Sri Lankans* (Portland, OR: Institute of Diaspora Studies of the USA, 2014), 79.

8 Paul J. Rutledge, *The Vietnamese Experience in America* (Bloomington: Indiana University Press, 1992), 4.

9 Enoch Wan and Thanh Trung Le, *Mobilizing Vietnamese Diaspora for the Kingdom* (Portland, OR: Institute of Diaspora Studies of the USA, 2014), 12.

10 Tin Nguyen, personal interview, Portland, OR, February 21, 2019.

11 "Vietnamese Women Now Account for Highest Number of Foreign Brides in South Korea," Hankyoreh, November 19, 2017, http://english.hani.co.kr/arti/english_edition/e_international/819733.html.

12 Wan and Trung Le, *Mobilizing Vietnamese Diaspora*, 129.

13 International Migration Statistics, Statistics Korea, 2010–2020, accessed September 1, 2021, http://kostat.go.kr/portal/eng/pressReleases/8/5/index.board.

14 Zhu Guohong, "A Historical Demography of Chinese Migration," in *Chinese Overseas*, ed. Hong Lui (London: Routledge, 2006), 1:140–42.

15 Célia Sakurai, "Japanese-Brazilians: Past and Present," trans. André Soares, Discover Nikkei, January 24, 2008, http://www.discovernikkei .org/en/journal/2008/1/24/copani-knt/.

16 Carolyn Kemp, "East Asians Living in Diaspora" (presentation made to OMF leaders, August 2017).

17 Richard R. de Ridder, *The Dispersion of the People of God* (Kampen, Netherlands: J. H. Kok, 1971); see Matt 28:15.

18 Andrew Harris, "Secrets of Ceylon: What Happened to the Jews of Sri Lanka?," eJewish Philanthropy, June 9, 2011, https:// ejewishphilanthropy.com/secrets-of-ceylon-what-happened-to-the -jews-of-sri-lanka/.

19 Barbara C. Johnson, "The Cochin Jews of Kerala," My Jewish Learning, July 27, 2010, 1–3, https://www.myjewishlearning.com/article/ the-cochin-jews-of-kerala/.

20 "Jews in Sri Lanka," Jewish Virtual Library, accessed September 1, 2021, https://www.jewishvirtuallibrary.org/sri-lanka-virtual-jewish-tour.

21 Acts 8:1–4; 9:29–31; 11:19.

22 C. W. Callaway, email, "Why Many Mien Have Turned to Christ," February 17, 2019.

23 Carolyn Kemp, "Multi-dimensional Discipling for Diaspora Communities," *Mission Roundtable* 12, no. 2 (May–August 2017): 22.

24 Alex Smith, *A Christian's Pocket Guide to Buddhism* (Fearn, Ross-shire, Scotland: Christian Focus, 2009), 31–68.

Bibliography

Guohong, Zhu. "A Historical Demography of Chinese Migration." In *Chinese Overseas*, edited by Hong Lui, 139–167. Vol. 1. London: Routledge, 2006.

Hazra, Kanai Lal. *History of Theravada Buddhism in South East Asia.* New Delhi: Munshiram Manoharlal, 1982.

Ridder, Richard R. de. *The Dispersion of the People of God*. Kampen, Netherlands: J. H. Kok, 1971.

Rutledge, Paul J. *The Vietnamese Experience in America*. Bloomington: Indiana University Press, 1992.

Smith, Alex. *A Christian's Pocket Guide to Buddhism*. Fearn, Ross-shire, Scotland: Christian Focus, 2009.

———. *Siamese Gold: The Church in Thailand*. Bangkok: Kanok Bannasan, 1999.

Wan, Enoch, and Ted Rubesh. *Wandering Jews and Scattered Sri Lankans*. Portland, OR: Institute of Diaspora Studies of the USA, 2014.

Wan, Enoch, and Thanh Trung Le. *Mobilizing Vietnamese Diaspora for the Kingdom*. Portland, OR: Institute of Diaspora Studies of the USA, 2014.

2

Hinduism in Diaspora

John Arun Kumar

Introduction

This chapter aims to sketch a brief portrait of Hinduism found outside of the Indian subcontinent. It explores a select group of nations and scholars who have written from their diasporic contexts about Hinduism. Hinduism embraces a wide diversity of religious beliefs and practices, and on account of differing histories of migration to different places, diaspora Hinduism is even more complex and has diverse trajectories of its development abroad.

Wherever Indians have migrated, they have taken their culture and religion with them.[1] The phenomenon of Hinduism outside India appears to be different from that in India and has many distinctive features. However, some scholars have argued that Hinduism found in diasporic settings is only different externally from the Hinduism of India but remains the same internally.[2] They influence each other in their ongoing processes of development and change continually due to transnational interactions and flows. This chapter focuses on diaspora Hinduism in terms of its essence, origin, features, and functions in light of current developments. Later I focus on two specific aspects of diaspora Hinduism—namely, (1) the increasing influence of right-wing Hindutva ideas and ongoing interactive processes of Hindus in the diaspora and (2) the role of caste and language among Hindus in the diaspora. In this chapter, I include references to Hindus in the United States, the United Kingdom, Mauritius, Fiji, Singapore, Malaysia, and the Caribbean.

The Term *Hinduism*

The term *Hinduism* is about two centuries old and is used as a common term to refer to all the religious beliefs and practices of the people of South Asia put together.[3] Hinduism is not a monolithic religion, and it will be too general to refer to it as the religion of the Hindus. This is because the term *Hindu* was itself coined some five centuries ago by outsiders based on the geographical location of the South Asian subcontinent by the basin of the Sindhu River. However, this term has come to be accepted by many in the subcontinent as their general identity marker, although they are stratified into caste, subcaste, and sub-subcaste groups. Some Hindus would identify Hinduism as a religion and some as a way of life. Others prefer to refer to it as *Sanatana Dharma*, or the Eternal Dharma.[4] Still others would say it is not a monolithic religion like Judaism, Christianity, or Islam. Hence for our purposes here, we could define Hinduism as an umbrella term used to discuss the various traditions and practices of Hindus not exclusively belonging to Buddhism, Zoroastrianism, Jainism, Sikhism, Judaism, Christianity, Islam, primal religions of

India, or any other religions and ideologies elsewhere in the world. Currently, the right-wing Hindus of India define Hinduism in terms of *Hindutva*, meaning "Hindu-ness."

Origin and Development of Hinduism in Diaspora

Although the term *Hinduism* is relatively new, its origin is traced to 3000 BCE and the interaction of the Vedic religion in its neighborhood of Persia with early Zoroastrianism and later with the Indus valley civilization, which existed in the general vicinity of current India. This point itself suggests that the origin of Hinduism is located in a diasporic community outside of present India. The historical influence of Hinduism is evident in Southeast Asia in places such as Thailand, Bali, Java, and Cambodia on account of trade links and marital alliances, which eventually led to Hindu priests being invited by rulers as well as the establishment of some aspects of the Hindu tradition and the building of temples.[5] However, the large-scale migration of Hindus from India to other lands can be traced back to the last two centuries only and is closely linked to British *Raj* in India. The migration occurred in two major periods: during the nineteenth- and early twentieth-century colonial period under indenture contracts and after World War II, when some students and businessmen migrated to Britain and later also to the United States, Canada, Australia, and the Gulf countries. There was also a movement of Hindus from diaspora locations to other places, such as from the Caribbean to Britain, Canada, and the United States; from Fiji to New Zealand; and from Surinam to the Netherlands.

Brian Hatcher suggests that the origin of modern Hindu thought could be traced to Raja Rammohan Roy, a socioreligious reformer of the nineteenth century during British rule in India. Hatcher first noted that many new Hindu movements prominent during the colonial period in India presented a variety of interpretations of what Hinduism really was or should be. He observes that "what passes for contemporary Hindu thought is a species of Western-influenced neo-Vedanta" propagated by the likes of Rammohan Roy, Mahatma Gandhi, and Sarvepalli Radhakrishnan.[6] Moreover, he questions whether there is one essential form of modern Hindu thought.

The nature of modern Hinduism, however, is complex and more than the inventory of various religious movements that account for the modern Hindu way of life. Such an attempt was made over one hundred years ago by John Nicol Farquhar, whose *Modern Religious Movements in India* (1915) sought to provide a handy scheme of categories for understanding the range of religious thought and activity in the India of his day. According to Farquhar, when surveying religious change in nineteenth-century India, one was confronted with (1) movements that favored "serious reform," such as the Brahmo Samaj in Bengal and the Prarthana Samaj in Bombay; (2) movements in which reform was "checked by the defense of the old faiths," such as the Arya Samaj in Punjab and the Radhasoami Satsang in northern India; and (3) movements that depended on a "full defense of the old religions," among which was placed not only older sectarian movements (such as Gaudiya Vaisnavism and Saiva Siddhanta) but also the figure of Ramakrishna Paramahamsa, a mystic from colonial Bengal. Upon reviewing Farquhar's work, Hatcher concludes that Farquhar was not "prepared to acknowledge the degree to which his system of classification was unable to contain the movements he surveyed."[7]

Upon abolishment of slavery in 1834, the British recruited nearly two million people from its largest colony in India to work in the plantations in Mauritius and Malaya in what came to be known as the indentured labor system. Until 1917, shiploads of Indians—most of whom were low-caste Hindus who were debt-ridden, marginalized, or starving villagers—were taken to far-flung colonies of the British Empire, such as Guyana, Trinidad, South Africa, Jamaica, the Fiji islands, and so on. They also worked as administrative "coolies" and as soldiers in the World Wars on behalf of the British. Among them, the religious sentiments and practices varied highly and waned over time without any connection with the ancestral homeland. However, the major impetus for the Hindu religious movement in the West came when Swami Vivekananda (1862–1902) made a persuasive presentation about Hinduism to the World's Parliament of Religions in Chicago in 1893. He was "first in a long line of proselytizing gurus who exported the ideals of reformed Hinduism to foreign soil"[8] and brought back some progressive Western ideas, such as equality (speaking against caste discrimination) and food habits (asking people to eat meat). Four years later, he returned to India with a small band of Western disciples and founded the Ramakrishna Mission, with branches in many parts of the world.

There are several other notable Hindu or quasi-Hindu movements in the United States. The Theosophical Society was started in New York City by a Russian, Helena Blavatsky, in 1875. After a trip to India, she established a headquarters in Chennai and incorporated many aspects of Hinduism into its doctrines. The US operation came about after the visit of Vivekananda and prospered under the leadership of Annie Besant. The Hare Krishna movement was founded by A. C. Bhaktivedanta (Prabhupada) and spread worldwide as the International Society for Krishna Consciousness (ISKCON). Transcendental Meditation was popularized in the West by Maharishi Yogi with the founding of the International Meditation Society in 1958. Swami Muktananda established the Siddha Yoga Dharma Associates (SYDA) Foundation in 1974. Bhagwan Shree Rajneesh (Osho) moved from Poona to Oregon in 1981 and established a global operation. In later years, Sathya Sai Baba, Shri Shri Ravishanker, Amritanandamayi Ma (known as Amma, a speaker at the 1993 World's Parliament of Religions in Chicago), Shri Karunamayi Ma, Sant Rajinder Singh Ji Maharaj, and many others became the face of Hinduism in the West. These movements have common features, including charismatic leaders; congregational gatherings; celebration of Hindu festivals; cultural programs focused on Hindu religious themes, festivals, and epics; mobilization of large amounts of funds; the practice of yoga in numerous new forms; and so on.

While Vedanta renders the path to liberation as a problem of right knowledge (*jnana*), there are others for whom devotion (*bhakti*) to God or service (*seva*) to the guru, as well as more esoteric practices of yogic alchemy, is seen to be the most efficacious means to salvation. One of the new values that Vedantists have adopted is religious tolerance, which many contemporary Hindus see as the only way to realize the dream of a secular Indian republic. Some individuals view the primary goal as bolstering the supremacy of the Hindu identity. The Arya Samaj strategy of reconversion (*shuddhi*, or purification) is a noteworthy example of an aggressive program of Hindu self-assertion. Religious groups like the Vedanta Society and Vishwa Hindu Parishad (VHP) are arising from diametrically opposed visions of Hinduism as tolerant versus intolerant.

Steven Vertovec explains the processes involving the construction, representation, and reproduction of Hinduism and Hindu identity in the diaspora.[9] Describing Hinduism in Great Britain and the Caribbean, he suggests that diasporic Hinduism has traveled very divergent historical trajectories and is significantly conditioned by a wide range of local factors. About the mutability of Hinduism, Vertovec notes, "The religious traditions of Hindus in the Caribbean are the outcome of over 150 years of inadvertent permutation, deliberate alteration, and structurally necessary modification."[10] The religious practices are re-created from memory and adapted to new local realities simultaneously at diasporic locations.

Diaspora Hinduism and Right-Wing Nationalism

Now that Hindus are dispersed globally and their overseas population has grown significantly in recent decades, Hindutva groups want to seize this opportunity to promote their agenda under the guise of teaching Hindu culture and Hinduism by sending its workers to various diaspora communities around the world. Hindutva groups are key proponents of Hindu right-wing nationalism, promoting India's true nature as Hindu. The activities of the Hindutva movement in the diaspora in the late twentieth century seem to be the major factor in its political ascendency in

India, thus proving close ties between the diaspora and their ancestral homeland.

Prema Kurien researched the emergence of California as the center of an aggressive Hindu nationalist movement, which in turn has caused the Muslims in that region to react defensively. She studied the activities of two different organizations in Los Angeles—the Federation of Hindu Associations (FHA) and the American Federation of Muslims of Indian Origin (AFMI). She found that they represent two different positions:

> The dominant Hindu and Muslim Indian American organizations, both in Southern California and in the rest of the country, have developed opposing constructions of "Indianness" and attempt to influence American and Indian politics in line with their own interests. Hindu Indian organizations view India as a Hindu society whose true nature has been sullied by the invasion of Muslims, the British, and the post-colonial domination of "pseudo-secular" Indians. Most of the major Hindu Indian American groups are working for the establishment of a Hindu *rashtra* (state) in India while most Muslims taught in Indian American organizations are striving to safeguard India's secularism.[11]

One can note that by the end of the last century, Hindutva proponents have strategically worked from outside India, especially in the United States, to achieve their ideological goals in India. This was possible because of the contradiction between America's official and unofficial policies. The Hindu and Muslim Indian Americans have separate, religion-based organizations and develop different constructions of "Indian" identity. On account of religious freedom laws and resources available for ethnic and minority communities, they compete with each other to have their definition of national identity recognized. Kurien suggests that America's official policy, which recognizes national origin as the criterion of ethnicity, and the unofficial policy, which views religion as the most legitimate mode of ethnic expression, have resulted in different constructions of Indian identity among Hindu and Muslim Indian Americans. This in turn has made religion and the need for ethnic recognition even more important for the group. This shows how the Hindu diaspora has played an important role in garnering support for the Hindutva cause of Hindu nationhood in India.

Rajesh Rai studied Hindutva activities in Singapore and Southeast Asia and observed that Hindu organizations have come to establish a formidable presence in the South Asian diaspora, particularly in the United States and the United Kingdom. He found that sympathy for the Hindutva movement in the Hindu diaspora extends well beyond members of Hindutva-affiliated organizations to also include large numbers of Hindu religious organizations that may not be directly affiliated with the Hindutva movement.[12] No British Hindu organizations have been publicly opposed to the *Sangh Parivar* (the family of Hindu nationalistic organizations). Most *sampradayiks* (radical foot soldiers) and the globe-trotting priests are vital to the religious practices of diasporic Hindu families as well as Hindu welfare organizations, both of which are greatly influenced by the *Sangh*. However, Rai observed that in recent years, Singapore, on account of the state's commitment to social cohesion and harmony, has curbed overtly political aspects of Hindutva ideology. As a result, there has been a concerted effort by Hindutva groups in Singapore to abstain from politically hard-line aspects of Hindu nationalism and avoid using all overt symbols, such as portraits of *Rashtriya Swayamsevak Sangh* (RSS) leaders or the proposed Rama temple in Ayodhya, India. Hindutva activities in the diaspora have been to gain support and consolidate its base in India.

Knut Jacobsen discusses yoga and gurus as a feature of Hinduism in the diaspora.[13] According to him, some of the elements of the process of globalization of Hinduism include (1) Hindu gurus with international success who have attracted followers worldwide, (2) the adoption of the Hindu practices by persons with a non-Hindu background, and (3) the popularity of yoga. Hinduism is commonly portrayed this way in popular media and film, and it has drawn many Western followers. Others have observed that "most of the Hindu diaspora are less zealous in spreading the religion and are more content with privately practicing their faith."[14] There is much attraction to the Eastern mystical elements of Hinduism in the West, while most remain oblivious to the political agenda of Hindutva advocates.

Due to religious nationalism and intense interactions with religious nationalist organizations and missionaries from the subcontinent, the split between Hindus and Muslims became so profound that by the 1940s, "Indo-Mauritians" became either "Hindu" or "Muslim." In everyday discourse, the label "Indian" (*endien* in Creole) has become a synonym for Hindus but is never applied to Muslims despite their Indian background. In the 1950s and 1960s, the "Hindu" community became further subdivided into "Hindus" as such—meaning Hindus of North India, mainly from a Bihari background, who are the great majority and considered to be "Hindi-speaking"—and the much smaller Tamil, Telugu, and Marathi groups.

Language and Caste among Diaspora Hindus

Again, in the Mauritius context, the Indian ancestral languages have played an essential role in the forming of identity and religion.[15] Hindus in Mauritius are from both South India and North India. The cultivation of ancestral language has emerged as one of the crucial mediating links to the homeland, and there is a history of fragmentation of the Hindu community based on ancestral languages and cultures in the diaspora. Hindi has become established as a rallying issue of Indian identity in Mauritius in the first decade of the twentieth century. The revivalist groups such as the Arya Samaj and the Hindu Maha Sabha were the main champions of Hindi. Standard Hindi was cultivated in religious contexts and frequently taught in Hindu temples. Those speaking Hindi are identified as Hindus, whereas those speaking Tamil, Telugu, or Marathi are identified by their respective languages. Hindi-speaking Hindus wield political power in the country, and they are politically well connected to Hindutva both globally and in India.

Among the fragmented Hindu community, the supremacy of the Hindi language, which is the language of the politically dominant majority Indo-Mauritians, is upheld over other Indian languages of Mauritius as the marker for religious and ethnic purity: "In the vision of the Hindu nationalist advocates of Hindi as an ancestral language of the Hindus of Mauritius, Hindi assumes an important role in concerns about religious and ethnic purity, which is sought to be maintained by links to an 'ancestral culture' located elsewhere spatially and temporarily. The fears about the disappearance of Hindi are linked to fears about the disappearance of the Hindu religion and the 'Hindu community' as a distinct ethnic group. According to this logic, the 'protection' of Hindi equals the 'protection' of Hinduism in Mauritius."[16]

Louis Dumont, in his classic study *Homo Hierarchicus*, claims that caste is the epiphenomenon of Hinduism. Discussions of caste among Hindus in the diaspora have not received adequate attention until recently. In making a case for the study of caste among South Asian diaspora, Valliammal Karunakaran argues, "Caste goes where South Asians go. As an institutionalized structure of oppression, it affects over one billion people in South Asia, but the numbers and narratives for the diasporas have always been fuzzy because while caste practices are upheld, discussion of caste is seen as taboo. Further what conversation on caste does exist, is unjustifiably centered only around the issues of Dalits, and never on the networks of privilege that sustain 'upper' caste power in the diasporas."[17] The above study was launched by the Dalit American Foundation and hosted in collaboration with the Ambedkar International Mission, the Ambedkar Association of North America, and the Dalit American Women's Association.

Indo-Fujians are often upheld as a casteless diaspora. As the original indentured laborers were mostly men, scarcity of women migrants resulted in many marrying across caste and racial lines. This is true of the Caribbean and South Africa. But the caste issue raises its ugly head even when it comes to the marriage of children, particularly in the more advanced Western societies. So when the Ravidassia religious sect of Indo-Fiji migrated to California, Fijian-Dalit women were rejected by Dalit and non-Dalit partners citing unsuitable gender-caste categories. They had to resort to marrying their daughters to Dalit men from India. The arranged marriage system is still practiced and widely popular in diasporic settings, even to third and fourth generations. Caste standing is featured prominently in matrimonial advertisements in nonresident Indian (NRI) newspapers and websites as well as media in their ancestral homelands.

Demelza Jones's study of Tamil Hindus in the United Kingdom points out that being Hindu is closely bound with a sense of ethnolinguistic identification. Jones discusses it in relation to an informant in the field data and argues that "being Hindu was closely bound with a sense of being Tamil. Tamilness is as important as Hinduness. Tamil Hindu traditions are mostly seen as part of Tamil culture." But the informant's relocation to a town where the number of Tamil families could be "counted on two hands, meant that temples which observed this specifically Tamil mode of Hinduness were not readily available. Any attempt to negotiate this absence by worshipping within a temple run by Vaishnavite Gujaratis (majority in that small local Hindu populace) proved unsatisfactory, and even emotionally unsettling, due to that temple's divergence from the aesthetic and ritual familiarity of the Tamil temples in which she [the informant] had worshipped in northern Sri Lanka and, later, in London."[18]

Though Islam is the official religion of Malaysia, there is a significant amount of minorities such as Hindus, Christians, and Buddhists in the country, and it is considered a multiethnic and multireligious society. A study on the Hindu minority in Malaysia, particularly focusing on the deity Muneeswaran in Malaysia and Singapore, shows how popular Hinduism is thriving.[19] This study notes how Tamils from Trichy, Salem, and its surrounding areas (where the deity was famous in the late nineteenth and early twentieth centuries) carried their practices with them to the Malay region. Vineeta Sinha notes that despite the lack of proper mythical antecedents in the Hindu religious texts, the deity Muneeswaran enjoins popularity in the Malay region. In addition, the deity Murugan's temples in Malaysia are famous for rituals of self-mortification, the main feature of the body piercing acts of piety.[20] Vertovec argues that "religion acts as a preferential device in the consolidation of the Hindu diasporic identity and simultaneously as a means of transformation and re-creation. Unlike Christianity or Islam, Hinduism assumes a strong association with a national territory, in the sense that virtually all Hindus are Indians."[21] Sam George calls Hinduism an imprisoned religion because of its scriptural prohibitions against going across large expanses of water (*Kala Pani*) and that all Hindu pilgrimage sites are situated in India.[22] The sense of bonding and reverence for India, ascribed sacredness to religious locations and leaders, and so on demonstrate the significance of India's civilizational heritage in the development and consolidation of Hinduism in the diaspora.

Vasudha Narayanan pleads for academia to bring into its discourse the new representative voices of Hinduism that have hitherto been ignored or muffled in the past. This includes lower-caste Hindus, women devotees, performers, and poets—common practitioners who did not have any say for centuries. She believes that it will provide "a better appreciation for the richness and the many dimensions of the Hindu traditions and a more expanded view of religion."[23] But it will also create many new problems and power struggles within the Hindu orders in the diaspora as well as in India.

Conclusion

From the above discussion, it is evident that Hinduism is widely varied across diasporic locations around the world. It is not monolithic in any sense and shows divergent traits depending on the history and development of Hinduism in different locations. The phenomenon of Hinduism outside India is increasingly influenced by right-wing Hindutva ideas and ongoing processes of adaptation and change due to transnational interactions. Though in many circles caste awareness is generally muted, the recent surge in out-migration of lower-caste people from India to overseas locations has brought this issue to the fore. There has also been a rise in freedom of expression for Dalits, especially at an international level, bringing caste dynamics in the Hindu diaspora into greater focus.

Some suggested lenses to explore further about Hinduism in diaspora would include the role of the family in the perpetuation of religious faith and practices;[24] religious identity of the next generation;[25] temple construction and religious activities of diaspora communities;[26] remittance sent toward religious activities;[27] the role of religion in Little India in different countries; historical and theological issues related to Hindu migration;[28] religious transformation through processes of adaptation, reinterpretation, and reification; Hinduism and Hindu organizations in different countries and regions of the world; and so on.

Notes

1 Raymond Hammer, "Hinduism outside India," in *Eerdmans' Handbook to the World's Religions*, ed. R. Pierce Beaver et al. (Grand Rapids, MI: W. B. Eerdmans, 1994), 174.

2 Anantanand Rambachan, "Global Hinduism: The Hindu Diaspora," in *Contemporary Hinduism: Ritual, Culture, and Practice*, ed. Robin Rinehart (Santa Barbara, CA: ABC-CLIO, 2004), 382.

3 Richard King, "Orientalism and the Modern Myth of 'Hinduism,'" *Numen* 46, no. 2 (1999): 146.

4 The term *religion*, as some have argued, does not capture all the meanings of dharma.

5 Rambachan, "Global Hinduism," 381.

6 Brian A. Hatcher, "Contemporary Hindu Thought," in Rinehart, *Contemporary Hinduism*, 179.

7 Hatcher, 180–81.

8 Wendy Doniger, *The Hindus: An Alternative History* (New York: Penguin, 2015), 637.

9 Steven Vertovec, *The Hindu Diaspora: Comparative Patterns* (New York: Routledge, 2000), 5.

10 Steven Vertovec, "Official and Popular Hinduism in Diaspora: Historical and Contemporary Trends in Surinam, Trinidad and Guyana," *Contributions to Indian Sociology* 28, no. 1 (1994): 123–47.

11 Prema Kurien, "Constructing 'Indianness' in the United States and India: The Role of Hindu and Muslim Indians Immigrants." Report, Department of Sociology, Southern California Studies Center, University of Southern California, 1997, 1–20.

12 Rajesh Rai, "Transnational Religious-Political Movements: Negotiating Hindutva in Diaspora," in *The Politics of Religion in South and Southeast Asia*, ed. Ishtiaq Ahmed (New York: Routledge, 2011), 235.

13 Knut A. Jacobsen, "Hinduism and Globalisation: Gurus, Yoga and Migration in Northern Europe," in *Routledge Handbook of Religions in*

Asia, ed. Bryan S. Turner and Oscar Salemink (New York: Routledge, 2014), 359.

14 J. Gordon Melton, "Emerging Religious Movements in North America: Some Missiological Reflections," *Missiology* 28, no. 1 (2000): 85.

15 Patrick Eisenlohr, *Little India: Diaspora, Time, and Ethnolinguistic Belonging in Hindu Mauritius* (Berkeley: University of California Press, 2006), 35.

16 Patrick Eisenlohr, "Language and Identity in an Indian Diaspora: 'Multiculturalism' and Ethno-linguistic Communities in Mauritius," *Internationales Asienforum* 33, nos. 1–2 (2002): 110.

17 Valliammal Karunakaran, Asmita Pankaj, Thenmozhi Soundararajan, and Prathap Balakrishnan, "Spearheading a Survey of Caste in South Asian Diasporas," Medium, August 11, 2016, https://medium.com/@Bahujan_Power/pioneering-a-survey-of-caste-in-the-diasporas-6e5a27cd82ef.

18 Demelza Jones, "Being Tamil, Being Hindu: Tamil Migrants' Negotiations of the Absence of Tamil Hindu Spaces in the West Midlands and South West of England," *Religion* 46, no. 1 (2016): 55.

19 Vineeta Sinha, *A New God in the Diaspora: Muneeswaran Worship in Contemporary Singapore* (Singapore: NUS, 2005), 43.

20 Sinha, 43.

21 Vertovec, *Hindu Diaspora*, 3.

22 Sam George, "Crossing Kala Pani: Overcoming Religious Barriers to Migration," in *Diaspora Christianities*, ed. Sam George (Minneapolis: Fortress, 2018), 71.

23 Vasudha Narayan, "Diglossic Hinduism: Liberation and Lentils," *Journal of the American Academy of Religion* 68, no. 4 (2000): 776.

24 See Inês Lourenço and Rita Cachado, "Hindu Transnational Families: Transformation and Continuity in Diaspora Families," *Journal of Comparative Family Studies* 43, no. 1 (2012): 53.

25 See Sam George, *Understanding the Coconut Generation* (Niles, IL: Mall, 2005).

26 See T. S. Rukmani, *Hindu Diaspora: Global Perspective* (New Delhi: Munshiram Manoharlal, 2001).

27 See Jeffery Jacob, "Remittance Trends in South Asia," in *Diaspora Christianities*, ed. Sam George (Minneapolis: Fortress, 2018).

28 See Sam George, *Desi Diaspora* (Bangalore: SAIACS, 2019).

Bibliography

Cachado, Rita, and Inês Lourenço. "Hindu Transnational Families: Transformation and Continuity in Diaspora Families." *Journal of Comparative Family Studies* 43, no. 1 (2012): 53–70.

Doniger, Wendy. *The Hindus: An Alternative History*. New York: Penguin, 2015.

Eisenlohr, Patrick. "Language and Identity in an Indian Diaspora: 'Multiculturalism' and Ethno-linguistic Communities in Mauritius." *Internationales Asienforum* 33, nos. 1–2 (2002): 101–114.

———. *Little India: Diaspora, Time, and Ethnolinguistic Belonging in Hindu Mauritius*. Los Angeles: University of California Press, 2006.

George, Sam, ed. *Desi Diaspora: Ministry among Scattered Global Indian Christians*. Bangalore: SAIACS, 2019.

———, ed. *Diaspora Christianities: Global Scattering and Gathering of South Asian Christians*. Minneapolis: Fortress, 2018.

———. *Understanding the Coconut Generation*. Niles, IL: Mall, 2005.

Hammer, Raymond. "Hinduism outside India." In *Eerdmans' Handbook to the World's Religions*. Grand Rapids, MI: W. B. Eerdmans, 1994.

Hatcher, Brian A. "Contemporary Hindu Thought." In *Contemporary Hinduism: Ritual, Culture, and Practice*, edited by Robin Rinehart, 179–212. Santa Barbara, CA: ABC-CLIO, 2004.

Jacob, Jeffery. "Remittance Trends in South Asia." In *Diaspora Christianities*, edited by Sam George, 234–252. Minneapolis: Fortress, 2018.

Jacobsen, Knut A. "Hinduism and Globalisation: Gurus, Yoga and Migration in Northern Europe." In *Routledge Handbook of Religions in Asia*, compiled by Bryan S. Turner and Oscar Salemink, 359–372. New York: Routledge, 2014.

Jones, Demelza. "Being Tamil, Being Hindu: Tamil Migrants' Negotiations of the Absence of Tamil Hindu Spaces in the West Midlands and South West of England." *Religion* 46, no. 1 (2016): 53–74.

Karunakaran, Valliammal, Asmita Pankaj, Thenmozhi Soundararajan, and Prathap Balakrishnan. "Spearheading a Survey of Caste in South Asian Diasporas." Medium, posted August 12, 2016. https://medium.com/@Bahujan_Power/pioneering-a-survey-of -caste-in-the-diasporas-6e5a27cd82ef.

King, Richard. "Orientalism and the Modern Myth of 'Hinduism.'" *Numen* 46, no. 2 (1999): 146–185.

Kurien, Prema. "Constructing 'Indianness' in the United States and India: The Role of Hindu and Muslim Indians Immigrants." Report, Department of Sociology, Southern California Studies Center, University of Southern California, 1997, 1–20.

Melton, J. Gordon. "Emerging Religious Movements in North America: Some Missiological Reflections." *Missiology* 28, no. 1 (2000): 85–98.

Narayanan, Vasudha. "Diglossic Hinduism: Liberation and Lentils." *Journal of the American Academy of Religion* 68, no. 4 (2000): 761–779. Accessed April 10, 2019. https://www.jstor.org/stable/1465856.

Rai, Rajesh. "Transnational Religious-Political Movements: Negotiating Hindutva in Diaspora." In *The Politics of Religion in South and Southeast Asia*, edited by Ishtiaq Ahmed, 225–241. Abingdon: Routledge, 2011.

Rambachan, Anantanand. "Global Hinduism: The Hindu Diaspora." In *Contemporary Hinduism: Ritual, Culture, and Practice*, edited by Robin Rinehart, 381–414. Santa Barbara, CA: ABC-CLIO, 2004.

Rukmani, T. S. *Hindu Diaspora: Global Perspective*. New Delhi: Munshiram Manoharlal, 2001.

Sinha, Vineeta. *A New God in the Diaspora: Muneeswaran Worship in Contemporary Singapore*. Singapore: NUS, 2005.

Solomon, Robert. "Hinduism, New Movements." In *A Dictionary of Asian Christianity*, edited by Scott W. Sunquis, 335–337. Grand Rapids, MI: William B. Eerdmans, 2001.

Vertovec, Steven. *The Hindu Diaspora: Comparative Patterns*. New York: Routledge, 2000.

———. "Official and Popular Hinduism in Diaspora: Historical and Contemporary Trends in Surinam, Trinidad and Guyana." *Contributions to Indian Sociology* 28, no. 1 (1994): 123–147.

3

Transnational Family Dynamics of Overseas Filipino Workers

Gerardo B. Lisbe Jr.

Filipinos are everywhere. Filipinos are one of the most scattered peoples of the world and are popularly known as Overseas Filipino Workers (OFWs). In 2019, over twelve million OFWs lived abroad and accounted for about 10 percent of the population of the Philippines.[1] Having highly employable skills, training, and aptitude, Filipinos are greatly sought after by foreign companies. Many are well educated and proficient in English. The overseas careers are more lucrative and provide upward social mobility. OFWs are considered global citizens. They provide substantially to their home country through remittances (about $32 billion in 2019 and 10 percent of the national gross domestic product) and integrate well socially in their places of work or settlement.

The large-scale, long-distance labor out-migration from the Philippines began in the mid-1970s on account of its population growth and the lack of employment prospects in the country. The government encouraged overseas jobs in order to secure foreign currency to pay off its debt crisis.

The labor shortage in the Gulf nations after the oil boom and the growth of new Asian cities attracted many Filipinos. About one-fifth of OFWs are seafarers, as Filipinos dominate the seafaring industry and account for 25 to 30 percent of all seafarers worldwide. Another feature of OFWs is a large number of women migrants who work as domestic helpers and maids; in some years, they even outnumber men in new recruits. The leading occupation of new hires was domestic work, and most of them went to the Middle East and other economic centers of Asia.

Among other motivating factors, economic considerations are likely to be the very top reason driving Filipinos to look abroad for their livelihood. The OFWs are called the new economic heroes because of the billions of dollars they infuse into the Philippine economy every year. They provide for their family's needs, build houses, send children to good

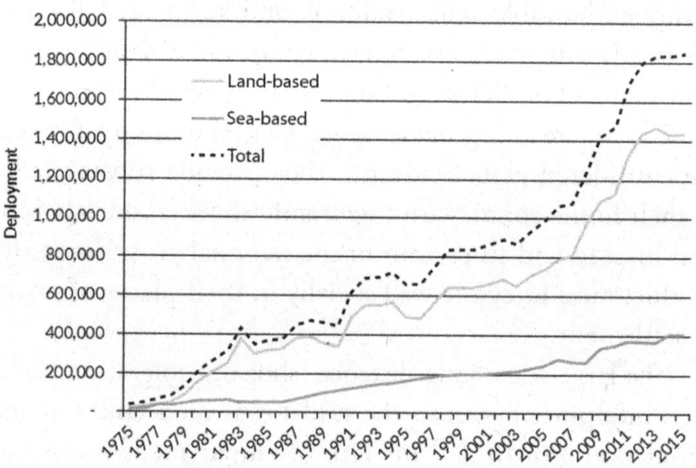

Figure 3.1. Annual deployment of Overseas Filipino Workers (OFWs), 1975–2015[2]

schools, and boost social status. Despite these positive benefits of migration of OFWs, the downside should not be overlooked. One of the unexpected consequences of the OFW phenomenon is the making of the transnational families among Filipinos, resulting in large-scale family disruptions.

Transnational families can be defined as "families that live some or most of the time separated from each other, yet hold together and create something that can be seen as a feeling of collective welfare and unity, i.e. 'familyhood,' even across national borders."[3] In transnational families, one or more members of a household live in a different country for prolonged periods. They are spread across time zones and have limited physical contact while connected virtually using modern gadgets. Affordable transportation and modern technology help them interact despite the distances that keep them separated.

Generally, Filipino families are considered closely knit, cohesive, and stable. Asian social values and Catholic heritage keep the family together and secure. But the last few decades of migration of Filipinos overseas has caused a severe strain on family relationships and intimacy. When Filipino fathers and/or mothers live for extended periods away from their children and each other, the overall family dynamics are permanently transformed. The new family form, where members are dispersed across geographical distances, results in more nuanced relational realities and constant flux daily, even when embedded within unyielding and stable household structures, and impacts all family members.[4]

This chapter explores the current state of the OFW phenomenon and analyzes in depth how transnational families try to create a sense of "familyhood" despite the distance. It presents a brief discussion of remittances and the views of Filipinos on handling finances. In the end, it offers arguments as to why churches should lovingly and missionally respond to the challenges faced by OFWs and their families using the diaspora mission as a paradigm to address this modern dilemma.

OFW Transnational Family Dynamics

The decision to work overseas is a bit easier for single Filipinos to make, but it is a much harder and more painful process for married people. For singles, it may be perceived as part of coming of age to leave home, but it is harder for their parents and siblings who are left behind, as they were tightly integrated in the past. However, thousands of fathers and mothers are forced to take up overseas employment in order to provide for their families. One OFW mother laments, "It is difficult to work abroad but the decision is more difficult when the family is left behind."[5] In several cases, young mothers have left behind their own children to work as caregivers of children of wealthy employers in the Gulf nations.

Moreover, the feminization of migration has made things much more complicated for OFW families. Scholars have examined "the unexplored consequences of globalization on the lives of women worldwide" as millions of women and mothers are moving around the globe as never before, and "this broad-scale transfer of labor associated with women's traditional roles results in an odd displacement . . . often to the detriment of the families left behind."[6] Whether a father/husband or a mother/wife leaves, migration has proven to be most damaging to those who are left behind.

Every member of an OFW family is affected by it, but in different ways. The phenomenon of transnational family (1) results in the transformation of households from a nuclear unit to transnational structures, (2) reconfigures traditional gender roles, (3) imposes the barrier of distance on marriages, and (4) affects intergenerational relations. These four principal lenses will serve as guides in this exploration of OFW transnational family dynamics.

Transformation of Households from Nuclear to Transnational Structures

Family is a foundational building block of a society. In traditional families, a married couple and their children lived together under one roof, each member acting according to the expected household roles and responsibilities. However, migration dramatically changes this notion and conventional norms undergirding it. Migration results in the breakup of families even when they are married, and physical distance transcends into emotional and relational realms. Marital oneness is threatened, and parenting styles are altered in adapting to new realities. Each member of a transnational family suffers distress arising from prolonged separation in unique ways, and separation considerably transforms interpersonal dynamics and understanding.

Reconfiguration of Traditional Gender Roles

Traditional gender roles between husband and wife have been reconfigured significantly in recent decades as women have entered the workforce. Traditionally, Filipino mothers/wives managed domestic affairs and were expected to fulfill the roles of housekeeper, cook, nursemaid, and so on. Fathers/husbands, on the other hand, specialized in livelihood and outdoor activities and were responsible for supporting the family.[7] Husbands/fathers who are working overseas still function according to the expected role as the primary breadwinner, but in a new place. However, when married women migrate abroad for employment, the traditional gender roles are dramatically reconfigured. They take on the provider role, and the left-behind husbands and fathers become "housebands"[8] taking care of children and household chores. Studies have found that this role reversal distorts men's sense of masculinity[9] and exacerbates their insecurity.[10]

The Barrier of Distance and Marital Relations

OFW transnational family dynamics impose the barrier of geographical distance on a marriage. When a husband or wife is employed abroad for prolonged periods, their marital relationship suffers, and separation is found to be detrimental due to "high emotional costs for both the mover and those left behind."[11] The separated couple may compensate through exchange of material things, frequent calls, and occasional visits, but the physical distance does take a toll over time and is deleterious to the physical, psychological, and spiritual oneness between husband and wife. Both are vulnerable to emotional and sexual infidelity. Extramarital affairs have strained relationships among many OFW families, and studies have found that marital infidelity is "a very common situation among many spouses of overseas workers."[12]

The Barrier of Distance and
Intergenerational Relations

When a father or mother lives abroad for work, parenting roles change considerably, and this trend is popularly called "long-distance parenting," "mothering by mobile," or "fathering from afar." All members of Filipino transnational families, the migrant parent and their children, suffer psychological and emotional difficulties due to the pain of separation. First of all, the decision to sacrifice family proximity to economic security affects both children and parents negatively. For a migrant parent, deciding to work abroad is not an easy decision to make, and children never fully understand the sacrifices made by their parents and never get to bond with the parent who is away. The trade-off between making a good living and the joys of happy family life is not simple, and the perspective on this choice differs in different stages of life. To secure a better future for their family and provide for better material comforts and educational opportunities for children, migrant parents end up sacrificing physical and emotional separation.[13] Second, migrant parents feel anxious and guilty for leaving their families behind. Studies have found that the priority of migrant Filipinos is their family back home, and this psychological burden that they carry every day creates considerable stress and strain.[14]

Another emotional and psychological effect on children is the sense of insecurity when parents are far away. On interviewing OFW children, Rachel Parrenas noted that children admitted feelings of insecurity, not knowing when they would see their parents again.[15] Migrant parents leave to provide financial security for their children in both the present and the future, yet by doing so, they leave their children to suffer psychologically. The children think their parents have abandoned them and experience a deprivation of parental love. The parents agonize that they are missing important stages in their children's lives and feel estranged from their own family. When these issues are left unaddressed and unresolved, they are likely to create greater emotional and relational problems in the future. Research has found that the longer a father is away from home, the more his bond with his children is weakened.[16]

When women migrate, it is harder for families, and they undergo many changes. Studies have found that the absence of a mother is "the most disruptive in the life of the children."[17] Children without mothers have more problems compared to other children. Seldom do the left-behind husbands become full-time caregivers to their children or do well in domestic roles, and migrant mothers suffer through the guilt of neglecting mothering duties and worry about their families. The role reversal is disruptive and most consequential to young children, as they do not see a healthy or stable family pattern. An offshoot of the feminization of migration is the issue of caretakers, as other relatives step in for the material welfare of the children of migrant mothers.

Technologies such as the internet and mobile phones are making possible an empowered experience of long-distance mothering.[18] Many mothers see the availability of the latest communication tools to have come to the aid of transnational migrant families in staying connected and carrying out their traditional roles in new ways.[19] It is possible to keep in touch with family, which creates a stronger sense of a shared social field, though virtual. The feeling of distance has diminished with frequent and repeated interactions between transnational families. Sometimes such regular communication without physical presence intensifies relational problems and ends in long-distance quarrels.[20] These families will continue to use all available modern gadgets to create some semblance of intimacy and a sense of familyhood, yet it is not the same as being there in person.

Remittances and Transnational Families

The primary motivation of migrants living transnationally is financial security. Such families are spread across time zones for the sake of boosting living standards and upward social mobility. Remittances are used to pay for durable goods, household improvements, children's education, and medical care. Unfortunately, many left-behind family members of migrants unwisely use the hard-earned money sent to them. The migrant parents spend their earnings on everyday expenses and not in income-generating ways. Many Filipino transnational families do not have substantial savings and are unable to pay the huge debts they incurred before and after migration, and many are forced to stay abroad because they cannot afford to return home or maintain a desired lifestyle by working locally. In the long run, relationships will suffer progressively and disintegrate unless these dysfunctions of Filipino transnational families are minimized.

A Christian Response to Transnational Families

It's not just the Philippine government that should be concerned about the plight of OFW transnational families;

Christian organizations should do something about this growing crisis and complex reality. What can churches do to preserve the health of all families and OFW transnational families in particular? How can churches and faith communities both at home and in destination countries come alongside to alleviate the struggles faced by and support OFW families? What are some of the biblical, ecclesiastical, missiological, and practical implications of the OFW phenomenon?[21]

Here are eight reasons the church should respond to the needs and challenges faced by OFW transnational families. First, God's design is for children to be born and raised by parents and families. Because God values families, Christians must also value families. When something threatens the stability of families in the congregation, churches must respond by helping to eliminate the threat or minimize its effects. The OFW phenomenon has deleterious effects on families in general, and churches need to prayerfully and wisely help OFWs and their families in order to lessen the harmful effects of the dysfunctions arising out of such family arrangements and totally eradicate those effects when possible.

Second, the consequences of sin affected not just the first couple but also their children and all generations until today. Each member of every family, including OFWs, is tainted with sin. In the case of OFWs, not everything about migration is necessarily sinful or caused by sins. But some sins have exacerbated the problems faced by migrant families. The sins that aggravate OFW family dysfunctions include marital infidelity, lack of financial stewardship, lack of love, laziness, pride, lack of concern for the welfare of others, selfishness, and so on. A ministry to and for OFW transnational families should be mindful of these spiritual problems so that they can address them appropriately and present sound biblical solutions.

Third, Filipino transnational families need to hear the gospel of salvation so that they too will have an opportunity to respond to Christ. The greatest problem that OFW families face is not financial or material but spiritual. They need to recognize that they are sinners and in need of God's mercy and grace to be saved. They must put their trust in Jesus as their Lord and Savior so that they too can partake of all the promises God has made for those who accept and believe in Christ. As the bearer of the gospel message, the church is God's hands and feet to reach out and minister to OFW transnational families. The ministry of the church can help Christian OFWs and their families overcome their sinful behaviors and the difficulties brought about by migration. This requires churches to reach out to and disciples OFWs and their families.

Fourth, God's spiritual family, the church, must strengthen families. As a community of faith, the church must strive to strengthen families, including OFW transnational families. One of the responsibilities of the members of the family is to relate to one another in a way that builds each other up and pleases the Lord. The disruptive effects of migration on husband-wife relationships, parent-child relationships, and overall family dynamics require churches to pay special attention to OFWs and their families. These families must be strengthened so that they can also contribute positively to the health of the entire congregation. If their condition remains the same and the church does not help them overcome their issues in life and family, then they can affect the numerical, emotional, and spiritual growth of the church in destructive ways.

Fifth, church leaders have an obligation to take care of God's flock. The responsibility of church leaders is to oversee and care for the needs of a congregation, and this shepherding role involves protecting, leading, guiding, feeding, and so on. As undershepherds, these leaders will be held accountable to the Chief Shepherd for how they oversee and care for the flock entrusted to them. And the Lord also expects them to do this willingly, eagerly, and without any compulsion. OFW families need someone, especially church leaders, to care for them, to lead and guide them as they make decisions, and to feed them God's word so that they will grow spiritually and will be able to make godly and wise choices in life. They need leaders who will eagerly and willingly minister to them and not those who are only after their money or material resources. They need pastors who can shepherd lovingly and intervene in the lives of troubled members of the congregation and not wait for these troubled members to come forward.

Sixth, as a faith community, the church must love and care for one another. The church's role in strengthening OFW transnational families is the scriptural command to carry each other's burdens. There are many people in the church, particularly OFWs or their families, who carry tremendous physical, emotional, and spiritual burdens. We cannot just watch them from a distance without getting involved in their lives. If we truly care for them, we must be involved. The local churches are ideally placed to care for their families and create a sense of mutuality within the community of believers. As members of God's family, we belong to each other, we are to carry each other's burdens, and we are obligated to love one another as a society of mutual love and service. John Baxter is right in his assertion that "the local church has the relational resources to adequately care for OFWs and their families."[22]

Seventh, the church must affirm parents' responsibility to provide for the needs of the family. The needs of the family involve not just the financial or material but also the emotional, psychological, and spiritual. A father who cannot find work locally will consider finding a job somewhere else, which may involve leaving his family behind so that he will be able to provide for his family's needs. A responsible family man will always find a way, even if it requires sacrifices on his part to ensure that his family is taken care of and their needs are met. Families must develop contentment to live with what they have rather than comparing themselves with other OFW neighbors.

Lastly, Christian OFWs can live out the Great Commandment and the Great Commission wherever they are. Many of these OFW Christ followers live and work among unreached people groups, among either the host population or fellow employees. When these Christian overseas foreign workers are trained for evangelism and church planting opportunities, the potential for diaspora missions is vast.[23] The churches that see this potential for diaspora missions will find appropriate ways to care for the flock, which includes OFW transnational families, so that they can do both—sending of diaspora workers and caring for the remnants.[24] This is a blessing to the OFWs so that they can become a blessing to the nations.[25] The churches that value God, families, and world missions will intentionally find practical ways to respond to the plight of Filipino transnational families as part of fulfilling both the Great Commandment and the Great Commission in the form of mission to and through dispersed Filipinos for a greater kingdom purpose.

Notes

1 All data are based on publications of the United Nations International Organization of Migration, *World Migration Report 2020* (Geneva: IOM, 2019), https://publications.iom.int/books/world-migration-report-2020; and the Philippines Overseas Employment Administration (POEA), "OFW Statistics," accessed December 4, 2019, http://www.poea.gov.ph/ofwstat/ofwstat.html.

2 Maruja M. B. Asis, "The Philippines: Beyond Labor Migration, toward Development and (Possibly) Return," accessed June 15, 2020, https://www.migrationpolicy.org/article/philippines-beyond-labor-migration-toward-development-and-possibly-return.

3 Deborah Bryceson and Ulla Vuorela, *The Transnational Family: New European Frontiers and Global Networks* (Oxford: Berg, 2002), 3.

4 Zlatko Skrbiš, "Transnational Families: Theorising Migration, Emotions and Belonging," *Journal of Intercultural Studies* 29, no. 3 (2008): 231.

5 Jazer Basan, "Working Abroad: The Joys and Challenges," *Smart Parenting*, February 26, 2011, https://www.smartparenting.com.ph/parenting/real-parenting/working-abroad-the-joys-and-challenges.

6 Barbara Ehrenreich and Arlie Hochschild, eds., *Global Woman: Nannies, Maids, and Sex Workers in the New Economy* (New York: Owl Books, 2004).

7 Belen T. G. Medina, *The Filipino Family* (Quezon City: University of the Philippines Press, 2001), 140.

8 Maruja Milagros B. Asis, Shirlena Huang, and Brenda S. A. Yeoh, "When the Light of the Home Is Abroad: Unskilled Female Migration and the Filipino Family," *Singapore Journal of Tropical Geography* 25, no. 2 (2004): 206.

9 Alicia Tadeo Pingol, *Remaking Masculinities: Identity, Power, and Gender Dynamics in Families with Migrant Wives and Househusbands* (Quezon City: University Center for Women's Studies, 2001), 33.

10 Phillip Gresham, "Heroes at Home? Disputing Popular Images of Non-migrating Husbands of Overseas Filipina Workers" (master's thesis, Radbourd University Nijmegen, 2011), 79.

11 Human Development Report 2009, *Overcoming Barriers: Human Mobility and Development* (New York: United Nations Development Programme, 2009), 72.

12 Francis Santamaria, "Problems Regarding Family Relations and Children of Migrant Workers," in *Filipino Women Overseas Contract Workers: At What Cost?*, ed. Mary Ruby Palma-Beltran and Aurora Javate De Dios (Quezon City: JMC, 1992), 71. See also Estrella Dizon-Aonuevo and Augustus T. Aonuevo, *Coming Home: Women, Migration, and Reintegration* (Manila: Balikkabayani Foundation, 2002), 63. Their survey revealed that "six out of 10 [left-behind] husbands had an extramarital affair while their wives were away."

13 Elspeth Graham and Lucy P. Jordan, "Migrant Parents and the Psychological Well-Being of Left-Behind Children in Southeast Asia," *Journal of Marriage and Family* 73, no. 4 (2011): 764. Also see Jorgen Carling, Cecilia Menjivar, and Leah Schmalzbauer, "Central Themes in the Study of Transnational Parenthood," *Journal of Ethnic and Migration Studies* 38, no. 2 (2012): 191–217.

14 Yuko Ohara-Hirano, "Cognitive Life Strains and Family Relationships of Filipino Migrant Workers in Japan," *Asian and Pacific Migration Journal* 9, no. 3 (2000): 372.

15 Rachel S. Parrenas, *Servants of Globalization: Women, Migration, and Domestic Work* (Quezon City: Ateneo de Manila, 2003), 135.

16 Parrenas, 149.

17 Graziano Battistella and Cecilia G. Conaco, "The Impact of Labour Migration on the Children Left Behind: A Study of Schoolchildren in the Philippines," *Sojourn: Journal of Social Issues in Southeast Asia* 13, no. 2 (1998): 237.

18 Mirca Madianou, "Migration and the Accentuated Ambivalence of Motherhood: The Role of ICTs in Filipino Transnational Families," *Global Networks* 12, no. 3 (July 2012): 277.

19 Cecilia Uy-Tioco, "Overseas Filipino Workers and Text Messaging: Reinventing Transnational Mothering," *Continuum* 21, no. 2 (2007): 253.

20 Raelene Wilding, "'Virtual' Intimacies: Families Communicating across Transnational Contexts," *Global Networks* 6, no. 2 (2006): 138–39.

21 Gerardo B. Lisbe Jr., "Church-Based OFW Family Care Ministry: An Ethnographic Study on the Structure and Activities That Filipinos Create That Significantly Reduce OFW Family Dysfunction" (DMin diss., International Theological Seminary, Los Angeles, CA, 2014), 40–52.

22 John Baxter, "The Local Church in Diaspora Missions," *Journal of Asian Mission* 11, nos. 1–2 (2009): 118.

23 Such training materials include Robert Clark's *A Higher Purpose for Your Overseas Jobs* and Joy Solina and Jojo Manzano's *Worker to Witness: Becoming an OFW Tentmaker*, both from Church Strengthening Ministry.

24 See Gerardo Lisbe Jr., "Taking Care of the Flock: A Case Study of the Role of the Local Church in Sending and Caring for Overseas Filipino Workers," in *Scattered and Gathered*, ed. Sadiri Joy Tira and Tetsunao Yamamori (Oxford: Regnum Books International, 2016), 506–12.

25 Ana Gamez, *Blessing OFWs to Bless the Nations* (Makati City: Church Strengthening Ministry, 2012).

Bibliography

Aonuevo, Estrella Dizon, and Augustus T. Aonuevo. *Coming Home: Women, Migration, and Reintegration.* Manila: Balikkabayani Foundation, 2002.

Asis, Maruja, Shirlena Huang, and Brenda S. A. Yeoh. "When the Light of the Home Is Abroad: Unskilled Female Migration and the Filipino Family." *Singapore Journal of Tropical Geography* 25, no. 2 (2004): 198–215.

Baxter, John. "The Local Church in Diaspora Missions." *Journal of Asian Mission* 11, nos. 1–2 (2009): 113–119.

Carandang, Maria Lourdes. *Filipino Children under Stress: Family Dynamics and Therapy*. Manila: Ateneo De Manila University, 2001.

Carling, Jorgen, Cecilia Menjivar, and Leah Schmalzbauer. "Central Themes in the Study of Transnational Parenthood." *Journal of Ethnic and Migration Studies* 38, no. 2 (2012): 191–217.

Ehrenreich, Barbara, and Arlie Hochschild, eds. *Global Woman: Nannies, Maids, and Sex Workers in the New Economy*. New York: Owl Books, 2004.

Gamez, Ana. *Blessing OFWs to Bless the Nations*. Makati City: Church Strengthening Ministry, 2012.

Graham, Elspeth, and Lucy P. Jordan. "Migrant Parents and the Psychological Well-Being of Left-Behind Children in Southeast Asia." *Journal of Marriage and Family* 73, no. 4 (August 2011): 763–787.

Gresham, Phillip. "Heroes at Home? Disputing Popular Images of Non-migrating Husbands of Overseas Filipina Workers." Master's thesis, Radboud University Nijmegen, 2011.

Lisbe, Gerardo B., Jr. "Church-Based OFW Family Care Ministry: An Ethnographic Study on the Structure and Activities That Filipinos Create That Significantly Reduce OFW Family Dysfunction." DMin diss., International Theological Seminary, Los Angeles, CA, 2014.

———. "Taking Care of the Flock: A Case Study of the Role of the Local Church in Sending and Caring for Overseas Filipino Workers." In *Scattered and Gathered: A Global Compendium* of *Diaspora Missiology*, 2nd ed. Edited by Sadiri Joy Tira and Tetsunao Yamamori, 597–606. London: Langham, 2020.

Madianou, Mirca. "Migration and the Accentuated Ambivalence of Motherhood: The Role of ICTs in Filipino Transnational Families." *Global Networks* 12, no. 3 (July 2012): 277–295.

Medina, Belen T. G. *The Filipino Family*. Quezon City: University of the Philippines Press, 2001.

Ohara-Hirano, Yuko. "Cognitive Life Strains and Family Relationships of Filipino Migrant Workers in Japan." *Asian and Pacific Migration Journal* 9, no. 3 (2000): 365–374.

Parrenas, Rachel S. *Children of Global Migration: Transnational Families and Gendered Woes*. Stanford, CA: Stanford University Press, 2005.

———. *Servants of Globalization: Women, Migration, and Domestic Work*. Quezon City: Ateneo de Manila Press, 2003.

Pingol, Alicia Tadeo. *Remaking Masculinities: Identity, Power, and Gender Dynamics in Families with Migrant Wives and Househusbands*. Quezon City: University Center for Women's Studies, 2001.

Santamaria, Francis. "Problems Regarding Family Relations and Children of Migrant Workers." In *Filipino Women Overseas Contract Workers: At What Cost?* edited by Mary Ruby Palma-Beltran and Aurora Javate De Dios, 69–78. Quezon City: JMC, 1992.

Skrbiš, Zlatko. "Transnational Families: Theorising Migration, Emotions and Belonging." *Journal of Intercultural Studies* 29, no. 3 (2008): 231–246.

Uy-Tioco, Cecilia. "Overseas Filipino Workers and Text Messaging: Reinventing Transnational Mothering." *Continuum* 21, no. 2 (2007): 253–265.

Wilding, Raelene. "'Virtual' Intimacies: Families Communicating across Transnational Contexts." *Global Networks* 6, no. 2 (2006): 125–142.

4

Kerala Nurses in Britain

Race, Gender, and Transnational Migration

Christy John Jacob

Research on migration out of India has largely focused on men who go abroad for work and the remittance they send to their families back home.[1] Much of the writings on Indian and South Asian Christian diasporas have emerged from the context of North America and less on the United Kingdom and Europe, primarily on account of the smaller migrant population and less scholarly work done on these communities, as most are working-class professionals.[2] Some researchers have studied women who are left behind as their husbands migrate in search of work, and others have probed Anglophone women writers of Indian origin.[3] However, most gender studies in migration have focused on trafficking, discrimination, and exploitation of unskilled or semiskilled workers and have omitted educated and professional women. Lately, some have paid some attention to Indian women who go abroad for work and on women-led migration from Kerala (India) to the

United States.[4] Yet little research has been carried out on the sociological and gender dimensions of Kerala nurses in the United Kingdom and the resulting socioeconomic, cultural, and religious ramifications, which this essay hopes to address to some extent.

Indian Women and Migration

After marriage, most Indian women are required to move out of the native homes of their parents and into their marital homes per patrilineal and patrilocal customs of traditional Indian society. According to ancient Indian civilizational laws, the householder stage of life requires women to move from their place of birth and upbringing with their parents and siblings to the house of their husband and become an integral part of it. It is a vital rite of passage for young women in India that once was linked to marriage and moves them from a parental to a conjugal home. However, with the increased emphasis on education for girls, an opportunity to work outside of the home, and better marriage prospects, the earliest departure from home for many young women now occurs as they leave for nearby cities or other states of India to pursue studies or when they find employment. The modern Western ideas of women's empowerment, feminism, and economic autonomy for women who have grown up in liberalized socioeconomic settings have raised the aspirations and ethos of a new generation of women in India.

Today, many women pursue education beyond secondary schooling in India, as it has become more accessible and affordable and allows women to secure lucrative job opportunities. In addition, they are willing to migrate to any corner of the globe. In most cities of India, it is common to find young women from rural places and other towns living with friends while pursuing college or professional education. To move to another city or nation for subsequent study or work becomes easier thereafter. Highly sought-after marriage alliances from abroad are another reason for the foreign migration of Indian women. Many new patterns and greater diversity have emerged in the labor market as employers have sought women's participation in the workforce. The presence of females is central to this process of diversification, and a record number of women are migrating abroad as health care workers, teachers, software programmers, service industry employees, and paid domestic workers.[5] Such a progressive outlook has enabled millions of Indian women to become financially independent and break free of the age-old customs and dependence on men, producing many dramatic transformations in household structures, family finances, interpersonal gender dynamics, sociocultural values, hierarchy, lifestyle options, and so on.

This chapter about the migration of women in search of work and a better standard of living focuses on Malayali[6] women nurses from the state of Kerala who have migrated to the United Kingdom to work in the hospitals of the National Health Service (NHS) and other health care companies. This is a fascinating tale of young Kerala women with training from nursing colleges in India who were from Christian backgrounds and pursued a dream to work in the foreign lands of their past colonial masters while seeking upward mobility. They nursed and cared for foreigners while their own elderly parents who sacrificed much for their education were left behind at the mercy of others or had to fend for themselves in their old age. This chapter primarily employs qualitative methods such as participant observation, interviews, and informal surveys on Kerala nurses and their families in the cities of Liverpool and Manchester in the United Kingdom over two years in 2018 and 2019.

Nursing in Kerala

Kerala is a southwestern state of India with the highest literacy rate in the nation and a very high migration rate. It also has the distinction of having an unbroken historic Christian presence since the arrival of the apostle Thomas in the first century and a relatively superior health care infrastructure. The development of schooling and encouragement for young women to pursue education and professional training in health-related fields could be attributed to Christianity and colonial connections. English missionaries opened schools and hospitals in Kerala and elsewhere in India, and these socioreligious institutions aggressively recruited young women to train and work in the hospitals by positioning nursing as a noble Christian service. The Christian worldview was not as biased against female infants, and they did not get aborted. Instead, the girls were encouraged to go to school to learn and work. Soon, education became a greater differentiator than caste and a way to gain socioeconomic upward mobility. It drove women to explore rewarding careers not limited by traditional gender-based roles and early marriage. Kerala women, in particular, sought careers in cities of India and later in other parts of the world. Christian communities were relatively more open to allowing women to work outside of the home, though nursing was deemed a low-status profession. Scholars have found a disproportionate share of Christians among the Kerala emigrants and particularly in the health care industries from the late 1960s through 2000 in the United States,[7] and the same could be said of Kerala immigrants to the United Kingdom.

Kerala is a land of nurses, as this profession remains among the top options among girls completing higher secondary schooling because of its affordability among middle- and low-income families, the potential to migrate overseas, and the economic security it provides. Nursing remains much in demand in Kerala because of the social status and prestige it brings, which is a more recent development. The Indian Nursing Council, a national regulatory body for nurses in India, reports that there are 2.1 million registered nurses and 879,508 auxiliary nurse midwives in India.[8] Kerala has a relatively large capacity to produce health workers, with 20 auxiliary nursing and midwifery training institutes (9 public), 204 general nursing and midwifery training institutes (16 public), 133 BS nursing institutes (8 public), 68 institutes offering MS degrees (6 public), 51 institutes offering postbasic BS degrees (6 public), and 36 institutes offering postbasic diplomas in nursing (11 public). The total intake capacity is 17,600 seats annually. Kerala students pursue nursing education in neighboring states like Tamil Nadu, Karnataka, Andhra Pradesh, Telangana, Puducherry, and other major cities of India, such as Mumbai, New Delhi, Kolkata, Pune, Bhopal, Baroda, Chandigarh, and so on. It is estimated that over 38 percent of nurses who studied in Kerala work in the United States, 30 percent in the United Kingdom, 12 percent in Australia, and 12 percent in the Middle East.[9]

Migration of Health Care Workers
from Kerala to the United Kingdom

Some amusingly claim that in any part of the world, if there is a hospital, you will likely see a nurse from Kerala. Around six thousand Kerala nurses went to work in Germany in the 1960s to meet shortages of health workers. After World War II, Germany needed trained nurses and requested the help of various churches in Kerala. The documentary film *Translated Lives* captures the tale of the migration of Malayali women to Germany and narrates the stories of a group of young Kerala women, some only in their midteens, who were trained in Germany as nurses. Draped in saris and with no training apart from saying "good morning" and "good night" in German, they landed in snowy Germany, which one nurse recalls as "cotton falling from the sky."[10] There are significant pools of Kerala nurses in Italy, Portugal, Belgium, France, the Netherlands, Switzerland, Spain, and other Scandinavian countries.

The migration of a skilled workforce from India, particularly doctors and nurses, began in the 1950s to the United Kingdom and European countries, then in the mid-1960s onward to the United States and Canada, and then after the oil boom in the 1970s to the Gulf. The trend continues with thousands of girls, predominantly from Kerala, joining nursing schools all over India with the intention to migrate overseas. They exchange skills, knowledge, and caring attitudes for better wages, living standards, and status in foreign countries, since the core skills of nurses in providing care are transferable to most parts of the world, especially the Western world, with advanced health care, and preferably in English-speaking nations. The United States,

Canada, United Kingdom, and Australia are the preferred destinations, as they can buy homes and retire in these countries, which is not possible in the Persian Gulf countries.[11] Many use Gulf nursing jobs as stepping-stones to reach the United Kingdom or other Western nations. Many hospitals and nursing homes in the United Kingdom are a Kerala microcosm.

The antecedents of migration for Kerala nurses to the United Kingdom include the historical legacy of the British Empire and long-standing trading links between Kerala and the Gulf.[12] British missionaries tried to redefine and professionalize nursing as a "respectable" vocational career. The mission hospitals established nursing schools and recruited poor women or widows from Christian communities in Kerala. The missionary nursing schools appointed Kerala nurses to senior positions due to their faith, English language skills, and work ethic. Early migration of nurses from Kerala was often facilitated by missionary networks, but it was not an organized movement in any way. The history of the NHS in the United Kingdom is closely associated with migration. The NHS began in 1948 to provide health care to the nation and from its outset suffered an acute shortage of staff. The deficit was handled by "importing" nurses, doctors, and medical professionals from abroad. The government launched recruitment campaigns in 1949 and brought thousands of nurses to Britain who were dispersed to hospitals all over the United Kingdom. The government targeted young women looking for a new life and opportunities, and they came from different parts of the erstwhile British Empire, including India. The Nationality Act of 1948 granted British citizenship to people from the Commonwealth, which boosted the influx of immigrants: more than eighteen thousand arrived in the United Kingdom. Today, India is the second biggest exporter of health care workers to the United Kingdom after the Philippines, and around thirty-eight thousand health workers migrated from Kerala alone in 2014 according to the Kerala Migration Survey.[13]

Sociology of Migration: A Nursing Perspective

As an Indian Christian minister's wife, I had the opportunity to interact with health workers in England, and my advanced training and research in sociology helped me analyze this migrant community closely. The decision to move is complex and is influenced by and in turn affects multiple spheres of the migrant's life. Most of the families in the northwest of England, Scotland, and Wales migrated from the Gulf after 2000. The reasons they mention include better salary, working conditions, access to superior health care technologies, job security, and greater opportunities for the family. However, becoming a nurse in Britain is not an easy task—the application process is long and arduous, requiring a lot of paperwork. Only qualified nurses with a nursing degree and at least a year of experience are wanted. They need to prove their English language skills by taking either IELTS (International English Language Testing System) or OET (Occupation English Test). Upon registering with the Nursing and Midwifery Council, they take a four-hour-long computer-based test, and after they pass the test and all documents are submitted, nurses have to wait for a decision letter to apply for a work visa in the United Kingdom.

Nurse migration is pushed, pulled, and shaped by a series of social forces. Nurses usually cite economic reasons as the main basis for migration to Britain. Yet this doesn't entirely explain the decision to move, as most of them had lucrative jobs in the Gulf already. Professional motives are a strong incentive behind their decision to migrate, like access to continuing education and relatively higher health care standards. The working conditions are better, as many nurses voiced happiness over the nonhierarchical working style, the critical thinking of treatment practices, and the respect of colleagues. Overtime payments and late-night working incentives were significant and attractive. The long-term job security, the flexibility of working hours, and the possibility of working fewer hours through the week were attractive to the nurses. Though the persistent winter cold weather conditions were initially hard for these nurses to surmount, they managed to settle well and network with other Indian nurses.

The root of British racism is heavily linked to its relationship with subjects of a former colony. Kerala nurses have seen racism at workplaces from their white patients and colleagues. Some informed me that their homes were stoned with bricks, and they feared the security of their small children. Others who were residing in the United Kingdom as refugees were called "Paki" (people from Pakistan). Many changed hospitals and looked for jobs with ethnic diversity. They believed that discrimination came from ignorance, so Malayali nurses tried to assimilate in order to be accepted as British Asians. Most became British citizens within five years of their arrival.

The relationship between economic change and family change is one of the most studied issues in social sciences. Scholars like Marx have commented on the transformation brought about by changes in the mode of production, especially by shifting to the capitalist order. The impact of the Western Industrial Revolution resulted in the biggest alteration in gender roles with the "shift of the locus of work from the home to somewhere else."[14] The desire to settle and stability outweighed career considerations for female workers. The Kerala nurses could settle permanently with their family, buy a house, and benefit from the public schooling system, free health care to all UK citizens, and plenty of social support for families in need.

Family support in the countries of origin and destination are important elements that are conducive to and supportive of migration. Keeping families together often meant the husband had to leave his employment in India or the Gulf and look for a new job in the United Kingdom. The husbands of nurses often did not find jobs commensurate with their education or past employment, leading to lifelong regrets and confusion. They ended up working in supermarkets or as manual workers in factories with basic wages. Nurses became the primary breadwinners and managed household finances. Since they arrived alone at first, they developed a level of independence, but when the family joined later, these behaviors became disruptive to the family. The division of household labor differed considerably from the norms in India. As they were no longer the primary breadwinners, the nurse's husbands did not have much say in household matters. As they did not want to leave their children in India or outside care or after-school programs because of expenses, men were forced to provide childcare. They experienced a role reversal similar to that of a homemaker, including cooking and child-rearing. This emasculation and the "loss of patriarchal power" cause status demotion and a psychological crisis of identity.[15] An opportunity to migrate and economic upward mobility intersect with a reconfiguration of gender by "undoing" the patriarchal norms.

Men and women alike participate in the long-term goal of familial progress, but working women sense a primary duty to ensure the well-being of their children. Thus many professionally employed migrant women focus not on career advancement and satisfaction but on the future of their children. Most Kerala nurses wanted their children to become medical doctors and even sent their wards to European Union countries to study medicine if they failed to get through the universities in the United Kingdom. Many nurses during the transition period of relocation encouraged their husbands to study through Open University or take civil service exams. This is due to internal competition among nurses to settle their husbands well. Some sponsored their husbands to nursing schools to become registered nurses or paramedics. Others worked in the NHS with their wives as health workers, carers, administrators, and kitchen staff or established their own small businesses as solicitors, real estate agents, or even travel agents to recruit foreign nurses on behalf of the NHS. Working in shifts and for long hours at a stretch provided flexibility and a way to balance the home front. Some wives preferred three- or four-night shift duty on weekends to allow husbands to have a regular weekday schedule. The nurse households were stable economically and had a better lifestyle, but their family life was troublesome.

Another major concern for these nurses was their health, as most of them had undergone either chemo, radiation, or surgery. Nurses preferred to do night shifts, as it helped them with childcare and guaranteed additional income. But night shift work is associated with an increased risk of cancer and complicated relational dynamics. Their newly adopted lifestyle, eating habits, and climatic conditions took a toll on their health. Nurses confessed changes in their diet and ways of cooking. Even though Indian cuisine ingredients were available in the market, neighbors would show discomfort over the smell of Indian cooking. At times, some regretted their decision to migrate to Britain and were concerned about their aged parents back in India. Some male migrants went back to Kerala at regular intervals to look after their ailing parents and relatives.

Moreover, the nursing profession is generally perceived as "dirty work," and nursing is associated with sexual transgressions. The work of nurses includes taking care of patients, requiring physical contact with men, close interaction with male doctors, working on night shifts, and so on, all of which raise the suspicion that nurses are morally loose. Per Indian religious beliefs, the nursing job is considered polluting on account of contact with blood and other bodily secretions. Any physical contact with men other than one's husband is seen as undermining the marital union. The Kerala nurses were eager to migrate overseas to escape such archaic sociocultural and religious taboos and to reclaim respectability elsewhere. They sent money home to family members and chose flashy lifestyles to prove their professional success and wealth. They were quick to sponsor family members to their adopted countries and support them regularly through remittances to buy their favor in an attempt to deflect degrading opinions of their profession.

Finding Solace in the Church

Religion has always been entwined with migration, identity, and the cultures of diaspora communities.[16] Religions spread because of the desire of a few devoted people to take their beliefs and practices to distant cities and other countries. Faith is a vital element to nurses in the United Kingdom, helping them deal with the hardships of migration and shaping values across places by offering a stable framework that connects the different parts of one's life. The Kerala nurses relied heavily upon a benevolent God who could eventually help them make the most of the prospects for themselves and their children. Christian families were less affected by stigma surrounding the nursing profession, and it explains why this profession and its migration are dominated by Christians. The migration of nurses from Kerala to Europe is embedded in the network of the Catholic Church, as it provided some sense of legitimacy and support for migration.[17] At the same time, some Kerala Christians do not want to credit nurses and their husbands in pioneering the Malayalam (the language of Kerala) congregations in their places of settlements because they lack the social status to undertake such religious tasks. However, as most of the nurses who migrated were Christians and their families were able to join them, they felt a need to establish their own places of worship even though they could have participated in local English churches.

These churches began as home-based prayer groups that spoke the same language but belonged to different denominations. Later, when any Kerala church group reached a critical size, they split to establish their distinctive denominational congregations.[18] Today, these Kerala churches in the United Kingdom are flourishing by providing spiritual nourishment to members and being involved in various ministries. Religion is the most common and acceptable basis of community formation and expression for immigrants. These congregations are built in a new setting to reproduce what has been left behind in their ancestral homeland even as they adapt to a new environment and the needs of the next generation. The worship is usually in Malayalam, and it is followed by meals, giving members enough time to socialize, which makes migrants feel less alien. The members gather not only for spiritual fellowship but also to show-case their status and prestige. Since the churches preserve traditional gender norms, they help the husbands of nurses claim their place in the community, develop a sense of belonging, and assert their importance, as identities are associated with church positions. These men seek out active participation and church leadership to counterbalance losses they have experienced in other spheres, and this is one of the underlying causes of much of the politicking in Kerala churches in foreign lands that are associated with the women-led migration of nurses.

In diasporic locations, the church becomes an "extended family" where kids roam freely, adults can gossip in their native language, and a feeling of togetherness is created. At the time of death or illness (even of kin in Kerala), church members provide a network of support by gathering at the home of the bereaved or the sick and offering spiri-tual consolation or material aid. Many prefer to be buried in Kerala beside their parents and siblings. The religious ritual is another significant reason for a migrant's deliberate exchange of economic capital, and Kerala nurse families actively participated in the process of commoditization of ritual practices. The local festivals and feasts are elaborated with food and a display of monetary power. Events like harvest festivals, feasts of saints, cultural festivals, ecclesial gatherings, youth fest, choir fest, Sunday school anniversa-ries, or ladies fellowship/conferences are all glamorous and filled with pomp, and these meetings are followed by *sadya* (a

Kerala-style meal). Even though they have accepted so many parts of their identity as English, the church is the place where they are truly Indian. The churches are like the jars of mango pickle on every dining table of a Kerala immigrant.

The sociology of religion states that religious institutions have played an important role in immigrant adaptation by facilitating the creation of community, the construction of ethnic identity, and the transmission of homeland culture and values to children.[19] Migrants lean on religious institutions for a sense of belonging and achieve social recognition when they face racial discrimination at work. They are not accepted as equals by white English society, and at the same time, they fear losing their Indian culture and values. Being unable to succeed themselves, they set their aspirations on their children. There are two kinds of second-generation Asian Britishers—the first category are those who came to the United Kingdom in their preteens along with their parents from the Gulf and are well versed in their ancestral language, and the second are those who were born or arrived in the United Kingdom as toddlers, who have very limited proficiency in their mother tongue.

The second generation is given the task to both achieve a high social and economic status in British society and remain Indian at the same time. In church activities and associations, special attention is given to the second generation. For the latter generation, Bollywood dances are part of the Indian culture and are performed almost everywhere, even for Christmas and Easter get-togethers. The paths that the second and third generations pursue are influenced by the framework provided by white British society and their Indian parents. They have to counter racism and othering while dealing with the values and norms shown by their

Indian parents. For this generation, *Kerala* and *India* are synonymous, as these terms are used interchangeably. They feel at home in Britain, hardly experience the crude racism their parents faced, and have friends from the white majority. Second-generation British Asians have small associations called *Vajaram* and *Kilukum* at the university level, which bring together students from different parts of the United Kingdom to share their experiences and the troubles faced by ethnic minorities. They host paid events to promote and showcase talent, with profits going to charity locally or in India. They are popular, and students dress as Malayalis and enjoy Kerala cuisines.

The raising of children in foreign cultures, along with the demands of establishing careers, becomes extremely challenging as the "coconut generation" assimilate into British Western culture.[20] The church plays a major role as a means by which migrants transmit culture and values to their children. The Britain-born and -raised generation stay away from traditions of the church that they find to be meaningless. Sunday school classes are made necessary and interactive to nurture children in the Christian faith and teach the faith and practices of the church. Church youth meetings—like Jesus Youth for Catholics, OCYM (Orthodox Christian Youth Movement) for the Orthodox churches, and youth fellowships for the Mar Thoma churches—are organized regularly to engage the next generation. Special English worship services are held on Sundays, and conferences are organized and led by leaders who can communicate well with them. A few members of the second generation have pursued seminary education, have entered ministries to cater to the needs of the British Asians, or are serving at British churches or Christian institutions.

Conclusion

This chapter briefly explored the inseparable axes of race, gender, and migration status and how they are intertwined for Asian Indian nurses who have come to live and work in the United Kingdom. Migration may have elevated the position of the nursing profession in India, but these nurses still experienced othering at workplaces. Nurses are the primary migrants, and their husbands are always considered as dependent, while children are forced to deal with the norms of a heteronormative society, reacting to expectations of the "white" English and their parents about their sexual relationships. Amid this turmoil, these migrants find solace in the church, where they can escape from othering for some time and can exchange their apprehension with others who are having similar experiences. Keralites have always roamed far away from home and adapted to alien cultures with ease, casting aside their *mundu* (traditional garment in Kerala) for pants and choosing pasta over *puttu* (steamed rice dish). The journey does not end here for many nurses, as UK migration is only a stepping-stone to migration to the United States or Australia, while some return to Kerala.

Notes

1 See Ajaya Sahoo, *Mapping Indian Diaspora: Contestation and Representations* (New Delhi: Rawat, 2017); Parvati Raghuram et al., *Tracing an Indian Diaspora: Contexts, Memories, Representations* (New Delhi: Sage, 2008); and Kerala Migration Survey, 2018, accessed January 15, 2020, https://cds.edu/endowments/international-mogration-from-kerala/.

2 See John Hinnells, "South Asians in Britain," in *The South Asian Religious Diaspora in Britain, Canada and the United States*, ed. Harold Coward, John R. Hinnells, and Raymond Williams (Albany: State University of New York Press, 2000); and Roger Ballard, ed., *Desh Pardesh: The South Asian Presence in Britain* (London: Hurst, 1994).

3 See Supriya Singh, "Transnational Family Money: Remittances, Gifts and Inheritance," *Journal of Intercultural Studies* 33, no. 5 (2019): 475–92; and Jasbir Jain, *The Diaspora Writes Home: Subcontinental Narratives* (Jaipur: Rawat, 2015).

4 See Sheba M. George, *When Women Come First: Gender and Class in Transnational Migration* (Berkeley: University of California Press, 2005); Prema Kurien, *Ethnic Church Meets Megachurch: Indian American Christianity in Motion* (New Brunswick, NJ: Rutgers University Press, 2018); and Sara Gabriel, "Malayali Nurses in America: Caring for Others," in *Malayali Diaspora: From Kerala to the Ends of the World*, ed. Sam George and T. V. Thomas (New Delhi: Serials, 2013), 137–48.

5 World Health Organization, "Women on the Move: Migration, Care Work and Health," accessed September 15, 2021, https://apps.who .int/iris/bitstream/handle/10665/259463/9789241513142-eng.pdf.

6 The people of Kerala speak the Malayalam language, and a person of the state is called Malayali.

7 Raymond Williams, *Religions of Migrants from India and Pakistan: New Threads in the American Tapestry* (New York: Cambridge University Press, 1988), 22; Sam George, *Understanding the Coconut Generation: Ministry to the Americanized Asian Indians* (Niles, IL: Mall, 2006), chap. 1.

8 Indian Nursing Council, "Annual Report 2018–2019," accessed April 1, 2020, https://indiannursingcouncil.org/uploads/annualreports/ 16002481139415.pdf.

9 Praveena Kodoth and Tina K. Jacob, "International Mobility of Nurses from Kerala (India) to the EU," CARIM-India, 2013, accessed April 1, 2020, https://www.mea.gov.in/images/pdf/ InternationalMobilityofNursesfromIndia.pdf, 3.

10 Shyni Jacob Benjamin, *Translated Lives: A Migration Revisited*, 2013, YouTube video, accessed April 1, 2020, https://www.youtube.com/watch?v=-JEocwW4SZY.

11 Filippo Osella and Caroline Osella, "Migration, Money and Masculinity in Kerala," *Journal of the Royal Anthropological Institute* 6, no. 1 (March 2000): 118.

12 Sindhu Thomas and Y. Srinivasa Rao, "Professionalization of Nursing Care in Colonial India," *Think India* 22, no. 3 (2019): 986–96.

13 See Kerala Migration Survey.

14 Kingsley Davis, "Wives and Work: The Sex Role Revolution and Its Consequences," *Population and Development Review* 10, no. 3 (1984): 401.

15 George, *When Women Come First*, 180.

16 Kurien, *Ethnic Church Meets Megachurch*, 8–9. Also see Raymond Brady Williams, *Christian Pluralism in the United States: The Indian Immigrant Experience* (Cambridge: Cambridge University Press, 2008).

17 Urmila Goel, "The 70th Anniversary of John Matthew: On 'Indian' Christians in Germany," in *South Asian Christian Diaspora: Invisible Diaspora in Europe and North America*, ed. Knut A. Jacobsen and Selva J. Raj (Farnham, UK: Ashgate, 2008), 57.

18 There are seven St. Thomas churches in the United Kingdom—namely, Syro-Malabar Catholic Church, Malankara Syrian Catholic Church, Mar Thoma Syrian Church, Malankara Orthodox Syrian Church, Malankara Jacobite Syrian Church, and Church of South India are in communion with the Church of England.

19 Williams, *Religions of Migrants*, 11–12.

20 See George, *Understanding the Coconut Generation*.

Bibliography

Ballard, Roger, ed. *Desh Pardesh: The South Asian Presence in Britain.* London: Hurst, 1994.

Benjamin, Shyni Jacob. *Translated Lives: A Migration Revisited.* 2013. YouTube video. Accessed April 1, 2020. https://www.youtube .com/watch?v=-JEocwW4SZY.

Davis, Kingsley. "Wives and Work: The Sex Role Revolution and Its Consequences." *Population and Development Review* 10, no. 3 (1984): 397–417.

Gabriel, Sara. "Malayali Nurses in America: Caring for Others." In *Malayali Diaspora: From Kerala to the Ends of the World,* edited by Sam George and T. V. Thomas, 137–148. New Delhi: Serials, 2013.

George, Sam. *Understanding the Coconut Generation: Ministry to the Americanized Asian Indians.* Niles, IL: Mall, 2006.

George, Sheba M. *When Women Come First: Gender and Class in Transnational Migration.* Berkeley: University of California Press, 2005.

Goel, Urmila. "The 70th Anniversary of John Matthew: On 'Indian' Christians in Germany." In *South Asian Christian Diaspora: Invisible Diaspora in Europe and North America,* edited by Knut A. Jacobsen and Selva J. Raj, 57–74. Farnham, UK: Ashgate, 2008.

Hinnells, John. "South Asians in Britain." In *The South Asian Religious Diaspora in Britain, Canada and the United States,* edited by Harold Coward, John R. Hinnells, and Raymond Williams, 75–88. Albany: State University of New York Press, 2000.

Jain, Jasbir. *The Diaspora Writes Home: Subcontinental Narratives.* Jaipur: Rawat, 2015.

Kerala Migration Survey. 2018. Accessed January 15, 2020. https://cds .edu/endowments/international-mogration-from-kerala/.

Kodoth, Praveena, and Tina K. Jacob. "International Mobility of
Nurses from Kerala (India) to the EU." CARIM-India, 2013.
Accessed April 1, 2020. https://www.mea.gov.in/images/pdf/
InternationalMobilityofNursesfromIndia.pdf.

Kurien, Prema. *Ethnic Church Meets Megachurch: Indian American
Christianity in Motion*. New Brunswick, NJ: Rutgers University
Press, 2018.

Osella, Filippo, and Caroline Osella. "Migration, Money and
Masculinity in Kerala." *Journal of the Royal Anthropological
Institute* 6, no. 1 (March 2000): 117–133.

Raghuram, Parvati, Ajaya Sahoo, Brij Maharaj, and Dave Sangha.
Tracing an Indian Diaspora: Contexts, Memories, Representations.
New Delhi: Sage, 2008.

Sahoo, Ajaya K, ed. *Mapping Indian Diaspora: Contestation and
Representations*. New Delhi: Rawat, 2017.

Singh, Supriya. "Transnational Family Money: Remittances, Gifts
and Inheritance." *Journal of Intercultural Studies* 33, no. 5 (2019):
475–492.

Thomas, Sindu, and Y. Srinivasa Rao. "Professionalization of Nursing
Care in Colonial India." *Think India* 22, no. 3 (2019): 986–996.

Williams, Raymond Brady. *Christian Pluralism in the United States:
The Indian Immigrant Experience*. Cambridge: Cambridge
University Press, 2008.

———. *Religions of Migrants from India and Pakistan: New Threads in
the American Tapestry*. New York: Cambridge University Press, 1988.

5

Spiritual Longing and Religious-Cultural Negotiation in the Indian Diaspora

Reflections from Indian Writing in English

Robbie B H Goh

India is a land of deep spiritual traditions, where the overwhelming majority of people identify themselves in religious-cultural terms. In the 2011 Census of India, only about 0.24 percent of the population failed to declare a religious affiliation, and of the more than 99 percent who profess to be religiously affiliated, the majority are Hindus (80 percent) and Muslims (14 percent), with Christians and Sikhs forming other minority groups at 2.3 percent and 1.7 percent, respectively. Religion underlies many of India's national milestones and events, from the partition of 1947 itself (which arose out of the need to provide a separate homeland for the Muslim population); to the state's clash with Sikh separatists, which led to the assassination of Prime Minister Indira Gandhi in 1984; to the overtly religious raison d'être and manifesto of political parties like the Bharatiya Janata Party (BJP); to the periodic eruptions of communal violence, such as over the Babri Mosque in 1992 and the "Godhra incident" of 2002.[1]

It is therefore unsurprising that religious issues feature frequently in Indian writing in English by authors in India as well as in the diaspora. Since this essay focuses on the diaspora, the body of texts examined will be those written in English, as the lingua franca of writers in the diaspora. In depicting Indian society (whether contemporary or dating back to about the mid-nineteenth century and the time of the partition), issues such as communal riots, interreligious social relations (including marriage), marginalization, religious persecution, or religious politics feature prominently. This is all the more true if we include caste issues as a subset of issues to do with the Hindu religion.

The situation is somewhat different when it comes to writing by the Indian diaspora, and particularly with novels set outside of India. Both religion and caste feature noticeably in Indian diasporic literature. However, in novels set in India, religion appears as a social and communal phenomenon; in the Indian diaspora, it tends to be an individual and personal one. The novels set in India depict religion as a cause for communal violence, discrimination against a community, inexorable social forces that act on different individuals, and politics playing out at a regional or national level. While of course the novels home in on the impact and consequences of religious forces on individual subjects, nevertheless the overall depiction is of religion as a large-scale phenomenon, generally acting on individuals in a forceful and even deterministic manner. Examples include the many partition novels that include depictions of communal violence between Hindu, Muslim, and (to a certain extent) Sikh communities (such as Vikram Chandra's *Sacred Games* or Salman Rushdie's *Midnight's Children*); local or regional scenes of religious traditions and how they conflict with groups of individuals (e.g., Arundhati Roy's *The God of Small Things* or David Davidar's *The Solitude of Emperors*); the oppression of Scheduled Caste groups by the Forward Castes (e.g., in Rohinton Mistry's *A Fine Balance* or Reeti Gadekar's *Bottom of the Heap*); and so on.

In the novels of the Indian diaspora, the theme of religion features more as an individual choice or struggle. The emphasis is on the individual's own religious condition, sometimes depicted in the context of a small diasporic community. There is much less of a sense of religion as a large-scale phenomenon affecting a vast community of believers and involving sociopolitical forces against which the individual is quite helpless. This contrast is understandable, given the fact that religious politics exert a much smaller force on the Indian diaspora than on those living in India and that even the influence of the surrounding religious community is much smaller in the diaspora (given the much smaller size of Indian communities in each location in the diaspora). Also, the influence of host societies (particularly in the liberal and often Christian-legacy societies of Global North countries) acts on diasporic individuals (particularly in second- and third-generation settlers) to offer individual choices in terms of religious-cultural practices that are less readily available to individuals in India.[2]

This is not at all to say that decisions to change aspects of one's inherited religious affiliation and practices come easily to individuals in the Indian diaspora. The religious influences of India on its diasporic citizens may not be as strong as on those living in India, but they do not entirely disappear either. Many diasporic Indians are temporary settlers without the option of remaining permanently in the host country: this includes the migrant workers in unskilled or semiskilled jobs in countries such as the Gulf Cooperation Council countries of Qatar, Oman, United Arab Emirates, and others. For such temporary migrants, whose longer-term goals involve returning to India and often marrying and starting a family with the income earned while overseas, the religious-cultural forces in India are very much in play. Even for more settled Indian migrants with the option to stay permanently, including those in liberal Christian-legacy societies like the US, the UK, and Canada, the religious influences of their country of origin do not completely disappear. Migrant families and surrounding communities (which often contain many of the same religion) continue to exert influence and even pressure on individuals to maintain their religious affiliation and practices. This can be seen, for example, in instances of forced arranged marriages in the Indian diaspora, where the subject is compelled to marry someone of the family's choosing in order to preserve caste or religious endogamy.[3] Outside the family, there are also religious organizations (like the Arya Samaj) active throughout the Indian diaspora that work to perpetuate the knowledge and practices of Indian religions such as Hinduism.[4]

Nevertheless, being outside of India and its religious context often leads individuals in the diaspora to explore and question various aspects of their identity, including their religious identity, beliefs, and practices. This is a theme that recurs in much of the Indian diasporic writing in English, particularly that set in liberal and Christian-legacy countries like the United States, Canada, and the United Kingdom. The second- and third-generation Indians in foreign lands, in particular, face competing pressures of conforming to the cultural and religious traditions of their families and adapting to the practices and beliefs of their host country peer groups (whether these be non-Indians or groups of Indian origin who have adapted and assimilated over time). Marriage and romantic relations are a particular stress point: the relatively small community in diasporic settings of those of the same religion or caste often means that individuals end up in romantic relationships with partners of a different race, religion, or caste; such matters of the heart are sometimes strong enough to override familial opposition and result in religious conversion or children brought up in bireligious households. Another stress point is the passing away of members of the older generation who are effectively the religious gatekeepers of the family; in the ensuing emotionally and psychologically vulnerable period, diasporic individuals may be more open to question inherited religious traditions and explore alternative ones.

These kinds of religious negotiations are explored in many of the works of Indian Anglophone writers like M. G. Vassanji, Manju Kapur, Shani Mootoo, Gautam Malkani, Manil Suri, Sanjeev Sahota, Bharati Mukherjee, and others. In such novels, individuals find themselves culturally and emotionally dislocated by migration and its consequences (including social relations with those of other races and religions, familial tensions, socioeconomic influences and pressures in the host country, racism, and other factors). In the course of coming to terms with these factors, protagonists explore the basis of their spiritual identities, asking hard questions that may lead to religious crises, the abandonment of certain aspects of their religious identities, and the exploration of alternative religions and religious values. Outright and explicit conversion is not normally the outcome in such novels; rather, what is depicted is a process of struggle with inherited and internalized religious beliefs and principles that are associated with family (particularly those of the older generations) and the country of origin.

Several types of spiritual-religious crises are explored in the Indian diasporic fiction in English: (1) the weakening of inherited religious identities and practices, abetted by the cultural influences of the new host society; (2) the questioning and transformation of inherited religious identities and practices, with the resulting creation of hybridized and syncretic ones; and (3) reactionary blowback, or the exaggerated affirmation of religious identity as a reaction against the fear of religious loss.

These modalities of crisis are not mutually exclusive, of course, and most novels depict different crises, although, in the final analysis, one will dominate the novel's narrative and the protagonist's development. It is notable that underlying these different depictions of religious crisis is a recognition of the inevitability of spiritual struggle and crisis for the diasporic Indian, the inescapably spiritual nature of this individual. Even for the more ironic and cynical depictions of spiritual crisis, the protagonists are never truly postreligious, their pose and attitude a kind of cover or shell for their inability to find a satisfactory religious position.

The weakening of inherited religious identities and practices is systematically and progressively depicted in Manju Kapur's *The Immigrant*. The novel depicts the lives of husband and wife Ananda and Nina, who grow up in India but both emigrate to Canada after Ananda goes there to study and is matchmade to Nina, who joins him as a transnational spouse. While both are Hindus, the gradual erosion of their religious certainties and practices begins with their leaving India. Ananda as a college student lives in Halifax with his uncle, who has married a white Canadian and whose Hindu practices have become extremely lax over time, reduced to the celebration of a "hybrid Diwali" once a year.[5] The most explicit way in which this is manifested is in the relaxation of the practice of vegetarianism, and Ananda, influenced by his uncle's family and the norms of his host society, gradually comes to relish the taste of meat, including the beef that is taboo to the Hinduism of his childhood upbringing. This change in personal practice is of course representative of a larger internal change, as Ananda struggles to come to terms with his new life in Canada, away from his remaining family (his sister in India), his marriage and sexual struggles with Nina, the materialism and individual freedom he experiences in Canada, and so on. As his uncle explains early in the novel, "Family here means different things . . . we help you be independent."[6] The greater degree of individualism and reduced familial-social interconnectedness in Canada when contrasted to India gradually fosters a hedonistic and materialistic streak in Ananda, as he avoids having children and instead embarks on a series of adulterous affairs.

For Nina, too, migration means the gradual questioning of her religious-cultural practices, in her case accelerated by Ananda's more advanced and more enthusiastic embrace of Canadian life. While at his encouragement she gradually comes to accept aspects of daily life, such as wearing Western clothes and adopting consumer culture, she is slower than her husband in abandoning the inherited conservatism of diet and behavior that comes from her Hindu and Indian upbringing. The transformation of her outlook is accelerated by the death of her mother in India and her extramarital affair and subsequent date rape that occur as she is busy expanding her career prospects and social horizons. Both these pivotal events, combined with the questioning of her identity, which comes with diasporic dislocation, finally result in the loosening of her Hindu identity and practices:

> In Halifax her vegetarianism was treated respectfully, as part of her beliefs, but she felt false every time she concurred with a picture of herself as a traditional, devout Hindu. Really, what did she care about a religion she never practiced? After she had had sex with Anton, it seemed especially hypocritical to hang on to vegetables.
> Down with all taboos. . . .
> . . . That weekend was spareribs, the real test. Red meat. Flesh. Mammals. Cow. Cows that looked into your eyes—cows that her mother worshipped on fixed days of the Hindu calendar.[7]

By the end of the novel, the marriage is effectively over, and both Ananda and Nina may be described as "reinventing" themselves, recognizing that as immigrants "there was no going back."[8] This renunciation of "going back" includes India both as a habitat and as a social-symbolic anchor conferring one's religious and cultural identity.

The weakening and eventual abandonment of inherited religion seem more clear-cut in *The Immigrant* but is more complicated in M. G. Vassanji's novel *Amriika* (1999). A Khoja Ismaili Muslim who has lived in Kenya, Tanzania, the United States, and Canada, Vassanji works his interpretation of that faith—syncretic, mystical, deeply communal, open-minded—into novels that explore the spiritual crises of diasporic Indian protagonists. While there is a similar weakening of the strong bonds of religious affiliation and practices that we see in Kapur's novel and a consequent questioning of the individual's religious identity, the outcome is by no means a movement away from inherited religion toward secular renunciation. Instead, a more complex and balanced outcome arises, in which religious identity gets negotiated, transformed, and also reaffirmed in its new form.

In *Amriika*, the protagonist Ramji, a diasporic Indian who comes to America by way of Dar es Salaam, explains the origins and some of the practices and beliefs of this religious community to which he belongs:

> Our ancestors were Hindus who were converted to a sect of Islam, and told by that refugee from the Mongols to await the final avatar of their god Vishnu. . . .
> . . . We sit cross-legged on the floor of the music library singing hymns to the Indian god Vishnu—whose other name is Allah, so our ancestors were taught several hundred years ago. Fearing persecution, they were secret worshippers, "guptis," who met in private with members of their new sect, the Shamsis. . . . We come endowed with a key to that inner truth, the secret answer to all questions and desires. Humbly worshipping our God, following the path of our ancestors, we will obtain salvation, escape the endless cycle of rebirth; so we've been taught. Let the others outside hustle and bustle around, wasting their precious births, pursuing illusion, maya.[9]

Founded by a mystical and mysterious Central Asian refugee from the Mongol invasion, carried by Indian traders and migrant workers from Gujerat in India to African states like Tanzania, and thence to Western countries like America and Canada, the Shamsi faith in Vassanji's novels focalizes the trials and transformations of Indian religious identity in a transnational era. Not incidentally, it serves as a figure for Vassanji's own intensely hybrid cultural identity: contrasting his own "complex, dynamic, and fluid" identity as an Indian with the distinct categories imposed by "Nationhood" and "academic departments," Vassanji insists, "I'm Indian by origin, but I've all these mixtures of faiths that have gone into my upbringing."[10] As a syncretistic faith, marrying aspects of Islam and Hinduism and characterized by a gentle open-mindedness with regard to matters spiritual, the Shamsi faith offers hope for accommodation and pluralism in the cultural clashes of transnationalism. However, by the same token, the Shamsi identity encounters the very problems that beset Indian-ness in the diaspora: the conflict between community and the individual, between cultural conservation and change, between faith and the rationality of modern secularism, and between romantic idealism and the ruthless realities of the transnational era.

These problems are enacted in Ramji's Indian African version of the "coming to Amriika" (the supposed Indian pronunciation of "America") immigrant story in *Amriika*. A sort of Asian immigrant version of Forrest Gump, he lives through and is to a certain extent implicated in the Vietnam war protests, America's New Age spiritual revolution, a sexual revolution of sorts in his trysts with various women (including white women, suspected revolutionaries, and the woman who helps end his marriage), and an era of terrorist fears evocative of 9/11, the Unabomber and Rushdie affairs, the "War on Terror," and related events.

All these tumultuous events and changes conspire to bring him to a crisis of his Shamsi faith: "I stopped praying a long time ago. I thought you knew that."[11] Yet his ostensible disavowal does not at all extricate him from the complex web of social relations, historical determination, and causality that comes with his Shamsi heritage. Working at the radical magazine *Inqalab* with his old mentor Darcy (whose parents were Shamsi missionaries to Tanzania), Ramji finds himself at the center of a crisis in American society, one that invokes the specter of Islamic fundamentalism, right-wing reactionary ideologies, and competition for (Arab-Islamic and American) imperialism.

Ramji's Shamsi faith thus epitomizes his condition of entangled hybridity, his inability to belong fully either to his traditional culture or to the modern rationality he sees in America. Near the end of the novel, he realizes "he had never belonged to any one place entirely, not stood behind a cause or movement without reservations; when he left a judgmental, jealous God for the cold thrill of reason, he still could not do without portents and symbols, always yearned for moral certainty."[12]

Amriika could thus be seen as a coming-of-age novel in which the identity of the diasporic Indian protagonist is shaped as he goes through the ideological crucible of America in the last four decades of the twentieth century. This is obviously not just a factor of Vassanji's (and his characters') Khoja Ismaili faith, although the syncretic nature of that faith over the centuries helps Vassanji in the development of that theme. Other Indian diasporic writers explore similar themes of religious-cultural questioning and negotiation with regard to other religions as well. One notable example is Gautam Malkani's novel *Londonstani* (2006). Set in London, it tells the story of a gang of Indian youths (and their white friend, the narrator, Jas, who adopts many features of their "*desi* [Indian] rudeboy" mannerisms and behavior). Jas's *desi* friends explore a range of attitudes toward their Sikh and Hindu faiths while Jas observes and comments as an (ostensibly) objective third party.

One of the more obvious ways in which Indian religious legacies are questioned in this novel is in the generational clashes between the youths and their parents. *Londonstani* depicts an older generation of Indian settlers in the United Kingdom that is unquestioningly comfortable with the religious identities and practices, which they have evolved, and a younger generation discontented with these and quick to challenge and even rebel against them:

> But even though Hardjit said all a this stuff, he din't like the way his mum had hung up pictures a Hindu Gods on their landing at home next to their pictures a Gurus. But then there isn't no point to talk to your mum or dad bout religion, innit. They don't know jack bout religion. I seen Hardjit win arguments with his dad by quoting bits a the Guru Granth Sahbi that his dad din't even know—like them hardcore Muslim kids who keep tellin their parents what it says in the Koran.
>
> If Hardjit din't like his mum's definition a Sikhism, Amit and his older brother Arun hated their mum's definition a Hinduism.[13]

While for the older generation, religious customs (no matter how syncretized with other religions and culture) are a means of holding on to racial identity in the diaspora, for the younger generation, their parents' form of religion is irrational, a rearguard action in a desperate and futile attempt to keep cultural change at bay. The clash in attitudes toward religious customs comes to a head when Amit's brother Arun, instigated in part by Jas (and in part by his mother's unreasonable demands), quarrels with his parents over the dowry and customs of his upcoming marriage. The quarrel takes an unexpectedly tragic turn when his parents' unyielding conservatism causes Arun's death by suicide and turns the rest of the gang against Jas. This rejection by the gang is also precipitated by Jas breaking one of the gang's taboos by dating a Muslim girl, Samira. At the same time, Jas becomes involved in a plot by his erstwhile mentor Sanjay, a wealthy but unscrupulous *desi* businessman who (somewhat like Ananda in *The Immigrant*) unapologetically rejects family and tradition to pursue a materialistic and hedonistic lifestyle, to rob Jas's father and participate in goods and services tax (GST) fraud. The novel ends with the seeming collapse of Jas's carefully constructed world: hospitalization from physical and psychological hurts, estrangement from his gang, a confrontation with his father, and the revelation (carefully concealed in the novel until that point) that he is really a white youth passing for a *desi*. Yet even at the very end of the novel, Jas is unrepentant, flirting with the *desi* nurse and throwing in a *Shukriya* (thank-you) to suggest a return to his former *desi*-imitating and self-serving ways.

Yet while there are copious examples of inventive and self-serving religious syncretism as well as secular materialism, the novel does not suggest that religious identities lose their hold completely. Jas and his friends exhibit a kind of religious reaction, in which their parents' (perceived) religious compromise prompts in them an exaggerated form of religious identity. Most noticeably, this takes the form of Hardjit's self-styling as a Sikh warrior, defending both

Sikhism and Hinduism from Islam (which in the novel is championed by Hardjit's nemesis, Tariq). Hardjit's big fight with Tariq, which is supposed to be the main event of the gang's life but becomes anticlimactic when it is quickly broken up by the police, nevertheless underscores how religion resurfaces as a badge of hypermasculine identity for the younger generation of South Asian immigrants. This is also emphasized by how Hardjit and the gang terrorize and brutalize whites who are perceived as being racist toward them as well as *desi* "coconuts" perceived as giving up their ethnicity in order to assimilate into white society.

This survey of some of the ways in which diasporic Indian writing in English deals with the issue of religion and religious identities is certainly not meant to be exhaustive. Many other works address these issues and many more complex expressions of the religious questioning (also negotiation and reaffirmation) that take place in the Indian diaspora. It is nevertheless possible to draw certain general conclusions from this survey. First, the diaspora contains a range of religious communities, not merely Hindus, and the transformation of religious affiliations and practices in the diaspora is a common concern across these religions. Second, while diasporic conditions involve an inevitable weakening of the stronger religious influences in India, this does not simply lead to secularism and other forms of spiritual abnegation. While this is a possibility (as expressed by novels like *The Immigrant*), in many cases more complex responses include religious negotiations like syncretism or hybridity as well as the reaffirmation of certain aspects of religion as a conservative reaction to religious change. Religion continues to be a major theme and dynamics and articulations differ in the two sites. dynamics and articulations differ in the two sites.

Notes

1 Edna Fernandes, *Holy Warriors: A Journey into the Heart of Indian Fundamentalism*, 8; Teesta Setalvad, "Godhra: Crime against Humanity," in *Critical Issues in Indian Politics: Religious Politics and Communal Violence*, ed. Steven I. Wilkinson, 101–30.

2 Sam George, *Understanding the Coconut Generation: Ministry to the Americanized Asian Indians*, 38–43; Mark A. Falzon, *Cosmopolitan Connections: The Sindhi Diaspora, 1860–2000*, 74, 93; G. S. Aurora, "Process of Social Adjustment of Indian Immigrants in Britain," in *The Indian Diaspora: Dynamics of Migration*, ed. N. Jayaram, 66–77.

3 Shinder S. Thandi, "Diversities, Continuities and Discontinuities of Tradition in the Contemporary Sikh Diaspora: Gender and Social Dimensions," in *Women in the Indian Diaspora: Historical Narratives and Contemporary Challenges*, ed. Amba Pande, 167–68.

4 See Vertovec, *Hindu Diaspora*; and Stig Madsen and K. B. Nielsen, "Hindutva and Its Discontents in Denmark," in *Migration and Religion in Europe*, ed. Ester Gallo, 155–70.

5 Manju Kapur, *The Immigrant*, 27.

6 Kapur, 29.

7 Kapur, 267.

8 Kapur, 330.

9 M. G. Vassanji, *Amriika*, 3, 27–28.

10 Susan Fisher, "History, Memory, Home: An Exchange with M. G. Vassanji," *Canadian Literature* 190, 49–61.

11 Fisher, 279.

12 Fisher, 399.

13 Gautam Malkani, *Londonstani*, 81.

Bibliography

Aurora, G. S. "Process of Social Adjustment of Indian Immigrants in Britain." In *The Indian Diaspora: Dynamics of Migration*, edited by N. Jayaram, 66–77. New Delhi: Sage, 2004.

Falzon, Mark Anthony. *Cosmopolitan Connections: The Sindhi Diaspora, 1860–2000*. Leiden: Brill, 2004.

Fernandes, Edna. *Holy Warriors: A Journey into the Heart of Indian Fundamentalism*. London: Portobello, 2007.

Fisher, Susan. "History, Memory, Home: An Exchange with M. G. Vassanji." *Canadian Literature* 190 (Autumn 2006): 49–61.

George, Sam. *Understanding the Coconut Generation: Ministry to the Americanized Asian Indians*. Niles, IL: Mall, 2006.

Kapur, Manju. *The Immigrant*. London: Faber and Faber, 2009.

Madsen, Stig Toft, and Kenneth Bo Nielsen. "Hindutva and Its Discontents in Denmark." In *Migration and Religion in Europe: Comparative Perspectives on South Asian Experiences*, edited by Ester Gallo, 155–170. Farnham, UK: Ashgate, 2014.

Malkani, Gautam. *Londonstani*. Toronto: HarperCollins, 2006.

Setalvad, Teesta. "Godhra: Crime against Humanity." In *Critical Issues in Indian Politics: Religious Politics and Communal Violence*, edited by Steven I. Wilkinson, chapter 4. New Delhi: Oxford University Press, 2005.

Thandi, Shinder S. "Diversities, Continuities and Discontinuities of Tradition in the Contemporary Sikh Diaspora: Gender and Social Dimensions." In *Women in the Indian Diaspora: Historical Narratives and Contemporary Challenges*, edited by Amba Pande, 161–176. Singapore: Springer Nature, 2018.

Vassanji, M. G. *Amriika*. Toronto: McClelland and Stewart, 1999.

Vertovec, Steven. *The Hindu Diaspora: Comparative Patterns*. London: Routledge, 2000.

6

Migration, Remittances, and the Asian Diaspora

Cherian Samuel

Migration and remittances make significant contributions to the economic growth and development of nations. The effects are more pronounced for developing nations and vary widely across different regions of the world, as is evident from the latest reports of the World Bank and the United Nations. There is a growing interest in understanding the role and contributions of diaspora populations in their ancestral home countries. This chapter explores these issues from an Asian perspective and can be divided into three parts. The first part outlines conceptual issues related to migration, remittances, and diaspora communities; the second part presents the current trends in Asian migration and remittances; and the third part presents some reflections. Finally, I conclude with a summary of key insights on remittances from Asian migrants globally.

I

International migration is a complex phenomenon that spans economic, social, political, legal, and security aspects in an increasingly interconnected and mobile world. Human migration encompasses a variety of movements and situations in an era of deepening globalization with increased human mobility and interconnectivity. Migration has helped improve the lives of people in both origin and destination countries. But in recent years, there has been a migratory surge on account of conflicts, wars, persecution, environmental degradation and catastrophes, and a lack of human security and opportunity. Migration is increasingly seen as a high-priority policy issue for many governments, given its importance to economic prosperity, human development, and security. The current scale and extent of migration are unprecedented in human history, and the controversies related to migration tend to dominate news headlines daily. There has been some progress in cooperation on migration, as many nations and the United Nations have committed to a global compact for safe, orderly, and regular migration, yet it is extremely difficult to manage migration entirely in any region of the world.

Migration generates large benefits for migrants, their families, and their countries of origin. The wages migrants earn abroad can be many multiples of what they could earn doing similar jobs at home. The wage differences and relative income gains are largest for lower-skilled workers, whose international movements around the world are the most restricted. The increase in migrants' earnings leads to considerable improvements in the welfare and human development of migrants' families who are with them in the host country or indirectly through remittances for those back home. Importantly, the benefits of migration for migrants and their families go beyond economic impacts and include improvements in education and health.

In addition to the benefits to migrants and their families, there are broader benefits of emigration for the countries of origin of the migrants. Emigration reduces unemployment and underemployment, reduces poverty, and fosters economic and social development in origin countries in several ways. For example, remittances sent by migrants to their countries of origin provide significant financial capital flows and a relatively stable source of income. They are generally less volatile and a more reliable source of foreign currency than other capital flows in many developing countries. They improve education, housing, health, and the overall well-being of family members back home. The emigration results in the transfer of skills, knowledge, and technology that are hard to measure but have sizable positive impacts on productivity and economic growth. Beyond these economic impacts, emigration can generate social benefits for countries of origin, including poor and fragile nation-states. For example, it is increasingly recognized that migrants can play a significant role in postconflict reconstruction and recovery efforts.

There is widespread agreement that migration generates economic and other benefits for destination countries. The precise nature and size of these benefits at a given time critically depend on the extent to which the skills of migrants are complementary to those of domestic workers as well as on the characteristics of the host economy. In general, immigration adds workers to the economy, thus increasing the gross domestic product (GDP) of the host country. There are a variety of ways in which migrants can have positive effects on labor productivity and GDP per head—for example, if migrants are more skilled than national workers and/or if immigration has positive effects on innovation and skills agglomeration. Migrants are more likely to be risk-takers, which has often led to significant contributions in many destination countries in areas such as technology, science, the arts, and a range of other fields. In addition to enhancing national income and average living standards in destination countries, immigration can have a positive effect on the labor market by increasing labor supply in sectors and occupations suffering from shortages of workers as well as helping address mismatches in the job market.

The diaspora of developing countries can contribute to development in their countries of origin by increasing trade and investment; providing market information and matching/referral services; improving access to technology; making remittances for health, education, and infrastructure projects; supporting philanthropic activities; and providing access to capital markets (such as through diaspora bonds). While some countries have devoted resources to fostering contacts with their diaspora, for many sending countries the diaspora remains a largely untapped resource. Policies that could help enhance benefits from the diaspora include providing dual citizenship and voting rights, working with overseas diaspora community organizations to improve contacts with origin communities, easing restrictions on foreigners' economic activities for diaspora members, and providing information to facilitate their return.

II

According to the *World Migration Report 2020*, the number of international migrants globally in 2019 was 272 million, about 3.5 percent of the world population. India had the largest number of migrants living abroad (17.5 million), and China held third place with 10.7 million in that year. The top destination country was the United States, with 50.7 million. Fifty-two percent of international migrants were male, and the remaining 48 percent were female. Nearly three-fourths (74 percent) of the international migrants were of working age, between the ages of twenty and sixty-four years.[1] As per the United Nations Refugee Agency, in 2019 there were 71 million forcibly displaced people in the world, which includes 41 million internally displaced people, 26 million refugees, and 3.5 million asylum seekers.[2]

International migrants accounted for a relatively small share of the total population worldwide, about 3.5 percent of the world's population in 2019 (272 million out of 7.7 billion), which amounts to 1 in every 30 persons. The proportion of international migrants with respect to the global population was only 2.8 percent in 1990, 2.9 percent in 2000, and 3.2 percent in 2010. According to the *World Migration Report 2020*, among the top ten nations with the largest number of international migrants were Saudi Arabia, in third place with 13 million people, and the United Arab Emirates, in sixth place with 9 million people.[3] The migration patterns show that most migrants remained within the region of their birth, and some nations were more susceptible to large-scale displacement due to war (Syria), political turmoil (Venezuela), and natural disasters (the Philippines) recently.

Asia and Europe combined hosted over 60 percent of all international migrants in 2019 worldwide, with nearly 80 million international migrants living in Asia and 78 million in Europe. North America hosted the third-largest number of international migrants in 2017 (58 million),

Table 6.1. Key figures from World
Migration Report 2000 and 2020

	2000	2020
Number of international migrants	192 million	272 million
Migrants as a proportion of world population (%)	2.8	3.5
Proportion of female migrants (%)	47.5	47.9
Proportion of children migrants (%)	16	13.9
Region with the highest proportion of international migrants	Oceania	Oceania
Country with the highest proportion of international migrants	UAE	UAE
International remittance	126 billion	689 billion
Number of refugees	14 million	25.9 million

Source: WMR 2020, page 10, accessed January 1, 2021, https://www
.un.org/sites/un2.un.org/files/wmr_2020.pdf (hereafter cited as
WMR 2020).

followed by Africa (25 million), Latin America and the
Caribbean (10 million), and Oceania (8 million). Between
1990 and 2017, Asia recorded the largest gain in the number
of international migrants, adding 31 million, followed by
North America (30 million) and Europe (29 million). Of
the 31 million international migrants added in Asia during
this period, 28 million, or 89 percent, were born in other
countries of Asia.

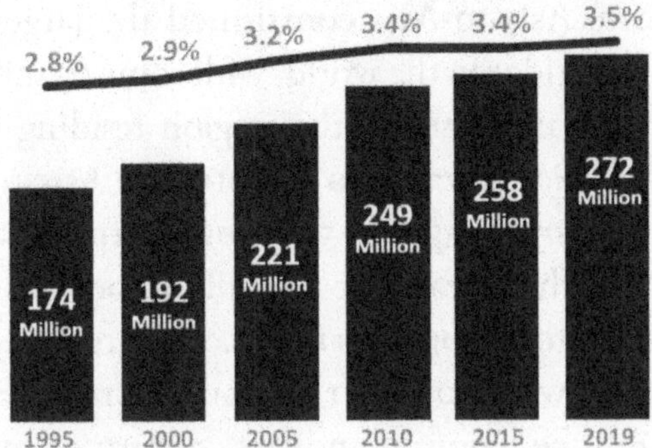

Figure 6.1. International migration (in millions and percentage of the population, 1995–2019)

Source: WMR 2020, page 22, accessed January 1, 2021, https://www.un .org/sites/un2.un.org/files/wmr_2020.pdf.

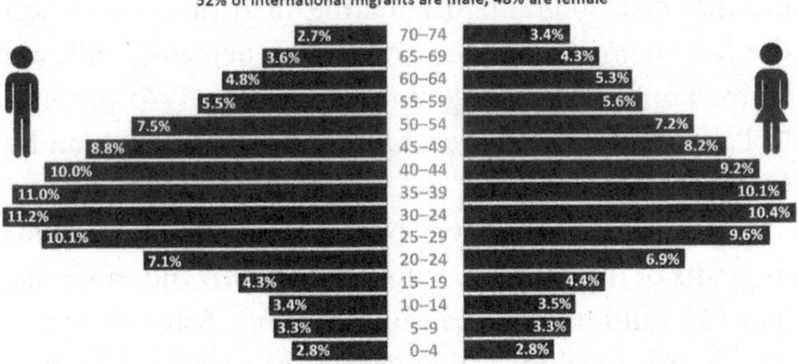

Figure 6.2. Age distribution of international migrants, 2020

Fifty-two percent of international migrants are male, and 48 percent are female. Age groups above seventy-five years are omitted (male 4 percent and female 6 percent). Most international migrants (74 percent) are of working age (twenty to sixty-four).

Source: WMR 2020, page 22, accessed January 1, 2021, https://www.un .org/sites/un2.un.org/files/wmr_2020.pdf.

In 2017, Asia-to-Asia constituted the largest regional migration corridor in the world, with some 63 million international migrants born in that region residing in another country of Asia. From 2000 to 2010, the Asia-to-Asia corridor grew by an average of 1.5 million international migrants per year, which increased to 1.7 million between 2010 and 2017. Europe-to-Europe was the second-largest regional corridor in 2017, with around 41 million international migrants born in Europe living in another country of Europe. The average annual increase in the Europe-to-Europe migrant stock has been around 0.6 million since 2000.

Between 2000 and 2019, the number of international migrants of Asian origin recorded the largest increase (41 million), followed by the migrant population born in Africa (15 million) and Latin America and the Caribbean (13 million). In relative terms, however, the number of international migrants originating in Africa experienced the largest increase since 2000 (+68 percent), followed by the population of migrants born in Asia (+62 percent), in Latin America and the Caribbean (+52 percent), and in Oceania (+51 percent).

Asia was the origin of 40 percent of the international migrants of the world in 2019 (111 million), and more than half (66 million) were residing in other Asian countries. The intraregional migration within the continent has risen significantly since 1990. Of those living in other parts of the world, the highest number of Asian migrants lived in Europe (22 million), followed by North America (17 million) and Oceania (3 million). The number of non-Asian migrants living in Asia has remained low since 1990, the largest amount being from Europe, and there is a substantial increase in the number of Africans living in Asia.

Globally, the twenty largest countries of origin account for almost half (49 percent) of all international migrants, while one-third (34 percent) of all international migrants originated in ten countries. India is now the country with the largest number of people living outside the country's borders, followed by Mexico and China. Of the twenty largest countries or the areas of origin of international migrants, eleven were located in Asia, six in Europe, and one each in Africa, Latin America and the Caribbean, and North America. In Gulf nations, migrants make up a large proportion of the total population of the country: 88 percent of the population of the United Arab Emirates, 77 percent in Kuwait, 79 percent in Qatar, and 45 percent in Bahrain. (See the appendix of volume 1 of the series, *Journeys of Asian Diaspora*.)

Asia also made up the largest share of forced displacement in recent years. As of 2019, most of the refugees of the world lived in neighboring countries. Wars in West and South Asia and the turmoil in Myanmar contributed significantly to the share of the current global refugee crises, all of which are in Asia. The Syrian Arab Republic and Afghanistan were leading originating countries for refugees in the world. Syrian refugees were mostly hosted in Turkey, Lebanon, and Jordan, while Afghani refugees are mostly in Pakistan, Iran, and India. The violence and persecution against Rohingya in Myanmar forced many to flee to neighboring Bangladesh and Thailand, and this is becoming the new epicenter of the global refugee crisis.

The remittances are financial or in-kind transfers made by migrants directly to families or communities in their countries of origin. Since 2000, remittances have exceeded developmental assistance received by many nations and have become a vital aspect of national budgets and economic policies. In 2019, the international remittances surged globally to 689 billion, and the top two remittance recipients were in Asia—India (USD 78.6 billion) and China (USD 67.4 billion)—while the top three remittance-sending countries were the United States (USD 68 billion), the UAE (USD 44.4 billion), and Saudi Arabia (USD 36.1 billion). Many Asian national economies, such as those of the Philippines, Nepal, Vietnam, Indonesia, Bangladesh, and others, have become utterly dependent on foreign remittances from their overseas residents. The actual exchange of resources may be much higher, as this does not include flows through informal channels and other means.

Globally, remittances accelerated in 2018.[4] Remittance flows to low- and middle-income countries (LMICs) grew by 9.6 percent in 2018 (up from the 8.8 percent rise in 2017) to reach a record US$529 billion. Remittance flows grew in all six regions, particularly in South Asia (12.3 percent) and Europe and Central Asia (11.2 percent). The rise in remittances was driven by higher growth in the United States and a rebound in remittance outflows from some Gulf Cooperation Council (GCC) countries and the Russian Federation. Central Asia saw incoming remittances grow by 11.2 percent in 2018 due to the recovery of the Russian economy. The remittances to East Asia and the Pacific increased by 6.7 percent, and the South Asian increase resulted from the remittances to both India and Bangladesh rising by double digits.

The remittances are now the largest source of foreign exchange earnings in the LMICs, excluding China. They are more than three times the size of official development assistance (ODA). Moreover, since foreign direct investment (FDI) has been on a downward trend in recent years, remittances reached close to the level of FDI flows in 2018. The growth rate of remittances from the Middle East remains strong to many other parts of Asia, like Southeast Asia, South Asia, Central Asia, and West Asia.

In 2020, in current US dollar terms, the top five remittance recipient countries were India, China, Mexico, the Philippines, and Egypt. As a share of gross domestic product (GDP) for 2020, the top five recipients were smaller economies: Tonga, Kyrgyz Republic, Tajikistan, Haiti, and Nepal. Data on remittance outflows typically get less attention than data on remittance inflows. The largest remittance-sending countries are a mix of high-income countries from the Organisation for Economic Co-operation and Development (OECD), GCC countries, and large middle-income countries. The United States was the largest sender in 2020, recording around $68 billion in outflows, followed by the UAE ($44 billion) and Saudi Arabia ($35 billion). Among middle-income countries, Russia is a large sender ($16 billion), given its sizable immigrant stock from Europe and Central Asia, while China also has large outflows ($18 billion), owing to money paid to expatriates working for multinational enterprises. The large immigrant populace in a small country like Kuwait explains its large outflow ($15 billion), and three major European remittance senders were Switzerland, Germany, and France, together amounting to $65 billion.

The remittances to East Asia and the Pacific held steady in 2018. Formal remittances to this region grew by 6.7 percent in 2018, 1.6 percentage points higher than the growth rate in 2017. The remittances to the Philippines rose by 3.1 percent in 2018 to reach $33.8 billion, down from the 5.4 percent growth seen in 2017. Growth was lower due to the significant drop of 15 percent in private transfers from the

Table 6.2. Top countries receiving remittances, 2005–20 (in USD billions)

2005		2010		2015		2020	
China	23.63	India	53.48	India	68.91	India	83.1
Mexico	22.74	China	52.46	China	63.94	China	59.7
India	22.13	Mexico	22.08	Philippines	29.8	Mexico	42.8
Nigeria	14.64	Philippines	21.56	Mexico	26.23	Philippines	34.9
France	14.21	France	19.9	France	24.06	Egypt	29.6
Philippines	13.73	Nigeria	19.75	Nigeria	21.16	Pakistan	26.1
Belgium	6.89	Germany	12.79	Pakistan	19.31	France	24.5
Germany	6.87	Egypt	12.45	Egypt	18.33	Germany	17.9
Spain	6.66	Bangladesh	10.85	Germany	15.81	Viet Nam	17.2
Poland	6.47	Belgium	10.35	Bangladesh	15.3	Nigeria	17.2

Source: WMR 2020, Table 3, page 36, accessed January 1, 2021, https://www.un.org/sites/un2.un.org/files/wmr_2020.pdf.

Table 6.3. Top countries sending remittances, 2005–20 (in USD billions)

2005		2010		2015		2020	
United States	47.25	United States	50.78	United States	61.86	United States	68
Saudi Arabia	14.3	Saudi Arabia	27.07	UAE	40.33	UAE	43.2
Germany	12.71	Russia	21.45	Saudi Arabia	38.79	Saudi Arabia	34.6
Switzerland	10.52	Switzerland	17.76	Switzerland	25.4	Switzerland	27.9
UK	9.64	Germany	14.68	China	20.42	Germany	22
France	9.48	Italy	12.89	Russia	19.69	Russia	16.9
South Korea	6.9	France	12.03	Germany	18.03	China	18.1
Russian Federation	6.83	Kuwait	11.86	Kuwait	15.2	Kuwait	15.3
Luxembourg	6.7	Luxembourg	10.65	France	12.79	France	15
Malaysia	5.68	UAE	10.57	Qatar	12.19	Luxembourg	14.2

Source: WMR 2020, Table 3, page 36, accessed January 1, 2021, https://www.un.org/sites/un2.un.org/files/wmr_2020.pdf.

Middle East in 2018. Remittances to Indonesia experienced double-digit growth in 2018 at around 24.7 percent after a muted performance in 2017. In contrast to the Philippines, flows from the Middle East (particularly Saudi Arabia) to Indonesia expanded by almost 50 percent in 2018.

Cambodia is sending its workers to Kuwait for the first time this year, though they signed an MOU (Memorandum of Understanding) over a decade ago. A target of 5,000 workers was agreed upon between the two countries. In Hong Kong, an initial batch of 14 Cambodian domestic workers arrived under a pilot program in January. The primary destination for Cambodian migrants is Thailand (an estimated 1 million), followed by Malaysia and the Republic of Korea. Myanmar officials stated in February that 5 million Myanmar nationals are working overseas, with about 3 million in Thailand, mostly in manual labor. Thailand continues to crack down on irregular migrants, with over 100,000 migrants deported in 2018. Japan is the fastest-growing destination for Vietnamese migrants. Official statistics indicated that 142,800 Vietnamese left for work abroad in 2018 (a 6 percent growth over the previous year), of whom 68,700 went to Japan, followed by 60,400 to Taiwan and China and 6,500 to Korea. In recent years, over 100,000 Vietnamese have left annually to work abroad, and an estimated 540,000 Vietnamese are currently working overseas.

The remittances to South Asia increased by an estimated 12.3 percent in 2018, a faster pace than the 5.7 percent growth seen in 2017. The upsurge was driven by stronger economic conditions in high-income economies (particularly the United States) and strong oil prices that had a positive impact on remittance outflows from some GCC countries. In India, remittances grew by over 14 percent in 2018 to $78.6 billion.

A flood disaster in the southern Indian state of Kerala is likely to have boosted remittances, with migrants sending financial help to families back home. In Pakistan, remittance growth remained moderate in 2018 (6.7 percent) due to significant declines in inflows from Saudi Arabia (the largest remittance source). In Bangladesh, remittances showed a brisk uptick in 2018 (14.8 percent), and Sri Lanka witnessed a remittance growth of 3.8 percent. For 2019, it is projected that remittances to the region will slow to 4.3 percent due to a moderation of growth in high-income economies and a slowdown in migration to the GCC countries. South Asia had the lowest average remittance costs of any world region (at 5.2 percent) in 2018, as it saw a fall in migrant worker deployments due to lower demand from the GCC countries, especially Saudi Arabia. In India, the number of low-skilled migrants seeking mandatory clearance for emigration dropped by 15 percent in 2018 (340,157) compared with 2017. In Pakistan, too, the number of emigrants dropped from a peak of 946,571 in 2015 to 496,286 in 2017 and fell again by 30 percent to 382,439 in 2018. The pace of migrant worker deployments from Bangladesh declined by 37 percent from 1,008,525 in 2017 to 734,181 in 2018 (largely due to a fall in deployments to Saudi Arabia by more than half).

On account of the global pandemic in 2020, there was a substantial drop in the demand for migrants worldwide, and many migrants were deported back to their home countries, especially from the Gulf nations, which will result in a significant decline in remittances to South Asian countries in particular and Asia at large in the coming years. This has caused large-scale disruptions in remittance flows and many Asian national economies that are dependent on remittances. Many economic and national policies concerning migrants will be revisited and are bound to change. However, global human migration cannot be stopped entirely, though its source, size, direction, and destination may dramatically alter depending on new economic realities after the pandemic.

III

The remittance makes a very tangible difference to the migrants and their families and the larger community in both their places of origin and settlements. It increases consumption and disposable income while improving the quality of life for most migrants and their families who are left behind in their homeland. It is proven as a currency of care and lifts the well-being of migrants' parents, siblings, and communities in many positive ways. It is used for the education of siblings, provides dowries for the marriage of sisters, and supplies capital to start small businesses. Remittances also go toward charities and religious activities in their ancestral homelands. They are used to start educational institutions, make improvements in sanitation, dig wells for water, build/renovate churches and temples, support missionaries and religious workers, and so on.

However, the sudden surge in revenue to family members through remittances has resulted in new problems. It creates socioeconomic disruptions in the community and develops new inequalities and rivalries between families. The remittances have also resulted in corruption, real estate booms, support to anticommunal elements, money laundering, and political lobbying. Most often remittances are spent unwisely and on consumables by family members.

They are seldom invested to generate future sources of revenue, and people remain ever dependent on migrants sending regular and increased remittances. Any disruption in the overseas job situation of the migrants results in a major crisis for the entire family, as is evident from the recent economic slump in some Gulf nations and the recent pandemic. Many political and even antinational entities in some Asian countries have sought financial support from their overseas residents to sustain their activities, as is evident from financial support garnered by terrorist organizations, radical Hindutva-based political parties in India, the liberation movement in Sri Lanka, the uprisings in the Middle East, and so on, all of which thrive on account of their diasporic financial linkages.

In conclusion, Asian diaspora communities have made significant contributions to the economic growth and development of their ancestral homelands through remittances. In the first two decades of the twenty-first century, the largest increase in international migration was from Asia and within Asia. Of the twenty largest countries or areas of origin of international migrants, eleven were located in Asia. The robust growth pattern in migratory trends has been matched by similar growth in remittances. The top five remittance recipient countries included three from Asia—India, China, and the Philippines—while Nepal was among the top five recipients of remittances as a share of GDP. Even so, the Asian diaspora will remain central in terms of their contributions to poverty reduction and economic growth and economic development in their home countries. India and China stand at the helm in terms of annual remittances received in recent years, and with a large population and the steady growth of their economies, both of these nations will continue to disperse a large number of their people beyond their national borders to within Asia and around the world in the coming decades.

Notes

1 United Nations International Organization of Migration, accessed December 1, 2019, https://www.iom.int/wmr/. Also see World Migration Data Portal, accessed December 1, 2019, https://migrationdataportal.org, for the latest migration data worldwide.

2 UNHCR, "Refugee Figures at a Glance," accessed March 1, 2021, https://www.unhcr.org/en-us/figures-at-a-glance.html.

3 Unless otherwise stated, statistics throughout are from *WMR 2020*, accessed January 1, 2021, https://www.un.org/sites/un2.un.org/files/wmr_2020.pdf.

4 See World Bank Remittance data (1970–2020), accessed January 1, 2021, https://data.worldbank.org/indicator/BX.TRF.PWKR.CD.DT.

Bibliography

Asian Development Bank. *Global Crisis, Remittance and Poverty in Asia*. Manila: Asian Development Bank, 2012.

Jacob, Jeffery. "Remittance Trends in South Asia: An Empirical Analysis." In *Diaspora Christianities*, edited by Sam George, 234–252. Minneapolis: Fortress, 2019.

UNHCR. "Refugee Figures at a Glance." Accessed March 1, 2021. https://www.unhcr.org/en-us/figures-at-a-glance.html.

UN IOM. *World Migration Report 2020*. Geneva: IOM, 2019. https://www.iom.int/wmr/.

World Migration Data Portal. Accessed March 1, 2021. https://
migrationdataportal.org/.

Zachariah, K. C., and Rajan S. I. "Emigration and Remittances:
Results from Kerala Migration Survey 2018." Center for
Development Studies. Accessed September 1, 2021. http://14.139
.171.199:8080/xmlui/handle/123456789/488.

7

From Bridging God and Human to Bridging the Digital Divide

Bill Tsang

Introduction

The word *missiology* may conjure up images of old professors discussing complex biblical concepts in a dimly lit seminary hall of a medieval gothic structure, perhaps with their silver cups of coffee on an antique table, while the word *technology* may summon pictures of young engineers clicking away at their MacBook computers in an open office with glass walls and huge info monitors, perhaps with coffee in their Google or Facebook mugs. The only connection one can probably find between these images may be the java in their cups.

However, if we take Chris Wright's view of *The Mission of God* (2006) in a grand narrative approach that incorporates the whole Bible regarding missions and a holistic view of missions, which includes not only the spiritual but the social and political aspects of our human existence, then it would be easier to connect missiology and technology. Indeed, mission is more than the Great Commission in its conventional sense—"making disciples of all nations, baptiz-ing them and teaching" them to observe Jesus's commands (Matt 28:19, 20). It involves the spiritual aspect as well as the social, emotional, and behavioral aspects of our redemption. In fact, it is more than the salvation of the whole person. The mission of God includes the redemption of individuals as well as communities—indeed of societies as a whole. The Bible regards the restorative act of God to be for the whole Creation. As the fall involves humans and the Creation, so does Redemption. Therefore, Wright sees that mission is for individuals as well as societies, the whole person as well as whole cultures and the whole of creation. From that larger picture, then, we see how the mission goes beyond preaching the gospel to caring for the larger community and society, from addressing spiritual needs to addressing the physical, social, and emotional needs of all. But how does technol-ogy fit into this larger picture? Is not technology only a tool to solve the problem or to increase our performance and efficiency?

Without getting into an intense debate over whether technology is good or evil or neutral in society, we first need to acknowledge that the medium can become the message, as Marshall McLuhan has prophesized, and technology can become central to a culture, so much so that it becomes the driver of culture.[1] Indeed, a form of technological theology as Neil Postman had proposed is becoming more prevalent in the internet age, where various forms of cultural life are under the sovereignty of technology. And those who have access to technologies to create and control information become an elite group with authority over those who have no such power or competence. It is clear that as the elite gets more powerful with technologies, the disadvantaged get more disempowered by their lack thereof—creating the digital divide. Thus the mission of God that is comprehensive in the redemptive narrative would need to address the technological aspect of our human condition. This chapter proposes a framework for an understanding of mission as a redemptive and reconciliation process in a fast-changing technological world—a world where individuals, communities, and cultures have degenerated, alienated, and divided.

Theological Foundation

I will use Daniel Groody's theology of migration to frame our discussion of missions in the digital age of the Asian diaspora.[2] This is a theology of reconciliation that balances justice and compassion and centers on developing the right relationships and healing the divides. This theological framework is pertinent and suitable because, first, it matches our more holistic view of the redemptive narrative, and second, it addresses missions in the context of migration. And lastly, the theology of migration provides a framework for bridging divides, one of which is the digital divide.

Migration theology was not developed originally to integrate migration and technology. But because of how technology has become an integral part of our culture and how it has created a divide between the haves and have-nots, a theology of reconciliation has great potential to provide a framework for integration. In this section, I shall attempt to summarize Groody's theology and outline particularly the parts that are relevant to the Asian diaspora and how the concept of reconciliation is understood in the redemptive act of God.

There are four pillars to the theology of migration. The first is the concept of *imago Dei* (image of God), which is introduced early in the Scriptures (Gen 1:26–27; 5:1–3; 9:6; 1 Cor 11:7; Jas 3:9). Human beings are created in the image, likeness, and glory of God, with dignity, creativity, and unique identities. They are created to be moral and relational in nature. God blessed man and woman. They were to enjoy the abundance together in the physical and social environment that God had created for them. But unfortunately, something—what some call the "Great Fall" in the Genesis narrative—happened. This led to segregation and alienation among people, from relational tension and rivalry in the family to betrayal and murder, from economic competition to systematic oppression (e.g., slavery). The distrust among people developed into the destruction of the community. In the process, people lost the basic things and building blocks of humans: the right to live freely; to have respect and dignity, privacy and security; to have a family, education, employment; and to have the freedom to act according to one's own conscience.

As a consequence of the Fall, people had to leave the perfect home that was created for them and wandered around the earth—the first migration. And at the end, people lost the identity and dignity given to them in the form of *imago Dei* in the beginning. They broke away from what was human to become "in-human." *To restore* the image of God, *the inhuman-human divide*, is beyond the ability of any created being.

So enters *verbum Dei*, the word of God. And the Word became flesh and lived among the people (John 1:14). Christ came down from a high position to live among people in a low position. Though Christ was in the form of God, he emptied himself and took the form of a servant and humbled himself (Phil 2:6–8). His action was a form of migration, from heaven to earth, resulting in a form of downward mobility. This is in contrast to what most earthlings seek in their social reality: upward mobility. Migration theology highlights Christ's initiation of a reversal of people's spiritual status, restoring them from a broken, alienated, and separated position back to one of restored union with God. Therefore, Christ became a model of a humble servant from that of a King of kings to jump-start a process of reconciling the divine-human divide so that humans can regain the *imago Dei*, an identity that is dignified and creative. He moved from a high position to low to effect a movement of those in a low position to high.

What was started by Christ needs to be sustained by the *missio Dei*, the third pillar of migration theology. The mission of God as understood by the church traditionally is to "go and make disciples of all nations, baptizing them in the name of the Father and of the Son and of the Holy Spirit" (Matt 28:19). This Great Commission is a mandate for Christians to preach the good news of redemption and restoration. But to unpack that message, it asks Christians to go out, to leave the places they are familiar with and go to places dissimilar from theirs, with people from different cultures, socioeconomic statuses, and values, separated not only from God but from each other. It requires them to engage with people from diverse backgrounds and bridge their differences and bring them back to Christ, and to each other—a process of healing the human-human divide.

In bringing people together to hear the good news of Christ, to live lives that reflect the image of God, Christians necessarily have to have a vision of God, *visio Dei*, to point people to the kind of community God has revealed to us: "Then I saw a new heaven and a new earth; for the first heaven and the first earth had passed away, and the sea was no more. And I saw the holy city, the new Jerusalem, coming down out of heaven from God" (Rev 21:1–2). This last pillar of Groody's migration theology points to bringing nations together to form the kingdom of God on earth—crossing over the country-kingdom divide. In our context, it would be the formation of a creative and restorative community where people from different cultures, ethnicities, races, socioeconomic statuses, and nationalities can come together and engage in building and sustaining this community and expressing their identities, creativity, and dignity to reflect the glory of God in *imago Dei*. This creative and restorative community in return would allow individuals to have the context and support to overcome the alienation, exploitation, and degradation in their lives and regain their dignity, creativity, and identity.

Mapping Migration Theology to Our Sociological Context

Before leaping from the missiological framework above to a specific technological context, let us connect this framework with a sociological perspective of the more general condition in our human society. What is our human condition in the twenty-first century? What are the major issues in our globalized, technologically driven, and connected society? What are some possible solutions? Are there common goals across the world, in Asia in particular? How can migration theology help us understand our world in tackling the major challenges to building and rebuilding our communities?

One of the major problems we see today is the glaring income gap in every part of the world. Economists such as Angus Deaton have pointed out that even though the absolute poverty of the global population has reduced, the relative poverty within each nation has increased.[3] Indeed, any keen observer can see the income gap in any major city today, in either Brisbane or Beijing, DC or Delhi, Madrid or Manila. In any of these megacities, we see the gap between those who are riding the technological waves and making economic gains with high computing power, information access, and mobile bandwidth and those who are still paddling with their hands to catch up to the waves with outdated devices and low-speed internet or being consumed by video games. This digital divide, combined with the income gap, has created a growing social divide, with a majority of the people struggling.

In a better world, we believe that everyone should be allowed to grow up in a safe place; to learn about themselves, others, and the world; to exercise their creativity; to express themselves; and to develop solutions to problems around them. But the world is not perfect, and individuals are often thwarted in the growing process, being isolated, perverted, exploited, deprived, and oppressed. So their true identities and full potentials cannot be realized—*imago Dei* unfulfilled. This social reality is often the result of how we structure our society. To counter the alienation, segregation, exploitation, deprivation, and the growing social divide, people need to know and have the concepts of justice and care within the community—*verbum Dei* revealed. People also need to learn and practice justice and care to initiate the integration of society, a society where we celebrate diversity, including the marginalized, and serve the disadvantaged.

But to sustain such communities in a society, people cannot just seek upward social mobility for themselves. They need to understand that resources have to flow around and be distributed among people from different social and economic backgrounds. Otherwise, the growth of the social divide will accelerate and metastasize. To bridge the divide, people need to step outside their comfort zones and interact with those different from themselves. The resourceful need to collaborate with the underprivileged. Some have to embark on downward social mobility as a path to cross the divide, to reach out to those below in the socioeconomic order and hierarchy, so that more can gain access and reach a higher ground—*missio Dei* in sociological terms.

The flow of resources can generate greater equality and opportunity for more people. The increase in interactions across boundaries and borders can create more diverse communities. Such communities necessarily inspire knowledge for the greater good and purposeful service for greater equality—*visio Dei*. The purpose is to construct a society that upholds justice and care and where individuals can express their creativity and develop solutions to solve their problems. A sustainable society is generative by definition. It allows individuals to be generative.

History reveals that a society where its members cannot fully express their humanity, creativity, and dignity will degenerate eventually. Individuals need the community to develop fully, just as communities need individuals to grow. The interactivity is ongoing and dynamic and keeps changing with the social context. The embrace and practice of justice and care to promote social mobility need to be creative and iterative. To sustain and scale the practice of justice and care, collaboration must be developed between the haves and have-nots, rich and poor, resourceful and underresourced, as well as technologically empowered and marginalized.

Tackling Poverty in the Technology Economy

The above discussion is theoretical and abstract. A real-life story comes across as more concrete to illustrate the complex issues involved. The story is about the Chen family (pseudonym) of six living at the margin of a dumpsite in Beijing's outskirt where they recycle trash. At the time I first met this family in 2008, there were only five of them, and they had lived there for over ten years in a shack they put together with rocks and wooden boards picked up in the dump. The oldest daughter, around age twenty, I was told, "got lost" while looking for a job in town a few years back. It was later that I learned that she was likely kidnapped by human traffickers. The father had a crude prosthetic leg and struggled with walking. A log had fallen and crushed his leg while he was collecting trash for recycling when he was young. The mother had a chronic headache and gastrointestinal problems and could only help with the recycling work sometimes. Their son was around twelve, and their twin daughters were sixteen. When I first visited them, they only had two years of schooling. The most distressing thing was that there was a brick wall constructed by other poor families at the dumpsite separating the Chens from the center of the site where fresh garbage was received. The Chens were pushed over to where the unrecyclable trash was disposed, next to toxic black sewage.

It was appalling to see how even among the poorest communities, vicious competition and segregation can distort human relations. This community of six or seven families at a dumpsite were migrants from rural China. They were among the three hundred million migrant workers who had moved from rural China to the cities looking for jobs and a better life. The waves of migration started in the 1990s after China's economic reform. These migrant workers took up mostly factory jobs working very long hours. Many work in low-paying construction, cleaning, garbage recycling, or other dirty, dangerous, and difficult jobs. Because of an anachronistic population control policy installed in 1958, the *hukou* system, that separates urban dwellers and rural peasants, these migrant workers do not have access to any government services such as housing, education, health care, or social welfare. Although some migrants might break out of poverty through hard work, luck, and ingenious means of pooling resources with relatives and clans, most of them are stuck with low-paying jobs even after having worked in the city for decades. They remain segregated in urban slums.

The Chen family is one of the hundreds of millions stuck in poverty as the other millions are becoming wealthy in China's fast-growing economy. They stand on the low end of the income gap and social divide that is a result of the blatantly unjust social system that allows only some people to access valuable resources. The twin sisters and their brother were once given free schooling for a couple of years by a good-hearted principal who founded an unregistered primary school for poor migrant students. Though the sisters and brother graduated at the top of their classes, no public middle school could take them because they had nonlocal *hukou*. The family got some support from us and some local philanthropists to send the brother to a private school in another province. But the twin sisters refused to go to a local private school that would take them in. They felt that it was an unacceptable luxury to go to school while their parents were toiling in the dumpsite to make a living for the family. So they decided to work to help support the family and their brother's education.

After working in grocery stores, food shops, microchip factories, and fruit processing plants, the twin sisters became very ill due to excessively long work hours and lack of nutrition. One had serious back pain and would need to take dozens of painkillers each day to keep herself sitting at the factory. The other sister was losing sight in one of her eyes. We paid for their medical treatments and wanted to get them into less hostile work environments. So we networked them with a small social enterprise in town that was helping poor youth. The owner tried to teach the twin sisters basic computer skills, such as using Microsoft Excel to do simple bookkeeping. This was an opportunity for the sisters to get into a growing sector with a better future in the finance and technology economy.

Imagine the gap the twin sisters had to overcome. They had two years of formal schooling in a substandard migrant school, had never touched a computer keyboard, and didn't know what an email account was. They had never worked in an environment where they had to interact much with people. So they were very anxious and kept questions to themselves. They tried very hard. But the gap was so huge and the mismatch between the person and the environment so great that despite some progress, they had to drop out after five months. The sisters just didn't have the basic digital literacy common among urban youth nor the social skills for working in an office setting. Both returned to work as waitresses in a restaurant on the outskirts of Beijing.

The Chen sisters represent a large group of underprivileged youth in our technology economy. How can we initiate upward social mobility, justice, and hope for the millions of migrant youth in China, across Asia, and even in other parts of the world when the gaps are so great? How can we provide technical and social skills on a community level? If it is so difficult to help even one family, is it possible to change the structure of the education system and to promote inclusiveness, diversity, care, collaboration, and a sense of community on a larger level?

Project C: An Experiment in Crossing Divides

When tackling the issues of the social and digital divide, the mission is first to make people aware of the injustice in the system and the inequality leading to the growing gaps in income, access, and opportunity. We then bring people from both sides of the divide together to work on restoring the community so that it is more equitable. In the process, people with more resources need to go to those with fewer resources. They need to impart skills and partake in interactions—practical skills that provide access to the technology economy and caring interactions that bring positive social development. The skill for the twenty-first century is digital literacy. While it is debatable if computer science will be a dominant subject of learning in the coming decades, there is little question that coding education is a growing global trend. Therefore, in an experiment to cross the divide, we focused on building coding skills.

Putting ideas into action, we started an experiment in Hong Kong in 2015 called Project C—a project inspired by our failure in helping the Chen sisters. Before describing the project, some contextual information is called for. Although Hong Kong is one of the richest cities in the world—ranked ten, with a GDP per capita of $64,488 in 2018, which is one notch higher than the United States ($62,641) and one lower than Switzerland ($68,943[4])—it has the highest income inequality of all developed countries, with a Gini Index (a measure of the gap between the rich and the poor) of 53.9 in 2021. For comparison, the same year Gini Index of the United States is 41.1, and Switzerland's is 32.7.[5]

In terms of the digital divide, a team from the Diocesan Girls' School of Hong Kong won the grand prize in a mobile app development competition at the 2017 Technovation World Pitch Summit at Google's headquarters. In the same school year, our colleagues found that some of the middle school students in one of the less resourceful schools did not even know how to type *A* on the keyboard. That is the digital divide in Hong Kong.

Many of the underprivileged students come from low-income families, ethnic minorities from South or Southeast Asia, and new arrivals who have migrated from the rural or small towns of mainland China. So migrant youth make up a large percentage of the underprivileged. In the past twenty-five years, there have been over 1.4 million new arrivals from the mainland, and over half of them are school-aged children. For a city of seven million, that is a large number.

Project C seeks to build an inclusive platform for bringing together underprivileged youth from underresourced schools with resourceful groups in the community to provide psychosocial development and computational skills through digital literacy and social integration. It takes *computing* to the underprivileged and brings mentors from the *community* who have *care* and *compassion* for these youth to *connect* with them and *coach* them to *code collaboratively* with *creativity* to *change* the *community* in the love of *Christ*.

The project is made up of two major parts: coding and mentoring. These two parts intend to produce three outcomes: computational thinking, psychosocial development, and community involvement. Computational thinking is taught through coding lessons and activities. Students learn to use a visual programming tool to develop mobile apps. The focus is on motivating students to observe their environment and identify practical problems they can solve with their coding skills. Psychosocial development is supported through mentoring, and mentors are mostly recruited from local churches. They do not need to have any computer programming skills—only a passion to care for and communicate with underprivileged youth. Mentors work with students to identify problems in their communities and then develop mobile apps to solve these problems. Students can also create mobile apps to showcase some unique landmarks or feature a well-known personality in their neighborhood. Through their interactions, mentors provide students with social support and enhance their confidence and motivation. Both mentors and mentees can develop a greater sense of belonging in the community and an attitude of service.

Project C has been piloted for two years in eight different schools with over 1,100 students. From our initial evaluation, we found that the students have made significant gains in perceived social support, sense of community, responsibility, and hope. In our interviews with the mentors and students, we collected numerous stories of how they have changed. Some of the mentors went the extra mile with the students and helped them improve academically. The math grade of one student went from 0 to 30 percent after only two tutoring sessions from a mentor and his volunteer. Some students did not think they had the aptitude for programming but were encouraged by their mentors to complete their projects. In the end, they felt a sense of confidence they never had. One mentor reported that after three months in the program, her students started to ask her about her faith because they were touched by her genuine care and support—the program discourages active preaching to students but encourages mentors to share their faith if students initiate the conversation. Eventually, these students were asked to go to church with the mentor. One of the students later committed her life to Christ.

Conclusion

In this chapter, we see how a practical program with a mission of providing creative technological skills to underprivileged youth and bringing social integration to the community can be impactful. Yet it is conceptually grounded in a holistic and comprehensive view of the mission of God. Surely there are limitations to Project C. There are questions of sustainability in terms of funding support, efficiency in the program delivery, and depth of impact in the community to bring wider social and cultural change. But just as our Christian lives go through the process of sanctification, striving to be more like Christ to regain the *imago Dei,* so do ministries that seek to transform communities to become more like the kingdom of God. Migration theology provides a rich framework for conceptualizing the mission for the underprivileged, especially among migrants marginalized in the technology economy.

To cross social and digital divides, we cannot just impart computing skills. Neither can we just provide social support. A holistic framework calls for an integrated approach, and it was a hard lesson we learned by working with migrant youth in Beijing. Our failure in getting the Chen sisters into the technology economy led to our coding project for the underprivileged. The twin sisters remain excluded from the technology economy despite our support. Fortunately, through a community of caring individuals and institutions, their brother graduated from college this year and got a job in finance in Beijing. Hopefully, that will pave the way for a better future for the family.

Project C seeks to engage a larger community, to be more effective in fighting poverty, to create the kingdom of God on earth through boundary crossing of various types. The project integrates education, technology, psychosocial development, and community service through coding. It allows the resourceful and underprivileged to cross the divides between them. The message of hope, care, and creativity has come through. But the work is complex and begs for a greater impact. So much more needs to be done, and there are miles to go before we sleep. Perhaps then I can dream of an old theology professor drinking cheap coffee in a slum café with a young start-up software engineer, talking about developing an app that provides jobs to the neighborhood youth in making animation videos of biblical stories.

Notes

1 See Marshall McLuhan, Quentin Fiore, and Jerome Agel, *The Medium Is the Message* (New York: Bantam, 1967); and Neil Postman, *Technopoly: The Surrender of Culture to Technology* (New York: Vintage, 1993).

2 See Daniel Groody, "Homeward Bound: A Theology of Migration," *Journal of Catholic Social Thought* 9, no. 2 (2012): 409–23.

3 See Angus Deaton, *The Great Escape: Health, Wealth, and the Origin of Inequality* (Princeton, NJ: Princeton University Press, 2013).

4 World Bank, "GDP per Capita, PPP (Current International Dollar)," accessed August 20, 2019, https://data.worldbank.org/indicator/NY.GDP.PCAP.PP.CD.

5 World Factbook, "Gini Index," accessed September 1, 2021, https://www.cia.gov/the-world-factbook/field/gini-index-coefficient-distribution-of-family-income.

Bibliography

Deaton, Angus. *The Great Escape: Health, Wealth, and the Origin of Inequality*. Princeton, NJ: Princeton University Press, 2013.

Groody, Daniel. "Homeward Bound: A Theology of Migration." *Journal of Catholic Social Thought* 9, no. 2 (2012): 409–423.

McLuhan, Marshall, Quentin Fiore, and Jerome Agel. *The Medium Is the Message*. New York: Bantam, 1967.

Postman, Neil. *Technopoly: The Surrender of Culture to Technology*. New York: Vintage, 1993.

World Bank. "GDP per Capita, PPP (Current International Dollar)." Accessed August 20, 2019. https://data.worldbank.org/indicator/NY.GDP.PCAP.PP.CD.

World Factbook. "Gini Index." Accessed September 1, 2021. https://www.cia.gov/the-world-factbook/field/gini-index-coefficient-distribution-of-family-income.

Wright, Christopher J. H. *The Mission of God: Unlocking the Bible's Grand Narrative*. Nottingham, UK: InterVarsity, 2006.

8

═══

Transnational Churches

Indian Denominations in the Persian Gulf

Sam George

It was a scorching early morning when I stepped outside the Doha International Airport in the late summer of 2017. I was flying on Qatar Airways from the United States to Kochi, India, and made a brief stopover for the weekend at the capital of this Persian Gulf nation. An Indian acquaintance who works in the banking sector and has lived in the city for nearly two decades came to pick me up, and we drove straight to his church. It was composed entirely of Kerala Christians, and service was in Malayalam, which made me wonder if I had landed in Kerala. Over the past few years, I had opportunities to visit many cities of Persian Gulf nations and interact with communities of diverse church traditions, denominations, languages, and nationalities. The vibrant diaspora churches in the Islamic heartlands of the world are a fascinating dimension of global Christianity and present many stimulating lessons for all Christians everywhere.

In this essay, I briefly survey the history of a particular Indian denomination in a lesser-known city of the Persian Gulf region—namely, Doha, Qatar—and explore various transnational dynamics, interactions, and transformative effects on the Indian church. Under the rubrics of diaspora or migration studies, there have been some publications on Indian migrants in the Persian Gulf in recent years and on Indian Christians in the region.[1] A few others have examined migration-led transformation in Indian denominational entities from a scholarly perspective and the missional impact of these diaspora communities.[2]

Indian Christianity in the Persian Gulf

Although Indians have been in contact with the Persian Gulf region for centuries because of trade links they had with the western port towns of India, only in the last five decades has the presence of Indian communities become considerable in the region. Since the oil boom of the 1970s, large masses from South Asian nations like Bangladesh, India, Nepal, Pakistan, and Sri Lanka began to migrate to the Persian Gulf nations. India records the largest share of migrant workers in the Persian Gulf, and people from Kerala constitute a large portion of it. The United Arab Emirates (UAE) is the largest destination of Indian migrants in the world, and there is a sizeable number of expatriates in Saudi Arabia, Kuwait, Oman, Bahrain, and Qatar. The Indian presence in Iran, Iraq, and Yemen has dwindled in recent years on account of wars, political instability, and the lack of job opportunities there. Indians work in oil, construction, shipping, health care, retail, technology, or other service sectors on a contractual basis. The construction frenzy of the region continues to draw a large number of laborers from India, many of whom live in labor camps and are forced to leave their families behind in India. There is widespread abuse and exploitation among Indian migrant workers in the region.

Indian migrant workers send a record amount of remittances back to their families year after year. Many national economies and households are dependent on regular remittances for their financial well-being. Being a shipping and trade center, the port cities of the Gulf require a large pool of migrant workers to man their operations, and the big cities of the region have emerged as global hubs with their world-class airlines and hosting of megaevents and conventions, all of which require a steady supply of personnel. In recent years, some Gulf cities have emerged as major technology, media, and retail centers by attracting investments, brand companies, and customers from around the world. By allowing several reputable Western universities to open their branches in the region, they keep their young from migrating abroad and attract young talent from around the world.

As Indians cannot settle permanently or become citizens in the Gulf States, they "live suspended in a state of permanent temporariness."[3] Some second- and third-generation Indians in the Gulf are called "temporary guest workers" and are treated as perpetual outsiders. With numerous daily flights from the Gulf to all major Indian cities, Indians have become a vital part of these countries and their economy but are treated as a second class no matter how well educated or financially successful they are. The alienation at workplaces and in the host society results in conflictual notions of belonging because they view themselves as being in the Gulf only to make money, while India remains their permanent home. As everyone eventually has to return to India at the expiration of their work contracts, they keep more in touch with their ancestral homelands and are less inclined to build any meaningful relations with the natives.

Since the turn of the millennium, religious activities among Indian migrants in the Gulf countries have become noticeable, particularly among radical religious groups. Muslim groups with strong Wahabi traditions such as the Jamaat-e-Islami, Hindu religiopolitical groups such as Rashtriya Swayamsevak Sangh (RSS), and religious cult groups like Mata Amritanandamayi have made inroads in the lives of immigrants. Many independent church groups with neo-Pentecostal slants and televangelists have emerged with a strong following and financial support from their Gulf patrons. Their lack of social interaction with the local people and the estrangement they feel as migrant workers in a foreign land deepen their quest for spiritual meaning and identity. Several Indian churches and denominations were quick to take advantage of this longing and have established thousands of churches and home fellowships across the Persian Gulf region, some formally organized but most small and secretive.

The churches in the Persian Gulf nations come in many sizes, colors, and stripes. Being diaspora congregations, most are organized along the lines of ethnicity, language, or nationality.[4] The English churches belonging to the Anglican or Western traditions cater to expatriates, and international churches offering services in English attract people of many nations. There is an ecumenical regional association of churches known as the Gulf Churches Fellowship[5] that comprises churches of Catholic, Eastern Orthodox, Episcopal, Protestant, Reformed, and Evangelical traditions. The vast majority of churches in the Persian Gulf nations belong to the Indians, and all major Indian denominations have established their branches there. They include the Indian Orthodox, Syro-Malabar Catholic, Malankara Catholic, Syrian Jacobite, Mar Thoma, St. Thomas Evangelical, Church of South India, Indian Methodist, Indian Lutheran, Indian Pentecostal Church, Indian Assemblies of God, Sharon Fellowship, Indian Brethren Assembly, New Life Fellowship, Church of God, Church of Christ, Apostolic churches of India, and so on. They conduct services in Malayalam, Tamil, Telugu, Hindi, Punjabi, Gujarati, Kannada, and Urdu. Some of them offer English services to cater to the needs of their young who have grown up in the Gulf and are studying in English medium or international schools. Numerous nondenominational and independent churches in the Gulf remain culturally Indian without any institutional affiliation with churches in India and have mushroomed all over the region in the last two decades.

Mar Thoma Churches in the Gulf

The Mar Thoma Church traces its origin to the apostle Thomas, one of the disciples of Jesus who is believed to have landed on the Malankara coast (modern-day Kerala) in 52 CE. This Indian denomination is an Eastern Oriental Reformed church that uses St. James liturgy translated into Malayalam for worship. All of its leaders hail from Kerala, and the church is headquartered in Tiruvalla in central Kerala. It emerged out of the ancient Malankara Syrian Orthodox Church of India when Reformation ideas reached the Indian shores in the nineteenth century.[6] It is an autonomous church that retains an ecumenical relationship with the Church of South India and the Church of North India and plays an active role in the ongoing activities of the World Council of Churches. The church defines itself as "Apostolic in origin, Universal in nature, Biblical in faith, Oriental in worship, Evangelical in principle, Ecumenical in outlook, Democratic in function, and Episcopal in character."[7]

The Mar Thoma Church has a significant presence in the Persian Gulf, with twenty parishes in five countries. The pioneers were doctors and nurses who came to work in British and American mission hospitals in the 1950s. Later, they were followed by engineers and semiskilled workers in the 1960s, and large-scale migration began in the 1970s and 1980s to work in the oil refineries and related industries. The earliest Mar Thoma parish was established in Kuwait in 1963, and now there are seven parishes in that small nation. It has the distinction of closing down during the Kuwait war in 1990 and reopening a year later. The Kuwait City Mar Thoma parish remains one of the largest parishes of the Mar Thoma Church, with nearly five thousand members. There are six Mar Thoma parishes in the United Arab Emirates (UAE)—one each in Abu Dhabi, Dubai, Sharjah, Fujairah, Al-Ain, and Ras-al-Khaimah. There are four parishes in the Sultanate of Oman and two in the island nation of Bahrain. There is only one Mar Thoma parish in Qatar, none in Yemen, and a few informal gatherings in Saudi Arabia, since Christian services are illegal in that nation. These parishes are administered under different dioceses of the church, and bishops are stationed in different places in India. The priests are sent by the church leaders in Kerala for a fixed term of three years, and churches are managed by local elected officials under the direction of priests.

The Mar Thoma parish in Doha began at the initiative of migrants who hailed from a Mar Thoma background and came to work in Qatar. The first church service was held in April 1967 by bringing a Mar Thoma vicar from Kuwait, and thereafter services were conducted once every three months. Subsequently, in the 1970s, the parish was helped by priests stationed across the Middle East as well as visiting evangelists, priests, and bishops from Kerala. The pioneers met at homes and villas at regular intervals as a Mar Thoma community and later met in a "cattle shed" and a local college for some time. They had to move around to different facilities and locations for church meetings and were at the mercy of local authorities and facility owners.

A full-time Mar Thoma priest was assigned to the Doha parish[8] in 1990 and secured land and permission to build a church facility in 2005. Currently, the parish is served by two resident Mar Thoma *achens* (priests or pastors) and comes under the Kottarakara-Punalur diocese of the church. They conduct Malayalam services every Thursday evening and Friday morning as well as an English service on second Fridays. With nearly two thousand active members, they are organized as prayer groups and hold a wide range of activities throughout the calendar year. A multitude of church leaders as well as preachers, missionaries, and singers from Kerala and elsewhere regularly visit the parish. They provide financial support for various projects of the diocese and the church.

A Transnational Church: Diasporic Dynamics

A church that was entirely confined to central Kerala for centuries has been transformed into a global church in the last five decades on account of the migration of its members. In the grand scheme of things, this makeover is remarkable and offers many insights into the role of migration in the remaking of Christianity itself. The ethnic culture and religion aid in asserting identity in a foreign land while diasporas act as a catalyst for ecclesial and institutional change in the homeland. The diaspora Mar Thoma churches have been agents of religious transformation by bringing new dynamism to an ancient order by leveraging their educational achievements, financial resources, and new ways of thinking. However, at times, this global church still operates like a parochial Central Travancore church of the nineteenth century.

At the time of India's independence, as a result of high literacy and unemployment levels in Kerala as well as the limitation of land and industrialization, many educated and ambitious young people of Kerala explored vocational opportunities in other parts of India.[9] They kept ties with their church hierarchies and established denominational churches wherever a sizeable number of them found employment. These locations became a launching pad for subsequent international migration, and these pioneers used the same logic to start distinctive denominational churches at their places of foreign settlement. A state- and language-based religious body gained a national presence and later dispersed worldwide, and because of this, a regional church was transformed into a national and global entity.

As large-scale, long-distance migration began toward the West and the Gulf, most Indian denominational churches did not have any vision to expand their operation or establish branches overseas. Unable to associate with people in host cultures or embrace their faiths, the migrant pioneers were quick to establish prayer and fellowship groups wherever they went, as it provided a way to meet their sociocultural and spiritual longings in a foreign land. The migrants carried their distinctive spirituality and religious culture with them to their chosen destinations and played a vital role in the formation and expansion of Indian churches beyond their shores. For example, the Mar Thoma Church leadership did not permit people to start churches outside of India in the 1960s despite many requests from Mar Thoma groups in Malaysia, the United Kingdom, Singapore, the United States, and the Gulf. They were encouraged to go to local Protestant churches but were asked to maintain ties with their ancestral churches in Kerala.[10] However, the priests who went to study at seminaries in the United States and the United Kingdom served the scattered believers there and later became advocates to senior church leaders in Kerala to start Mar Thoma churches in foreign lands.

The cyclical nature of migration and temporary employment in the Gulf significantly restructures the social hierarchy, economic class structure, family dynamics, and religious practices in Kerala.[11] The rotational system of church leadership works well in the Gulf context and helps maintain close ties to institutional structures in the ancestral homelands. These congregations remain culturally closer to Kerala, as people do not see their future locally beyond their working years. However, this arrangement does not afford church leaders any longitudinal insights, and church culture is continually refreshed to that of their ancestral homelands every three years. The consequence is more obvious among Indian diaspora churches in the West than in the Gulf.

Most Gulf parishes of the Mar Thoma Church tend to be large and are beyond the reach of one or two priests. Without adequate pastoral care, many parishioners are drawn to other vibrant groups and teachings of charismatic leaders. An elected official of the Doha parish informed me that over time, people are less connected to or involved with the church and are induced into incorrect beliefs and practices. The reciprocal influence on Kerala Christians includes the rise of the prosperity gospel and televangelists who beam their programs widely to dispersed masses in the Gulf and solicit financial support to grow their work further in India. Mar Thoma clergy and people consider Gulf appointments as a financial reward posting by bishops to older and needy priests at the end of their term who cannot serve effectively in the new context with younger members. They cannot handle the increased pace of life and ministry and are found to be very rigid in their ways and unable to cope with such a ministry assignment.

The Indian denominations in the Gulf are generally seen as a major source of financial support for mother churches in India, and commitment seems to be limited to offering minimal support for the highest returns without any long-term vision or ministry in the Islamic host society. The denominational leaders make coercive demands on a portion of remittances from their scattered members. Kerala parishes make appeals through letters, emails, and phone calls to solicit money for building renovations and mission projects from their nonresident members, reminding them of their ministry to family members and their eventual return. Many migrants are found to donate generously to church and charitable projects from their newly acquired wealth out of a sense of gratitude to God, to repay their debt to religious leaders back home, and for missionary work. The public proclamation of foreign donation provides prestige and prominence back home and is used to motivate other members to solicit support from overseas family members. The migrants gain legitimacy and power by acquiring currencies of respectability in a highly communitarian society.

The Gulf migrants and returnees donate to secure their place in venerable church bodies for social upward mobility and have become a force for change within religious polities and ministries. For example, Mar Thoma leaders in several Gulf nations have been demanding the status of a diocese for many years in order to create more positions and greater representation in the affairs of the church in the region. Church leaders are opposed to a permanent Gulf diocese because of the lack of freedom for Christian activities in a predominantly Islamic theocratic society, the transient nature of Gulf expatriates, and the fear of undermining the current arrangement of monetary support of each parish to various dioceses in India. Gulf parishes and the mother church seem to be in an unhealthy codependent relationship that both cannot live without.

Moreover, Indian churches in the Gulf have no or little interaction with the host society or other migrants. Due to laws against proselytizing and fear of deportation, the migrants keep their faith to themselves and do not want to jeopardize their livelihood or their prospect of reentering the country. They remain an ethnocentric social club without any evangelistic fervor to share the gospel with others. Often Syrian Christians preserve caste-like ethnocultural exclusivity and are opposed to creating space for people unlike themselves in their churches. However, there are many "conversions" among Indian Christians in the Gulf, mostly from one church to another, as many charismatic groups have been successful in veering people away from traditional faith and denominational affiliations. People abandon sterile religious ritualism for more intimate fellowships and deeper spiritual experiences. There is a proliferation of new-generation churches with neo-Pentecostal leanings that are led by self-proclaimed pastors or apostles who have no theological training or ministerial accountability. A Mar Thoma church leader in Doha bemoaned the fact that some church members have joined other churches after taking adult baptism and how priests are expected to keep the flock from straying to greener pastures or becoming prey to the work of Pentecostal pastors. Conversely, an Indian Pentecostal pastor in Doha apprised me of how so many traditional Kerala Christians are getting "saved after coming to the Gulf" as they experience relational and spiritual intimacy with other Spirit-filled believers. Some are drawn to the new-generation churches after experiencing miracles or healing, and switching churches does not cause any social ostracization as in Kerala. There are several cases of Hindus, Muslims, and Sikhs who have embraced Christianity in Qatar and are active in Indian evangelical or Pentecostal churches but are less likely to join a traditional church. Overall, it is true that after migrating to the Gulf, Indian Christians are revived in their faith and have a positive impact on families and communities back home. They also play an instrumental role in transforming ecclesial bodies in their places of origin and destination.

Conclusion

As a result of the migration of people to foreign countries, geographically confined and culturally defined church denominations are transformed into global entities. Both migrants and their ancestral religious institutions reciprocally support and influence each other through many sustained interactions. Their transnational exchanges facilitate cross-cultural diffusion and alter ecclesial practices and institutional structures. As migrants strive to reproduce their ancestral faith in foreign lands, they also borrow faith expressions from local realities and other churches. The diaspora Christians are two-way mediators for change in both sending and receiving places, as seen in the example of the Mar Thoma parish in Doha.

Notes

1 See three chapters on Indian Christians in Kuwait, UAE, and the Gulf at large in Sam George, ed., *Desi Diaspora: Ministry to Scattered Asian Indians* (Bangalore: SAIACS, 2019). Also T. V. Thomas, "South Asian Diaspora Christianity in the Persian Gulf," in *Diaspora Christianities: Global Scattering and Gathering of South Asian Christians*, ed. Sam George (Minneapolis: Fortress, 2018).

2 For example, see Prema Kurien, "The Impact of International Migration on Home Churches: The Mar Thoma Syrian Christian Church in India," *Journal for the Scientific Study of Religion* 53, no. 1 (2014): 109–29. Also Stanley V. John, *Transnational Religious Organization and Practice: A Contextual Analysis of Kerala Pentecostal Churches in Kuwait* (Leiden: Brill, 2018).

3 Neha Vora, *Impossible Citizens: Dubai's Indian Diaspora* (Durham, NC: Duke University Press, 2013).

4 For a history on churches in UAE and Oman, see Andrew Thompson, *Christianity in the United Arab Emirates: Culture and Heritage* (Abu Dhabi: Motivate, 2014); and Andrew Thompson, *Christianity in Oman* (London: Palgrave Macmillan, 2019).

5 See Gulf Churches Fellowship, accessed February 29, 2020, http:// gulfchurches.org.

6 For a wider history of Indian Christianity, see Robert E. Frykenberg, *Christianity in India: From Beginning to the Present* (Oxford: Oxford University Press, 2008).

7 See the Malakara Mar Thoma Syrian Church website, http://marthoma.in. For more on the history of the church, see Zac Varghese Kanisseril and Mathew A. Kallumpram, *Glimpses of Mar Thoma Church History* (New Delhi: Kalpana, 2003). On its transformation into a global church, see M. J. Joseph, ed., *In Search of Christian Identity in Global Community* (Tiruvalla, India: Christava Sahitya Samithi, 2009).

8 Known as Immanuel Mar Thoma Church in Doha. See Immanuel Mar Thoma Church, accessed December 31, 2019, https://www.imtcdoha.com.

9 For an account of global dispersion of people from Kerala, see Sam George and T. V. Thomas, eds., *Malayali Diaspora: From Kerala to the Ends of the World* (New Delhi: Serials, 2012).

10 Annamma Thomas and T. M. Thomas, *Kerala Immigrants in America* (Cochin, India: Simons, 1984); T. M. Thomas and Abraham Mattackal, eds., *In the Beginning: Formative Years of Mar Thoma Parishes in North America* (Tiruvalla, India: Christava Sahitya Samithi, 2008).

11 Ginu Zacharia Oommen, "Gulf Migration, Social Remittance and Religion: The Changing Dynamics of Kerala Christians," accessed January 31, 2020, https://www.mea.gov.in/images/pdf/GulfMigrationSocialRemittancesandReligion.pdf.

Bibliography

Frykenberg, Robert E. *Christianity in India: From Beginning to the Present*. Oxford: Oxford University Press, 2008.

George, Sam, ed. *Desi Diaspora: Ministry to Scattered Asian Indians*. Bangalore: SAIACS Press, 2019.

———, ed. *Malayali Diaspora: From Kerala to the Ends of the World.* New Delhi: Serials, 2012.

John, Stanley V. *Transnational Religious Organization and Practice: A Contextual Analysis of Kerala Pentecostal Churches in Kuwait.* Leiden: Brill, 2018.

Joseph, M. J., ed. *In Search of Christian Identity in Global Community.* Tiruvalla, India: Christava Sahitya Samithi, 2009.

Kanisseril, Zac Varghese, and Mathew A. Kallumpram. *Glimpses of Mar Thoma Church History.* New Delhi: Kalpana, 2003.

Kurien, Prema. "The Impact of International Migration on Home Churches: The Mar Thoma Syrian Christian Church in India." *Journal for the Scientific Study of Religion* 53, no. 1 (2014): 109–129.

Thomas, Annama, and T. M. Thomas. *Kerala Immigrants in America.* Cochin, India: Simons, 1984.

Thomas, T. M., and Abraham Mattackal, eds. *In the Beginning: Formative Years of Mar Thoma Parishes in North America.* Tiruvalla, India: Christava Sahitya Samithi, 2008.

Thomas, T. V. "South Asian Diaspora Christianity in the Persian Gulf." In *Diaspora Christianities: Global Scattering and Gathering of South Asian Christians*, edited by Sam George, 110–126. Minneapolis: Fortress, 2018.

Thompson, Andrew. *Christianity in Oman.* London: Palgrave Macmillan, 2019.

———. *Christianity in the United Arab Emirates: Culture and Heritage.* Abu Dhabi: Motivate, 2014.

Vora, Neha. *Impossible Citizens: Dubai's Indian Diaspora.* Durham, NC: Duke University Press, 2013.

9

Adventures of the Lebanese Diaspora

Mental Well-Being in Foreign Lands

Naji Abi-Hashem

Introduction

Lebanese people have always had a desire to travel and explore the world. By nature, they are very enthusiastic wanderers with roots going back to the Phoenicians, who roamed the Mediterranean Sea on large ships made of the cedars of Lebanon. Geographically, Lebanon is a tiny nation with a beautiful landscape and many natural resources. Its main revenue sources are tourism, banking, education, small industries, and agriculture. In 1943, Lebanon became an independent nation and is governed by a parliamentary democracy. Its cities are cosmopolitan and have an international atmosphere, as the three languages of Arabic-Lebanese, French, and English are commonly used in daily life, education, and business.

As of 2020, the population of Lebanon was about five million people, but there are at least an additional two million foreign migrant workers and refugees in the country. The number of Lebanese living and working outside the country is estimated to be between ten and sixteen million, which makes Lebanon one of the few countries in the world whose expatriate population far exceeds its residents.[1] Lebanon is truly a mosaic of subcultures, mentalities, religious traditions, educational backgrounds, and integrated worldviews, balancing Middle Eastern with Western values, customs, social norms, and lifestyles.

Migratory Waves from Lebanon

In the past 150 years, many waves of Lebanese migrants left for West Africa and the Americas. The first known wave of migration is documented around 1860, and subsequent waves followed during the First World War and especially after the Second World War. Between 1870 and 1930, about 330,000 migrants left the East Mediterranean area—Mount Lebanon and Syria (including Palestine at the time)—for the Americas.[2] Since the 1960s, migration to North America has been steady, at first from the Christian communities of Lebanon and Syria but later from other groups, like Sunnis, Shiites, Druze and Jews, and other Arabic-speaking countries in the Middle East.[3]

Although many Lebanese uprooted themselves and migrated with no intention of returning, they kept their heritage and tradition alive and stayed in close contact with their homeland. Others left Lebanon mainly to establish a foreign base where life is more stable, predictable, and secure. They sought additional citizenship in case the situation in Lebanon deteriorated further. Many foreign embassies made applications for permanent visas easier than usual because their respective countries liked the Lebanese population due to their middle-class status, higher educational skills, and smaller family size.

In addition, there are seasonal travelers who live and work in two countries—for example, the Gulf area, North and West Africa, and parts of Europe—and return at the end of the work season. Not to mention the multitude of students pursuing education abroad, businesspeople, diplomatic delegates, academics and research scholars, and family members and friends all spending long periods abroad. The circular movement of the Lebanese diaspora is fluid, and it is difficult to ascertain the exact number of resident-nationals inside versus the migrant-internationals outside Lebanon. Likewise, it is difficult to determine the psychological, sociopolitical, and cultural impact of the returnees (with their newly adopted ideas, habits, norms, innovations, views, skills, etc.) on local Lebanese dynamics, mentalities, and society at large.[4]

People of Lebanese descent are found in almost every corner of the earth (except perhaps the two poles). Thus every resident in Lebanon has a family member, relative, or close friend somewhere else in the world. Lebanese emigrants are found in large numbers in the following countries (highest concentration first): Brazil, the United States, Argentina, Venezuela, Colombia, Mexico, Australia, France, Canada, the Arabic Gulf countries, western Asia, North and West Africa, Syria, and so on.[5] These are sample statistics but not a comprehensive count, because people of Lebanese ancestry are present in virtually every nation, from South

Africa to Scandinavia, China to Japan, Moscow to Alaska, and so forth, and consequently, they keep expanding and settling in every frontier possible.

There are various motives and causes for leaving one's hometown and migrating internally or internationally to a nearby country or a faraway land. (Those who live in foreign lands or are members of the Arab diaspora are called *mahjar*.) For the Lebanese, the reasons include a desire to explore or seize new educational or business opportunities, a need to seek a better life or escape from troubles at home, or simply an innate love for adventure. The quest to travel, conquer, and resettle is somehow in the Lebanese DNA. In addition, severe economic crises, social unrest, and political turmoil, mainly during and after the Ottoman Empire rule and the First World War, caused some Lebanese to look westward to the open sea to escape the seemingly painful and hopeless living conditions at home.

The Christian communities in Mount Lebanon were marginalized, mistreated, heavily taxed, and oppressed. The collapse of silk production and industries resulted in famine in the region. Scores of peasants from poor towns and villages spread across the hills of Lebanon or boarded large ships toward West Africa (as did my own father in the 1930s, heading to Ghana, then known as the Gold Coast) or sailed to Brazil, Mexico, and Venezuela as their favorite destinations with only a one-way ticket and the clothes on their back.[6]

During the recent decades and up to our modern days, Lebanese of all classes and backgrounds have been journeying out by invitation to join family members or to begin new lives. They sell their properties and transfer all their assets abroad. They translate their official documents into foreign languages and secure necessary visas, at times after years of waiting and spending a lot of money. The majority of them do well in foreign lands, but unfortunately, some still struggle and have never been able to fully integrate, find their particular niche, or thrive as they had hoped. They suffer constantly from family tensions, cultural shocks, insufficient revenue, and a lack of support from the community.

Life in Lebanon is pleasant and meaningful, with strong family ties, wide social connections, delicious cuisine, natural recreation, free media, and a lively cosmopolitan culture. However, Lebanon has many instabilities, ills, anguishes, and agonies. The endless geopolitical tensions in the area, severe financial crises, political turbulence, accumulated burdens and traumas, major outside interferences, irreconcilable divisions among the ruling parties, limited opportunities, high unemployment rates, need for economic reforms, and the presence of a huge number of foreign workers have been some push factors for Lebanese out-migration, and they have strained the institutions beyond their utmost limits mentally, physically, socially, financially, and psychologically.[7] Political instability and wars in the region recently have only resulted in a record number of migrants and refugees into and out of the country.

My Journey and International Services

I grew up in a mountain town above Beirut, went to a Catholic school, and then spent most of my early adulthood in the state capital, pursuing more education, working, undergoing seminary training, and serving a large church as a junior pastor in West Beirut (1980–83). The years spanning from the late 1970s to the early 1990s were full of sporadic episodes of street violence, political turmoil, and armed-militia conflicts, which was broadly known as the Lebanese civil war (but more accurately should be called other people's wars on our land). During those years, many migrated abroad, especially young people, business owners, and intellectuals. When foreign embassies opened their offices, long lines were formed quickly outside by people seeking permanent visas. The preferred destinations were Canada, Australia, and the United States because they appreciated the industrious minds, assorted skills, and social adaptation of the Lebanese people.

I have known scores of individuals and families who were desperately trying to leave. Once they obtained a visa (any visa), they completely uprooted themselves and impulsively left. I have served people in times of extreme troubles and tragedies and have seen them experience the chronic stresses, fears, and agonies of domestic conflicts, widespread violence, emotional despair, trauma, and deep social devastation. I have observed massive migration out of Lebanon, resulting in a painful brain drain and internal displacement of large groups who lost everything in their hometowns. They were forced to move elsewhere and squeeze into small quarters, and they struggle with severe losses, anxieties, and depression. I also saw the remarkable resiliency of many Lebanese who were coping and surviving well, as each community mobilized their resources, sharing, and caring in remarkable solidarity.[8]

In the early 1980s, I went to the United States, not to escape from the troubles in Beirut, but to pursue graduate education in pastoral care and eventually in clinical psychology and counseling. I got involved in the development and ministry of the Evangelical-Protestant Arabic Middle Eastern congregations and trained leaders for churches in California. I specialized in cross-cultural counseling and focused on the multicultural dynamics and psychosocial functioning of minorities. I began speaking and writing on these and other related topics while actively participating in many national and international conferences.

I spend several months a year in my homeland of Lebanon, helping in community service, college and church teaching, seminary training, trauma care and counseling, and public lecturing and mentoring leaders; supporting orphanages; and performing other activities. There are about two million Syrian migrants and refugees in Lebanon due to the ongoing wars within Syria that began in 2011. The waves of displaced Syrians flooded Lebanon and overwhelmed its resources and infrastructure. The government agencies, private sector NGOs, churches, and other religious groups mobilized their resources to help these newcomers; the majority of Syrians are from rural areas. Some were not directly war victims but came to work or to improve their prospects, as many surrounding nations considered Lebanon a paradise. However, after a few years of helping and providing, teaching and healing, and retraining and resettling them, the Lebanese suffered from compassion fatigue. The ambivalence toward newcomers started growing, with a mixture of feelings and embedded resentment. The Syrian presence, along with some Iraqi and Palestinian refugees, compounded by the geopolitical dynamics and internal mismanagement, has contributed to past and current instability, financial crises, and increased joblessness and has ultimately exhausted the country's resources and hindered its growth.

Lebanon now has the highest refugee-migrant-displaced population per capita in the world. Its cultural, political, demographic, and socioeconomic health is weak, and its overall internal balance is fragile. This tiny country has been historically pushed and pulled by regional troubles and surrounding powers. The combined effect of all these factors and other unseen forces has led Lebanese nationals—particularly young university graduates—to revolt by staging ongoing strikes and massive demonstrations since mid-October 2019. Scores of Lebanese professionals and skilled workers have left to the nearby Gulf States, as they have been on a major recruiting spree over the years. Rarely have I encountered a Lebanese family that is totally intact! Almost every family has lost a home or an asset or a relative during the previous years of militia fighting, civil strife, and armed conflicts (1975–90) and now has one or more members living somewhere abroad in the diaspora.[9]

Surviving and Thriving in the Hosting Societies

The majority of the Lebanese abroad continue to be outstanding and excel in their fields. They have embraced challenges and found creative ways of adapting, problem-solving, and striving (not merely surviving). They spot new opportunities and are quick to seize them. That is partly due to their cultural disposition, multilinguistic ability, innate resiliency, warm social skills, strategic networking, and remarkable flexibility. In addition, and as is the case with other immigrant groups, they sense an increased level of freedom from home country restrictions like family demands, social obligations, moral boundaries, and cultural expectations.

Being in a foreign land has its advantages and disadvantages. For some, it is a fresh beginning and a new launching pad for mobilizing their energy and creativity. Yet for others, it is a crippling reality and almost a gravesite for their talents and aspirations. Some who cannot cope or function properly pack up again and return home. Others cannot send money or any positive reports as expected of them. They become stuck and caught between a rock and a hard place. They keep a low profile and manage life from day to day. These migrants fail to cope, belong, or integrate in a timely or healthy manner. Forming a new, expanded identity and a reference-point community is not easy amid all the mental stressors, survival challenges, and societal barriers. They do not expect to face such psychosocial challenges, especially young, inexperienced, and single travelers. Individuals and small family units lack the emotional training and adaptation skills needed for cross-cultural adjustment and the ability to form a newly balanced and integrated sense of belonging.[10]

For immigrants who originated in more collective societies or traditional cultures and who travel to more individualistic societies, the task of *acculturation* can be overwhelming.[11] Some newcomers who feel shy and intimidated by totally different settings minimize their exposure and remain unassertive. Others take risks and become highly motivated to establish themselves—for them, only the sky is the limit! The fact that most international travelers, foreign students, businesspeople, immigrants, displaced people, refugees, or asylum seekers are not well known upon arrival can itself be a positive asset. They can live anywhere, eat any food, work any job, wear any clothes, speak in a broken accent, and so on without being judged, ridiculed, or shamed. Such behaviors or qualities can never be shown back home, among their family, friends, or colleagues.

During my life and work in the United States, I have observed, trained, dealt with, and treated many foreigners from various backgrounds and nationalities who struggled with or got lost in the larger North American multicultural society. An unplanned or complicated migration process can lead to serious mental and emotional distress, like severe anxiety and clinical depression, substantial social-cultural maladjustment, familial-intergenerational conflict, and major professional impairment.[12]

On the other hand, scores of Lebanese migrants have become well known as business executives, academicians, researchers, scientists, politicians, inventors, community leaders, scholars, educators, clergy-pastors, social activists, health care providers, and the like. Both Lebanese men and women have made substantial contributions to their host societies, in different disciplines and on all social levels. They have earned the highest respect of their institutions, communities, and governments. Numerous Lebanese writers, thinkers, poets, philosophers, and artists have traveled during the last century to the West and other Arabic-speaking countries, where they have settled temporarily or permanently. They have produced outstanding literature, poetry, scripts, analyses, books, and monographs in English, French, Arabic, or other adopted local languages.

Thus the Lebanese diaspora is broad and vibrant. The majority of its settlers—either first, second, or third generation—fare quite well and become highly accomplished. They tend to excel in their respective fields, and many become well-known leaders, move up the corporate echelons, influence strategic spheres, and are occasionally elected to powerful executive-senior roles and key political positions, even as prime ministers and heads of state, as is the case in some Central and South American countries.

Lebanese Diaspora and Transnational Connections

Lebanon has one of the longest histories of *emigration*. Even today, the outward flow continues to be significant despite national efforts to slow it down. However, the recent conflicts in Lebanon have overburdened its domestic and foreign policies, including its migration agenda or the benefits of its widespread and resourceful diaspora. The Lebanese diaspora remains the backbone of the Lebanese economy and a lifeline for countless families and institutions.

The vast majority of Lebanese expatriates care deeply about the recovery of their homeland. They follow the local and regional news passionately; contribute to worthy social, educational, and humanitarian causes; and enthusiastically celebrate national holidays as well as religious feasts. Wherever they settle, they establish local foundations and advocacy groups, like the Lebanese American Association (LAA), the American-Arab Anti-Discrimination Committee (ADC), and the Arab American Institute (AAI).[13] Recently, the Lebanese government established an agency to look after the concerns of its diaspora and coordinate their support for Lebanon. For the first time, it extended the right to vote from afar to them, and many reclaimed their Lebanese nationality.

Working with immigrants, minorities, and refugees of all types—and especially Arab American individuals, families, and groups—I have observed repeatedly their relational dynamics and psychosocial struggles, different coping styles and survival skills, and varying levels of emotional functioning and mental adaptation and how they handle the inevitable internal-intrapsychic versus external-intercultural tensions. These forces unfold and arise during any *cross-cultural immersion* and become more acute when accompanied by preexisting psychological issues and emotional struggles.

Migrants coming from urban settings who are educated and exposed to a Western lifestyle and mentality fare better in their host countries than those coming from rural areas or traditional settings. Acculturation is a demanding process, and moving into a different environment creates substantial challenges and mental shocks. These dynamics often fail during the adaptation-assimilation cycle and the formation of a cohesive identity. Usually, elderly and traditional people hold on to their customs and refuse to adapt (in matters like dress code, social norms, religious practices, habits, rituals, etc.). They become rigid and controlling, afraid of losing their heritage, which leads to more tension, confrontations, and conflicts with the hosting society as well as with their offspring, who usually adapt to local lifestyles rather quickly. The noticeable rise of anti-Arab and anti-Muslim sentiments in the West, commonly known as *Islamophobia*, and the surge of misconceptions and stereotypes, especially after 9/11, have made life difficult for Lebanese in North America. In the United States, there are approximately three to four million Arab Americans and seven to eight million people who identify as Muslims. Until recent years, Lebanese migrants constituted the majority of the Arab American groups.

Those who migrate from troubled areas, where they have experienced political turmoil, social unrest, persecution or torture, armed conflicts, natural disasters, war tragedies, and multiple losses, face a double-edged challenge in the host society: (1) the task of dealing with their sense of loss, grief, bereavement, and unresolved traumas and (2) the task of learning about, adapting to, and functioning within the new world system, a strange and complex environment. To help with these struggles, a lot of culturally appropriate counseling, coaching, and in-depth psychotherapy are needed to facilitate their healing and recovery as well as to help them acquire the necessary insights and skills for healthier accommodation and navigation in the new reality. Culturally sensitive, socially competent, and spiritually aware caregivers should provide these interventions, counseling, and treatments.

Many immigrants employ one or more strategies to cope with the migratory challenges:

1. *Isolation:* They retreat to self-preserve and deal with the host society on a minimum basis, which could lead to significant loneliness, seclusion, and eventual psychosocial alienation.
2. *Fusion:* They completely merge into the new culture, adopt everything it offers, and forget their heritage, identity, memories, and values. They blindly copy behaviors and attitudes to embrace new social norms without objective questioning or rational screening.
3. *Splitting:* They flip back and forth between two modes, displaying two personas and living in two ego states, such as living one version at home and another outside among peers and colleagues. Teenagers are particularly vulnerable, as they are often forced into such a fragmenting role. Parents and

elders impose strict traditional rules at home, which cause mental-emotional splitting and personality compartmentalization.

4. *Integration:* They expand rather than restrict their identity and psychosocial repertoire. They learn to function well within the host society and cultural system without losing their authentic personhood, historical roots, and ethnic-national uniqueness. They can adequately reconcile the internal versus external differences, integrate various polarities, and balance conflicting mentalities and lifestyles. Hopefully, they can do all that with ingenuity, grace, inner peace, and visible harmony.[14]

In terms of *transnationalism*, the Lebanese diaspora is somewhat unlike other migrant groups in that there are no clear boundaries between those inside and outside Lebanon. They constantly overlap as they move in and out. Therefore, their *transnational* relationship is quite integral, organic, and interdependent. This connection (both physical and virtual), along with the fluid movement of travel (carrying multiple passports) and the easy transfer of funds (providing billions of dollars annually), makes that relationship special and alive, as it provides substantial moral and commercial support to the motherland. The Lebanese diaspora has created a long-distance sense of nationalism and decentralized Lebanese geography. The trends of globalization and internationalization have greatly helped in this worldwide process.[15]

In terms of religious involvement, first- and second-generation Lebanese are active in one or more communities of faith for social and spiritual reasons. Many Christians, Muslims, and Druze belong to churches, mosques, or community centers, which could be exclusively Lebanese or mixed Arabic–Middle Eastern congregations. Such communities provide a source of solidarity, refreshment of faith, and cultural continuity for the participants. There are Islamic centers that are mostly Shiite or Sunni and churches that are mostly Orthodox, Catholic (Maronite), or Protestant. Many people float around within these broader community groups (overlooking denominational differences) to get the best ethnic exposure, social nurturance, and religious experience.

Lebanese evangelicals are very active and well received in the diaspora. Some are pastors, theologians, and leaders of humanitarian organizations, denominational bodies, and mission agencies. Others are professors at Christian universities or seminaries, and a few with special training have returned home as international aid workers or cross-cultural missionaries. Numerous television, satellite, and internet broadcasts of spiritual programs in Arabic reach wide audiences worldwide. The Evangelical Association of Arab Ministers in North America (RABITA) provides networking opportunities and resources for Protestant churches through conferences, consultations, and bilingual literature.[16]

Conclusion

As the scattered Lebanese around the world maintain a vital affinity toward their homeland, they have a mental awareness and an emotional bond with anything related to Lebanon in a very nostalgic way. That feeds into the roots of their heritage and informs their newly acquired cultural identity and expanded international mentality. This is true on social, psychological, professional, and existential levels.

They try to operate from an integrated sense of public self and a balanced worldview, moving naturally between the immediate local and extended global spheres. Being raised with a Lebanese mindset, progressive outlook, and multilingual abilities has enabled them to become truly global citizens.

Lebanese expatriates abroad and residents inside Lebanon alike keep hoping and praying that their beloved country will recover from its many wounds, be released from its regional entanglements, recuperate from its financial and political troubles, heal from its past misfortunes and injuries, and be free once again to reclaim its role and status as the modern-day Phoenicia, the land of the cedars, and the Switzerland of the Middle East. Lebanon has played a key role in Christian work in the region and continues to be a major leader and keeper of Christianity in the Near East. Finally, as Pope John Paul II, who loved Lebanon and took upon himself the mission of saving this country from disintegration, eloquently declared during his last historical visit, "Lebanon is more than a country. It is a message."[17] That still resonates around the world, as Lebanon could return as a model of coexistence, a beacon of peace and freedom, and a vibrant example of multicultural harmony.

Notes

1 A. Pukas, "Lebanese across the Globe," *Arab News*, 2018, accessed June 1, 2020, https://www.arabnews.com/node/1296211/middle-east; J. Skulte-Ouaiss and P. Tabar, "Strong in Their Weakness or Weak in Their Strength? The Case of Lebanese Diaspora Engagement with Lebanon," *Immigrants and Minorities* 33, no. 2 (2015): 141.

2 M. Humphrey, "Lebanese Identities: Between Cities, Nations and Trans-Nations," *Arab Studies Quarterly* 26, no. 1 (2004): 32; A. Khater, "Phoenician or Arab, Lebanese or Syrian—Who Were the Early Immigrants to America?," Khayrallah Center for Lebanese Diaspora Studies, 2017, accessed June 1, 2020, https://lebanesestudies.news.chass.ncsu.edu/2017/09/20/phoenician-or-arab/; A. Khater, "Why Did They Leave? Reasons for Early Lebanese Migration," Khayrallah Center for Lebanese Diaspora Studies, 2017, accessed June 1, 2020, https://lebanesestudies.news.chass.ncsu.edu/2017/11/15/why-did-they-leave-reasons-for-early-lebanese-migration/.

3 N. Abi-Hashem, "Working with Middle Eastern Immigrant Families," in *Working with Immigrant Families: A Practical Guide for Counselors*, ed. A. Zagelbaum and J. Carlson (New York: Routledge, 2011), 151–80.

4 See Humphrey, "Lebanese Identities"; W. Pearlman, "Emigration and Power: A Study of Sects in Lebanon 1860–2010," *Politics & Society* 41, no. 1 (2013): 103–33; and Khater, "Phoenician."

5 M. Cumoletti and J. Batalova, "Middle Eastern and North African Immigrants in the United States," Washington, DC: Migration Policy Institute, 2018, accessed June 1, 2020, https://www.migrationpolicy.org/article/middle-eastern-and-north-african-immigrants-united-states; Pukas, "Lebanese."

6 Cf. Pearlman, "Emigration and Power."

7 N. Abi-Hashem, "Pastoral and Spiritual Response to Trauma and Tragedy," in *Tackling Trauma: Global, Biblical and Pastoral Perspectives*, ed. P. A. Barker (London: Langham Global Library, 2019), 152; Humphrey, "Lebanese Identities"; Khater, "Why Did They Leave?" Also see P. Tabar, "Lebanon: A Country of Emigration and Immigration," 2010, accessed January 1, 2021, https://documents.aucegypt.edu/Docs/GAPP/Tabar080711.pdf; and P. Tabar and J. Skulte-Ouaiss, *Politics, Culture and the Lebanese Diaspora* (Newcastle, UK: Cambridge Scholars, 2010).

8 Abi-Hashem, "Pastoral," 165.

9 N. Abi-Hashem, "Trauma, Coping, and Resiliency among Syrian Refugees in Lebanon and Beyond: A Profile of the Syrian Nation at War," in *Human Strengths and Resilience: Developmental, Cross-Cultural and International Perspectives*, ed. G. Rich and J. Sirikantraporn (Lanham, MD: Lexington, 2018), 105–30; D. Eldawy, "A Fragile Situation: Will the Syrian Refugee Swell Push Lebanon over the Edge?," Migration Information Source, 2019, accessed June 1, 2020, https://www.migrationpolicy.org/article/syrian-refugee -swell-push-lebanon-over-edge.

10 Abi-Hashem, "Working with Middle Eastern Families"; N. Abi-Hashem, "Immigrants," in *Encyclopedia of Cross-Cultural Psychology*, ed. K. D. Keith (Malden, MA: Wiley-Blackwell, 2013), 688; N. Abi-Hashem and J. R. Brown, "Intercultural Adjustment," in *Encyclopedia of Cross-Cultural Psychology*, 745; Humphrey, "Lebanese Identities," 34; Pukas, "Lebanese."

11 M. Aprahamian, D. Kaplan, A. Windham, J. Sutter, and J. Visser, "The Relationship between Acculturation and Mental Health of Arab Americans," *Journal of Mental Health Counseling* 33, no. 1 (2011): 82.

12 Abi-Hashem, "Working with Middle Eastern Families"; Abi-Hashem, "Immigrants"; Abi-Hashem, "Pastoral"; N. Abi-Hashem, "Cross-Cultural Psychology and Counseling: A Middle Eastern Perspective," *Journal of Psychology and Christianity* 33, no. 2 (2014): 156–63; Aprahamian et al., "Relationship."

13 See the Arab American Institute, accessed December 1, 2020, http:// www.aaiusa.org.

14 Cf. Abi-Hashem, "Immigrants," 690; Abi-Hashem, "Trauma, Coping and Resiliency," 120; Abi-Hashem, "Pastoral," 152; Aprahamian et al., "Relationship," 90.

15 Cf. Humphrey, "Lebanese Identities"; Skulte-Ouaiss and Tabar, "Strong in Their Weakness."

16 Evangelical RABITA, accessed June 1, 2020, http://www.evangelical
rabita.org.

17 Celestine Bohlen, "Pope Calls on Lebanon to Resume Special Role
for Peace," *New York Times*, May 12, 1997, https://www.nytimes.com/
1997/05/12/world/pope-calls-on-lebanon-to-resume-special-role-for
-peace.html.

Bibliography

Abi-Hashem, N. "Cross-Cultural Psychology and Counseling:
A Middle Eastern Perspective." *Journal of Psychology and
Christianity* 33, no. 2 (2014): 156–163.

———. "Immigrants." In *Encyclopedia of Cross-Cultural Psychology*,
edited by K. D. Keith, 688–691. Malden, MA: Wiley-Blackwell,
2013.

———. "Pastoral and Spiritual Response to Trauma and Tragedy." In
Tackling Trauma: Global, Biblical and Pastoral Perspectives, edited
by P. A. Barker, 151–172. London: Langham Global Library, 2019.

———. "Trauma, Coping, and Resiliency among Syrian Refugees
in Lebanon and Beyond: A Profile of the Syrian Nation at
War." In *Human Strengths and Resilience: Developmental, Cross-
Cultural and International Perspectives*, edited by G. Rich and
J. Sirikantraporn, 105–130. Lanham, MD: Lexington, 2018.

———. "Working with Middle Eastern Immigrant Families."
In *Working with Immigrant Families: A Practical Guide for
Counselors*, edited by A. Zagelbaum and J. Carlson, 151–180. New
York: Routledge, 2011.

Abi-Hashem, N., and J. R. Brown. "Intercultural Adjustment." In
Encyclopedia of Cross-Cultural Psychology, edited by K. D. Keith,
744–746. Malden, MA: Wiley-Blackwell, 2013.

Aprahamian, M., D. Kaplan, A. Windham, J. Sutter, and J. Visser. "The Relationship between Acculturation and Mental Health of Arab Americans." *Journal of Mental Health Counseling* 33, no. 1 (2011): 80–92.

Cumoletti, M., and J. Batalova. "Middle Eastern and North African Immigrants in the United States." Washington, DC: Migration Policy Institute, 2018. Accessed June 1, 2020. https://www .migrationpolicy.org/article/middle-eastern-and-north-african -immigrants-united-states.

Eldawy, D. "A Fragile Situation: Will the Syrian Refugee Swell Push Lebanon over the Edge?" Migration Information Source. Accessed June 1, 2020. https://www.migrationpolicy.org/article/ syrian-refugee-swell-push-lebanon-over-edge.

Humphrey, M. "Lebanese Identities: Between Cities, Nations and Trans-Nations." *Arab Studies Quarterly* 26, no. 1 (2004): 31–50.

Khater, A. "Phoenician or Arab, Lebanese or Syrian—Who Were the Early Immigrants to America?" Khayrallah Center for Lebanese Diaspora Studies, 2017. Accessed June 1, 2020. https://lebanesestudies.news.chass.ncsu.edu/2017/09/20/ phoenician-or-arab/.

———. "Why Did They Leave? Reasons for Early Lebanese Migration." Khayrallah Center for Lebanese Diaspora Studies, 2017. Accessed June 1, 2020. https://lebanesestudies.news.chass .ncsu.edu/2017/11/15/why-did-they-leave-reasons-for-early -lebanese-migration/.

Pearlman, W. "Emigration and Power: A Study of Sects in Lebanon 1860–2010." *Politics & Society* 41, no. 1 (2013): 103–133. https:// www.researchgate.net/publication/258174806.

Pukas, A. "Lebanese across the Globe." *Arab News*, 2018. Accessed June 1, 2020. https://www.arabnews.com/node/1296211/middle -east.

Skulte-Ouaiss, J., and P. Tabar. "Strong in Their Weakness or Weak in Their Strength? The Case of Lebanese Diaspora Engagement with Lebanon." *Immigrants and Minorities* 33, no. 2 (2015): 141–164.

Tabar, P. "Lebanon: A Country of Emigration and Immigration." 2010. Accessed January 1, 2021. https://documents.aucegypt.edu/Docs/GAPP/Tabar080711.pdf.

Tabar, P., and J. Skulte-Ouaiss. *Politics, Culture and the Lebanese Diaspora*. Newcastle, UK: Cambridge Scholars, 2010.

10

Navigating Hyphenated Identities

Missional Communities of Global Indians

Prasad D R J Phillips

Introduction

The apostle Paul is a fascinating character in the New Testament who navigated his life and ministry by affirming his multiple identities. He was a Jew by birth, Roman by citizenship, educated in Jerusalem, and a Pharisee by profession, and he hailed from the city of Tarsus, where he was influenced by Persian art and literature and Greek philosophy. Moreover, he was raised in the province of Cilicia, which had an Armenian heritage that can be traced back thousands of years.[1] Yet in his letter to the church in the Roman colony of Philippi, Paul argues that Christians are heavenly citizens (Phil 3:20), saying our ultimate home is in heaven, and here on earth we are a colony of heaven's citizens. Just as Roman colonists never forgot they belonged to Rome, we must not forget that we are citizens of heaven, and our conduct must match our heavenly citizenship, bringing a piece of heaven every day to all our dealings with everyone. Such a view of our faith is profoundly transformative and gives new meaning to all our earthly allegiances.[2] Christians living in diaspora are torn between the realities of the universal church, holding the citizenship of heaven, and the local factors of the world here and now. In this chapter, I focus on Indians in the United Kingdom and their transnational connection between host and home countries using an interdisciplinary lens with a missiological emphasis.

According to Thomas Faist, the notions of diaspora and the transnational refer to cross-border processes; the diaspora has been often used to denote religious or national groups living outside an (imagined) homeland, whereas transnationalism is often used both more narrowly to refer to migrants' durable ties across countries and more widely to capture not only communities but all sorts of social formations, such as transnationally active networks, groups, and organizations. Moreover, while diaspora and transnationalism are sometimes used interchangeably, the two terms reflect different intellectual genealogies.[3]

Alongside diasporic transnationalism, this chapter interacts with identity theories. Identity can be understood as a set of meanings that a person has while occupying a particular role in society or a group that has certain characteristics. The concept of identity seeks to explain specific meanings that individuals have for the multiple identities they claim, how they relate to each other, and how they influence their behavior, thoughts, and feelings while relating to society at large.[4] Since this chapter is missional in focus, I use the framework of diaspora mission, which is "a missiological framework for understanding and participating in God's redemptive mission among diaspora groups."[5]

Using these foundational understandings of concepts, this chapter explores the "religious transnational identities" of the Asian Indian Christian diaspora in the United Kingdom. This chapter is reflective, stemming from my interactions with various Indian churches and families based in different cities of the United Kingdom. They find themselves navigating their "Indianness" across the fluid and overlapping layers of being an Indian, a nonresident Indian, a British resident, and a practicing Christian. These notions are always contextual, constructed, and contested. The study takes an interdisciplinary approach and engages with diaspora, transnationalism, and identity studies and tries to interpret these from David Bosch's missiological understanding of "creative tension" to identify how global Asian Indians in Britain are navigating their diasporic hyphenated identities to become a missional community.

This chapter has three sections besides the introduction and conclusion: first, it locates the transnational Asian Christian Indian identity in the contemporary context; and the second section goes on to problematize the notion of identities, which is contextual, constructed, and contested; and the final section articulates how Asian Indians living in the United Kingdom navigate hyphenated identities in three places—home, church, and community, particularly as a missional community.

Transnational Asian Christian Indian Identity

Since the start of the third millennium, much attention has been given to transnational and diaspora studies.[6] Some have studied Indian migrants before and after the independence of India,[7] and more recently, some focused writings have emerged on mission among the global Indian diaspora.[8] Most studies are from the context of North America; relatively less work has been taken up in the United Kingdom. Interestingly, much attention has been paid to other religious communities, such as Muslims, Jains, Sikhs, and even sects of Buddhism, but little research is done on South Asian or Indian Christians in the United Kingdom.[9] However, in order to narrow down my study, I focus on the professionals who have come to the United Kingdom for their higher education studies and found employment, or on intercompany transfer visas, or even as specialized professionals, such as doctors, nurses, and engineers.[10] My engagement in this chapter comes as an insider who falls into this category and has engaged with this group and is involved in diaspora missions through local churches and Christian organizations.

According to the Government of India's official records, there are around 351,000 nonresident Indians (NRIs); 1,413,000 persons of Indian origin (PIOs); and a total of 1,764,000 overseas Indians living in the United Kingdom.[11] My chapter will broadly focus on the first group of NRIs in the United Kingdom, who still have a strong connection with India, since most of them were born in India and are only recent migrants to the United Kingdom. This group plays an essential role by providing services, and they are regular taxpayers. Among the UK NRIs, it is reported that there are around 654 companies that have a turnover of over £100,000 and generate a cumulative annual turnover of £36.84 billion. These companies provide jobs for more than 174,000 people in the United Kingdom.[12] Christians are a small group among these NRIs, and the vast majority are health care professionals or software engineers or work in the banking sector.

Locating identity for Indians living in India is itself a challenging task because of the diversity in language, race, caste, religion, and so on. This challenge is amplified due to external factors such as trade, migration, and colonization. The issue is further intensified by the presence of multinational companies in India, affordability of the internet, telephony, and global travel. The impact of globalization is experienced by Indian Christians through transnational links in a very typical way. For example, parents who live in Bangalore pray for their children who are scattered around the world—one may be in the United Kingdom, while the other is in America or Australia. The children visit their parents regularly, and parents visit children to take care of grandchildren. Many travel from one child in one place to another while living in India for a significant part of the year. Most of their adult children have dual church membership—one in their birth country, where they were baptized, married, and even want their children to be baptized or confirmed, and the other in their host country. These children in the diaspora engage in Christian missions in different ways. They are active in their Christian faith simultaneously in two places—transnational ethnic churches and local British churches. The questions I want to explore are, first, why do Indian Christians, after relocating to the United Kingdom, continue to have sustained connections with their home country? Second, do these connections result in the formation of multiple identities? If so, what kind of negotiations happen while they juggle these identities?

Most Indian Christians living in the United Kingdom not only have transnational connections but strive hard to claim connections to both their host country and their birth country. Most NRIs make a deliberate choice to move to the United Kingdom for socioeconomic reasons but maintain strong links to the country of their birth because of parents, siblings, relatives, and friends who are still in India and may have land, property, assets, or investments there. But their children do not have any such strong bonds, and these relations weaken over time and with every generation that grows up in a foreign land. To keep these connections active and the memory of the Indian identity alive, immigrants try to preserve language, food, ethnic wear, and cultural and religious festivals. Very often these elements are revived in the environment of a church and its ministries. For Indian diaspora Christians, ethnically exclusive churches become a space to reclaim, relish, and celebrate their ethnic identity and culture. This phenomenon attracts new immigrants to join and experience their displaced identity. These fellowships serve as nursery beds to practice and teach younger generations their "mother tongue," to cook and eat Indian food, and to share their common heritage. These communities are like surrogate families and provide a support system for families nuclearized by migration. Moreover, religion has proven to be an effective agency to preserve ethnic culture and establish transnational links to ancestral homelands. Strangely, in these gatherings, the ministry and mission of immigrant Christians flourish while they encounter numerous unexpected challenges.

The Problem of Identities: Contextual, Constructed, and Contested

Indians living in the United Kingdom need to, first of all, accept the facts of their inherited identity for contextual reasons. Indians in the United Kingdom have a commonwealth status, which enables them to exercise their franchise in British elections. This includes the fact that India was a colony, and we share a common history, which has good, bad, and ugly sides but is interpreted differently.[13] The history parents learned in India is different from the history their children are taught in the United Kingdom. For example, 1957 in British history is known as the date of the Sepoy Mutiny and in Indian history as the first independence war. Second, the present political system in India is a colonial gift, and the past interferes with our perception of British history and politics; a memory of preindependence India is slowly being reshaped by postcolonial scholars and writers. India has one of the largest English-speaking populations in the world; "Indian English" is officially recognized, and numerous Indian words are part of the English language and vice versa. However, most Indian migrants to the United Kingdom have difficulty with both spoken and written British English. Pronunciation, accents, and usage hinder communication for the first generation especially. In the Asian context, importance is given to people and relations, but in Britain, struggles for survival keep people disjointed. The contextual realities that Indians bring with them become a barrier to integrating into the host society.

While inherited and immutable elements are vital to identity, one cannot deny that the majority of them are constructed, shaped, and reshaped continually. These constructions can be viewed as assimilations and can happen in a variety of ways. From a missiological point of view, this could be understood to some extent with studies of contextualization. For transnationals, it becomes a mode of cultural production, where cultural objects, images, and meanings go back and forth, constructing new and different social and cultural phenomena. British Indian youth growing up in diaspora play a major role and become vendors and agencies of cross-cultural "goods" in the form of music, language, literature, and values.[14] They mediate between both the host and home countries, giving new meanings to old notions, and often have the capability of interpreting new ideas in place of traditional concepts. Moreover, the Indian diaspora lives in changing contexts while being part of global and local histories. This dynamic process provides a space to construct (deconstruct and reconstruct) attitudes toward the birth country, the host country, and the diasporic community itself. In other words, it is important to understand that any kind of transnational Asian Indian identity develops in a process controlled by contextual realities in both time and space. This leads to diaspora Asian Indians living in the United Kingdom or perhaps anywhere else having multiple identities.

Transnational Indian identities are contextual and constructed in a very vigorous process that remains a contested space. They are kept in "creative tension" with each other, seen not as mutually exclusive but as complementary principles that can assist Indian Christians in the United Kingdom in their goal of being missional.[15] Although there seem to be existing multiple identities emerging from ethnic, linguistic, religious, regional, professional, economic, and several other backgrounds, transnational connections have a unique place during such negotiations. It is important to recognize that all transnational negotiations happen in a context. For example, Tamil Indian Christians who live in the United Kingdom will find themselves attracted to a church that serves the Tamil ethnic community, where language and ethnic identity take a dominant role and other elements, such as denomination, nationality, professional background, and personal beliefs, become peripheral. Interestingly, several subtle negotiations happen from multiple ends. For example, because of diversity found within a congregation, a Tamil church of a specific denomination is forced to make every effort to accommodate the needs of all of its members. Ethnic networks play a critical role in establishing and sustaining the diaspora community churches. They become cultural havens or social networks providing comfort, belonging, support, and nostalgia in a foreign land. The result of these contestations weakens the bond to the local community or host nation. Very often, church provides a neutral third space for such negotiations. One of the biggest challenges resulting from such loose connections and strong identity is the frequent conflict and breakup of these churches, which results in the formation of multiple ethnic-language-specific congregations in the same city.

Global Asian Indians
Navigating Hyphenated Identities

Andrew Walls, a British scholar of World Christianity, in his recent book focuses on the two great migrations—namely, the "Great European Migration" to the world and the "great reverse migration"—and how they significantly shaped the expansion of the Christian faith by giving birth to multiple centers and diverse churches. Nevertheless, he further poses a particularly relevant question to the global church: Will Christians, whether of the West or in the diaspora, be able to follow the New Testament bicultural model of having a multicentric and global Christian faith?[16] This is important for Indian diaspora Christians to answer. From this perspective, it seems that the Indian diaspora church in the United Kingdom is still in its incipient stage. With this question as a basis of interrogation, let us examine how and why the Asian Indian Christian diaspora in the United Kingdom, with their multiple identities, can continue to be part of God's mission.

Interestingly, the children of the Asian Indian diaspora living in the United Kingdom are uniquely positioned compared to their first-generation migrant parents to be multicentric and have a global faith. They predominantly associate with churches that speak English rather than their "mother tongue." They grew up differently from how their parents grew up in their ancestral homeland. Parents often must come to terms with the fact that their and their children's attitudes, customs, beliefs, and language constantly mutate in response to many factors so that children often represent a hybrid identity, forming a unique and distinct pattern of Christian identity, worship, witness, or even missions compared to that of their parents' culture of origin.[17]

It is very difficult to deny that the Indian diaspora brings with it rich experiences from pluralistic contexts and engagement in India that, when shared, can benefit them and the host country, which is also equally becoming pluralistic. From a missional point of view, there are possibilities for diaspora Asian Indians in the United Kingdom to enrich the secular yet pluralistic context. Indians have always lived in a pluralistic and multicultural context. Second, they have lived in a very spiritual and religious environment that stands in stark contrast to the notion of secularism in the West. They can share their lived experiences even though there are significant differences; they can accommodate and respect the spirituality of other religious practices and beliefs. Indians have learned to celebrate diversity and the changing landscape of Britain—from being largely a monocultural, racial, linguistic, and religious context to being a diverse and pluralistic context. Moreover, Christians feel like a minority and often powerless, something that Indian Christians are familiar with. These inherited traits of Indians put them at an advantage to engage in prophetic dialogue and contextualization as part of their missional engagements in the host country as well as in their birth country.

Similar to the notion of "reverse mission," the diaspora people become social actors of the missionary movement in their host country. However, there are challenges for members of the Indian Christian diaspora who form monocultural churches as described earlier in this chapter. Very often these churches try to keep their "unique" identity and celebrate an experience of worship like that of their native country in order to preserve a memory that they want to continue and transfer to the next generation in the host country. The mission of such a church is very often exclusive, as it focuses on catering to the spiritual, cultural, and emotional needs of a particular ethnic community. This is similar to the homogenous model of church growth developed by the American missiologist Donald McGavran, which has a certain practical advantage[18] but has been equally criticized for its theological and ecclesiological incompatibility. Thus there is a need for a strategic and deliberate effort for these churches to move from ethnic uniformity to multiethnic unity, from homogeneity to heterogeneity, from monocultural churches to multicultural churches. This would require Indian churches to come out of their comfort zone and be relevant to the context they are living in.

In one of his early books, Patrick Sookhdeo, a South Asian British scholar, describes an interesting predicament that South Asians face while slowly assimilating into the British context. He identifies that not only is there a cultural divide between different migrant groups, but the host society seems to experience an uneasy tension to accommodate them.[19] With both groups having several preconceived notions about each other, there is a kind of coterie formed with other ethnic identities to protect and survive themselves. One of the distinct characteristics that South Asians generally have, including Indians, is the importance of people over time or punctuality. This can be seen in their hospitality, marriages, family functions, or even funerals. Second, Indians prioritize family and honor as compared to individual life and freedom. These are often believed to be strengths that they have culturally inherited and make every effort to preserve. Finally, most Indians give a lot of value to careers and work, which is seen in their high achievements in academics or even business. Most are ambitious and work hard to achieve upward socioeconomic mobility. Yet because of displacement, they try to find a new kind of transnational identity that connects their home country and host country. This new identity would be best only if they move from their "cultural and religious ghetto" to a new identity formed in Christ and in Christian faith.

As Christians, our faith has a greater purpose and meaning. We are called not just to preserve our faith but to live it and share it with others. If the host nation has provided a certain degree of comfort and stability, immigrant Christians, alongside their services through various kinds of work in the host country, must make a conscious effort to live out their faith. This will challenge their traditional understanding of themselves and the British understanding of them and all that they bring with them. This requires space for prophetic dialogue. If Indian Christians are known for their hospitality and the importance given to people and life, then the Indian Christian community in the United Kingdom cannot hide under the bushel but must come out and participate, an act that must be undertaken with mutual respect and humility.

In such contested spaces, the negotiation of the transnational identity provides many rich encounters. It seems that when you are closer to your birthplace, the narrower and finer differences are amplified and subtle differences are identified. Likewise, the farther you are from your place of origin, the more your local differences begin to blur, and other general identities become dominant. In such situations, negotiations are always fluid; the subtle differences rarely become a point of contention, and one lays aside their identity in terms of race, color, caste, language, denomination, or even being an Indian as secondary in order to become an advocate of a global kingdom citizenship, where Indian identities have fluid boundaries and all specific identities are hyphenated. This sense of self becomes more prominent with the second and third generations of immigrants. It is similar to how Paul finds his identity primarily in his common heavenly citizenship as a follower of Christ. This identity should be more permanent and valued, while earthly citizenship should be kept hyphenated, knowing it is only temporary. This unique position will enable globalized Asian Indians in the United Kingdom to establish a distinctive form of missional diaspora community. They can be a missional community in at least three ways:[20]

1. *Missions to the diasporas:* Here members of the Christian diaspora become evangelists to other diaspora communities within the host country, which could be fellow Asian Indians who live in the same neighborhood in the United Kingdom, and they are much more open to the gospel in a foreign country than in their homeland. Immigrant churches become missional in reaching out to others in similar contexts who would be able to easily connect and relate. Missions here are pastoral and very evangelistic in nature, taking the gospel of the kingdom of God to their kindred and fellow immigrants living in their context.

2. *Missions through the diasporas:* Here members of the Christian diaspora become missionaries, where through their missional calling they support and send missionaries to other parts of the world, including their birth country. Usually this happens in at least two ways: by inviting mission agencies to their churches to share and be encouraged and then through an invitation to participate in the mission of churches and mission agencies. This allows the diaspora church to be part of the missionary work to their own country. The constant visits and missionary giving to the home country revitalize their memory and connect them to their birth country, people, church, and missions.

3. *Missions beyond the diasporas:* Here members of the diaspora community go beyond their ethnic or monoculture identity to a multicultural identity. This is unfortunately not a default position but requires a deliberate departure to become a representative of

the universal church and beyond. The diaspora community sees themselves as missionaries to evangelize the host country (reverse mission), and the ethnic monocultural church attempts to become a multicultural church where diversity is celebrated and unity is found in the body of Christ. The "catholic" nature of the church is exhibited and truly becomes missional, as seen in the high priestly prayer of Jesus (John 17:21).

Conclusion

This chapter has tried to address the issue of identity for an Asian diasporic community. It is an attempt to understand a few major issues that a particular group, Asian Indian Christians living in the United Kingdom, navigate in their hyphenated identities and diasporic transnational connections. This chapter focused on how missional this group is and has the potential to be. Their transnational connections with the host country, home country, and global community empower them to play an important role. This group has its own context and challenges but within their contested space can forge a unique Christian identity that is perhaps typically characteristic of the universal church. One must realize that having this niche space enables them to be religious and social actors as a diaspora community.

Diaspora missiology provides a new means of engagement in world missions, and it does not replace traditional missions but complements them. Nonetheless, I would have to accept the remarks of British historian Brian Stanley in his latest book that states that in the twentieth century, "migrant churches had limited impact outside their ethnic constituency."[21] However, I sincerely believe that God has divinely positioned the Indian and other diaspora Christian communities in the United Kingdom to create a different history in the twenty-first century in which they can make an impact outside their ethnic constituency and contribute to world missions and the growth of the kingdom of God.

Notes

1 Paul D. Gardner, "Paul," in *New International Encyclopedia of Bible Characters: The Complete Who's Who in the Bible* (Grand Rapids, MI: Zondervan, 2015).

2 Roji Thomas George, *Philippians: A Pastoral and Contextual Commentary* (Carlisle, UK: Langham Creative Projects, 2019).

3 Thomas Faist, "Diaspora and Transnationalism," in *Diaspora and Transnationalism*, ed. Thomas Faist and Rainer Bauböck (Amsterdam: Amsterdam University Press, 2010), 9.

4 Peter J. Burke and Jan E. Stets, *Identity Theory* (Oxford: Oxford University Press, 2009), 3.

5 Enoch Wan, *Diaspora Missiology: Theory, Methodology, and Practice* (Portland, OR: Institute of Diaspora Studies: Western Seminary, 2011).

6 Carolin Alfonso, Waltraud Kokot, and Khachig Tölölyan, *Diaspora, Identity and Religion: New Directions in Theory and Research* (London: Routledge, 2004); Rogers Brubaker, "The 'Diaspora' Diaspora," *Ethnic and Racial Studies* 28, no. 1 (January 1, 2005): 1–19.

7 John R. Hinnells, ed., *Religious Reconstruction in the South Asian Diasporas: From One Generation to Another* (New York: Palgrave Macmillan, 2007); Roger Ballard, "South Asian Presence in Britain and Its Transnational Connections," in *Culture and Economy in the Indian Diaspora*, ed. Bhikhu Parekh, Gurharpal Singh, and Steven Vertovec (London: Routledge, 2003).

8 See Sam George, *Understanding the Coconut Generation: Ministry to the Americanized Asian Indians* (Niles, IL: Mall, 2006); Sam George, *Diaspora Christianities: Global Scattering and Gathering of South Asian Christians* (Minneapolis: Fortress, 2018); and Sam George, ed., *Desi Diaspora: Ministry among Scattered Global Indian Christians* (Bangalore: SAIACS, 2019).

9 See Ballard, "South Asian Presence"; and Patrick Sookhdeo, *Sharing Good News: The Gospel and Your Asian Neighbours* (London: Scripture Union, 1991).

10 See Faizal bin Yahya and Arunajeet Kaur, *The Migration of Indian Human Capital* (London: Taylor and Francis, 2010).

11 See Ministry of External Affairs, Government of India, "Population of Overseas Indians," accessed February 1, 2020, http://mea.gov.in/images/attach/NRIs-and-PIOs_1.pdf.

12 "New Report Quantifies Indian Diaspora's Contribution to UK Economy," *Economic Times*, February 5, 2020.

13 See Shashi Tharoor, *Inglorious Empire: What the British Did to India* (London: Allen Lane, 2018).

14 Gijsbert Oonk, "Global Indian Diasporas: Exploring Trajectories of Migration and Theory," in *Global Indian Diasporas*, ed. Gijsbert Oonk (Amsterdam: Amsterdam University Press, 2007), 18.

15 See David Bosch, *Transforming Mission: Paradigm Shifts in Theology of Mission* (Maryknoll, NY: Orbis, 1991), 431–32.

16 Andrew F. Walls, *Crossing Cultural Frontiers: Studies in the History of World Christianity* (Maryknoll, NY: Orbis, 2017), 60.

17 Emma Wild-Wood, "Mission, Ecclesiology and Migration," in *Mission on the Road to Emmaus: Constants, Context, and Prophetic Dialogue*, ed. Cathy Ross and Stephen B. Bevans (London: SCM, 2015), 59.

18 See Donald McGavran, *How Churches Grow: The New Frontiers of Mission* (London: World Dominion, 1966).

19 Sookhdeo, *Sharing Good News*, 76–84.

20 For more on these mission paradigms, see Wan, *Diaspora Missiology*.

21 See Brian Stanley, *Christianity in the Twentieth Century: A World History* (Princeton, NJ: Princeton University Press, 2019).

Bibliography

Alfonso, Carolin, Waltraud Kokot, and Khachig Tölölyan. *Diaspora, Identity and Religion: New Directions in Theory and Research.* London: Routledge, 2004.

Ballard, Roger. "South Asian Presence in Britain and Its Transnational Connections." In *Culture and Economy in the Indian Diaspora,* edited by Bhikhu Parekh, Gurharpal Singh, and Steven Vertovec, 197–222. London: Routledge, 2003.

Bosch, David Jacobus. *Transforming Mission: Paradigm Shifts in Theology of Mission.* Maryknoll, NY: Orbis, 1991.

Brubaker, Rogers. "The 'Diaspora' Diaspora." *Ethnic and Racial Studies* 28, no. 1 (January 1, 2005): 1–19.

Burke, Peter J., and Jan E. Stets. *Identity Theory.* Oxford: Oxford University Press, 2009.

Faist, Thomas. "Diaspora and Transnationalism." In *Diaspora and Transnationalism,* edited by Thomas Faist and Rainer Bauböck, 9–34. Amsterdam: Amsterdam University Press, 2010.

Gardner, Paul D. "Paul." In *New International Encyclopedia of Bible Characters: The Complete Who's Who in the Bible,* edited by Paul D. Gardner. Grand Rapids, MI: Zondervan, 2015.

George, Roji Thomas. *Philippians: A Pastoral and Contextual Commentary.* Carlisle, UK: Langham Creative Projects, 2019.

George, Sam, ed. *Desi Diaspora: Ministry among Scattered Global Indian Christians.* Bangalore: SAIACS, 2019.

———, ed. *Diaspora Christianities: Global Scattering and Gathering of South Asian Christians.* Minneapolis: Fortress, 2018.

———. *Understanding the Coconut Generation: Ministry to the Americanized Asian Indians.* Niles, IL: Mall, 2006.

Hinnells, John R., ed. *Religious Reconstruction in the South Asian Diasporas: From One Generation to Another.* New York: Palgrave Macmillan, 2007.

McGavran, Donald A. *How Churches Grow: The New Frontiers of Mission.* London: World Dominion, 1966.

Ministry of External Affairs, Government of India. "Population of Overseas Indians." Accessed February 1, 2020. http://mea.gov.in/images/attach/NRIs-and-PIOs_1.pdf.

Oonk, Gijsbert. "Global Indian Diasporas: Exploring Trajectories of Migration and Theory." In *Global Indian Diasporas*, edited by Gijsbert Oonk, 9–27. Amsterdam: Amsterdam University Press, 2007.

Sookhdeo, Patrick. *Sharing Good News: The Gospel and Your Asian Neighbours.* London: Scripture Union, 1991.

Stanley, Brian. *Christianity in the Twentieth Century: A World History.* Princeton, NJ: Princeton University Press, 2019.

Tharoor, Shashi. *Inglorious Empire: What the British Did to India.* London: Allen Lane, 2018.

Walls, Andrew F. *Crossing Cultural Frontiers: Studies in the History of World Christianity.* Maryknoll, NY: Orbis, 2017.

Wan, Enoch. *Diaspora Missiology: Theory, Methodology, and Practice.* Portland, OR: Institute of Diaspora Studies: Western Seminary, 2011.

Wild-Wood, Emma. "Mission, Ecclesiology and Migration." In *Mission on the Road to Emmaus: Constants, Context, and Prophetic Dialogue*, edited by Cathy Ross and Stephen B. Bevans, chapter 4. London: SCM, 2015.

Yahya, Faizal bin, and Arunajeet Kaur. *The Migration of Indian Human Capital.* London: Taylor and Francis, 2010.

11
===

Diasporic Hybridity and Its Potential for Mission

Koreans, Chinese, and Japanese in the United States

Byoung Ok Koo

When God called Abraham from Ur into the unknown land of Canaan as a stranger, he initiated a solemn mission that he designed to be a pathway for God's blessing for all of humanity (Gen 12:1–3). Exodus tells a similar story that reveals God's redemptive love both for the Israelites and also for people who do not yet know God, asserting that the nations will come to him through Israel's priesthood (Exod 19:5–6). Looking at the repeated patterns of migration in the Bible, one can see that migration is both a means for spreading God's love throughout the earth and an expression of God's love as he works to lead all nations to their eternal Savior. God precisely designed a redemptive plan for a particular people who migrate from one location to another. God's people in migration are both an object of blessing and a tool to be used to reach others. Though migrants can experience hardship, God is with them, and they are promised God's blessing. The vital thing to understand is that until the people understand God's will and purposes for their migration, they cannot fully realize God's blessings.

In 2017, the United States had the largest immigrant population in the world: over forty-four million people, approximately 20 percent of the world's migrants.[1] Asian Americans (of thirty-four different ethnicities) now comprise the fastest-growing segment and are projected to be the largest immigrant group in the United States by 2055.[2] Therefore, if a person wants to fully grasp multicultural America (both now and in the future), then understanding Asian Americans is not merely an optional task but central to church and mission activities in the United States, especially in regard to the mission to, through, and alongside diasporas.

In this discussion of the importance of understanding Asian immigrants in the United States and their significance for the mission, I will focus on immigrants coming from Korea, China, and Japan. There are mainly three reasons for choosing these particular East Asian groups. First, dealing with all thirty-four Asian American ethnicities at one time in this limited chapter is almost impossible because they are too many and too diverse. Second, just six ethnicities (Chinese, Indian, Filipino, Vietnamese, Korean, and Japanese) make up 85 percent of all Asian Americans.[3] Understanding three of the six groups is a significant step toward an overall grasp of Asian Americans. Third, among these ethnicities, Koreans, Chinese, and Japanese are strongly related and share many similarities. As a part of the Global South, Korea and China are rapidly increasing in power and importance to global Christianity, while their neighboring country Japan needs special attention in mission. I begin with a brief overview of the immigration history of these three groups, then highlight some similarities and differences as well as groups' general characteristics, and finally list some implications of these immigrants for their roles for diaspora missions.

Korean, Chinese, and Japanese Immigration History

Among these three East Asian countries, China has the longest history of immigration to the United States. As early as 1794, Hawaiian sugar plantation owners brought in Chinese people for farm labor.[4] In 1848, there were 325 Chinese, and as per US census data, by 1884, 17,068 Chinese men and 871 Chinese women were living in Hawaii.[5] At that time, the number of Chinese men outnumbered Hawaiian men and reached about half of the total adult male population. On the mainland, when the gold rush in California took place in the mid-1800s, people in China were struggling with economic hardship due to increasing British power over China (after their victory in the Opium War of 1839–42).[6] As a result, many Chinese men came to the United States in pursuit of gold. Many Chinese also worked for the transcontinental railroad project that started in 1865. By 1880, the number of Chinese in the United States rose to over three hundred thousand, and alongside it, the anti-Chinese atmosphere began to spread, which ultimately resulted in the Chinese Exclusion Act of 1882. This law blocked Chinese immigrants coming to the United States and barred US citizenship for Chinese people who were already living in America. In addition, it banned them from "owning land, intermarrying with Whites, owning homes, working in many occupations, getting an education, and living in a certain part of the city," and it caused them to isolate themselves within their communities.[7]

The Japanese followed as a replacement for Chinese workers and began to immigrate to the United States on a large scale. The West forced Japan to open for trade in 1853, and as a result, Japan experienced Western military oppression and economic hardship. In 1868, the Meiji restoration movement in Japan played an important role in opening Japanese migration to Hawaii and other parts of the United States.[8] Unlike the Chinese migrants, the government of Japan provided supervision for workers; however, despite these efforts, Japanese migrants experienced similar discrimination, resulting in the 1907 Gentlemen's Agreement.[9] With this agreement, Japan stopped issuing passports and stopped new Japanese workers from going to the United States in exchange for increased protections for those who had already arrived and retained the right to issue visas for nonlaborers.

The first large-scale Korean immigration to the United States began in 1903, starting with work on the Hawaiian sugar plantations. In 1902, there were less than fifty Koreans in the United States.[10] Due to the boycotts and demonstrations conducted by Japanese workers, sugar plantation owners wanted a replacement. At that time, Korea had been experiencing severe famine for years and was faced with its imminent colonization by Japan. As a result, and due to the crucial role played by two American missionaries, 121 Koreans left Incheon for the United States in 1902.[11] Until Japan compelled Korea to ban immigration to Hawaii to protect Japanese workers there, 7,226 Korean immigrants went to Hawaii by 1905.[12] They were mostly male workers, and four out of ten were Christians.[13]

Since there were mostly male workers from these countries, a unique immigration group of "picture brides" accompanied them. These picture brides came to Hawaii to become wives of men who had only seen their photographs. Between 1910 and 1925, approximately 1,100 picture brides came to the United States from Korea, while about 3,000 Korean male workers in the United States remained bachelors.[14] About 45,000 Japanese picture brides came to the United States and dramatically changed Japanese communities.[15] By 1924, 200,000 Japanese had come to Hawaii and 180,000 Japanese had come to the mainland.[16]

Due to anti-Asian sentiments among the whites, the Immigration Act of 1924 (the Johnson-Reed Act) blocked all Asian immigration and altered immigration history. After the Pearl Harbor attack in 1941, the American government relocated about 120,000 Japanese Americans to internment camps until 1945 or 1946.[17] This unique and traumatic experience damaged Japanese cultural traditions and brought intermarriage, residential and occupational integration, and so on.[18] Because of the War Brides Acts of 1947, Japanese and 6,500 Korean war brides entered the United States.[19] The Immigration and Nationality Act of 1965 gave 20,000 equal quota limits annually per country.[20] Since 1965, Asian immigration to the United States has grown considerably compared to European immigration, which has declined dramatically. As of 2015, the population of Chinese in the United States was 4,948,000; Korean, 1,822,000; and Japanese, 1,411,000.[21]

This brief history of Chinese, Japanese, and Korean immigration to the United States shows similar historical experiences, such as escaping from political and economic hardship, male dominance, racism, and discrimination. The volume of Korean immigrants is small, but their missionary and Christian migration had a long-term effect on the Korean community worldwide. The Japanese internment experience and restoration process enormously impacted their assimilation and Christianity.

Chinese Americans: Ongoing Assimilation and Hybridity

Ongoing Assimilation. Due to the continuous and massive influx of Chinese migrants, the ongoing work of assimilating as newcomers has become an inevitable characteristic of Chinese Americans. Since 1965, the proportion of first-generation immigrants remains high, and according to the 2013–15 American Community Survey, about two-thirds (63 percent) are foreign-born Chinese.[22] The majority of the Chinese population in America is somewhere in the beginning stages of their assimilation process of adjusting to American life. Chinese American immigrants have some uniqueness and distinctiveness concerning their assimilation.

Growing by a Diverse Population. With the continuously increasing population of Chinese immigrants to the United States, the growth of Chinese churches in America is another characteristic and example of cultural assimilation. In 1952, there were only 66 Chinese churches in America, but this number grew to 700 by 1994.[23] Two decades later, the number of Chinese churches in America reached 1,679 by 2014. In terms of proportion, about 31 percent of the Chinese population in America identify themselves as Christians.[24] As the number of Chinese immigrants and students increased, many Chinese churches were planted by Chinese, who were originally from Taiwan and Hong Kong.[25]

Westernization and Ethnic Detachment. Several factors have contributed to the conversion of Chinese and the growth of Chinese churches in the United States. As a result of Western capitalism and the modernization of China, many young people are drawn to Christianity and more receptive to it.[26] Unlike previous immigration waves, the newer "Chinese immigrants have bypassed the urban ghetto Chinatown and settled in ethnically mixed suburbs."[27] They were confined to ethnic enclaves but exposed to and fully immersed in the American culture: "This ethnic detachment from other Chinese . . . plays an important role in their eventual increased receptivity to the Chinese Christian community."[28]

Japanese Americans: High Assimilation but Permanent Foreigners

Among Asian immigrants to the United States, Japanese Americans are characterized by the highest level of assimilation into American culture for several reasons: the low influx of Japanese immigrants, scattered residency, proficient English skills, and high intermarriage.

Low Influx of Japanese Immigrants. In contrast to China and Korea, since 1965, Japanese immigration to the United States has remained small. In 2015, the ratio of the US-born Japanese population to the Japanese immigrant population was exceptionally high (73 percent), twice that of Chinese (37 percent) and Koreans (38 percent).[29] The low migration rate is due to economic improvement in Japan, especially in the 1960s and 1970s: "The improvement of the socioeconomic conditions in Japan in the 1960s—with the Olympics in Tokyo in 1964, the World Exposition in Osaka in 1970, followed by another Olympics in Sapporo in 1972—contributed to a lower volume of Japanese emigration during the post-1965 era."[30] However, when the Japanese economy shrank in the 1990s and many US operations were downsized, many Japanese families returned home.[31] As a result, "third- or higher-generation Japanese Americans make up the majority of their population,"[32] unlike other Asian groups.

Scattered Residency and Proficient English Skills. Scattered residency is a unique feature of Japanese Americans. While most immigrants naturally tend to live together in certain areas to protect themselves, due to the internment experience, Japanese Americans scattered and mixed well into the host society. Additionally, Japanese Americans did not have enough new immigrants continually arriving from Japan. Accordingly, the proportion of proficient English speakers among Japanese Americans is 84 percent[33] as compared to Chinese (59 percent) and Korean immigrants (63 percent), primarily because the majority of the Japanese population was born in the United States.

High Intermarriage Rate. Among all Asian American newlyweds who got married between 2008 and 2010, more than half of Japanese Americans (55 percent) married someone who was not Asian. Of those Japanese Americans who did marry an Asian, 9 percent of them married an Asian who was not Japanese. Between 2008 and 2010, the intermarriage rate of Japanese Americans reached 64 percent, the highest intermarriage rate among all Asian American newlyweds.[34] All in all, Japanese Americans are "highly assimilated into the mainstream U.S. culture."[35]

Permanent Foreigners. Despite high assimilation, there is an unbreakable barrier—their racial status as Asians in America. Japanese Americans tend to seek Japanese social networks and communities because they often experience social boundaries that push them from mainstream society. Daisuke Akiba raises an important question: "Why do Japanese Americans cherish their Japanese roots despite their obvious social and socioeconomic assimilation?"[36] He provides two reasonable explanations. First, "unlike white immigrant groups, even third- or fourth-generation Japanese Americans will never be allowed to be fully integrated into the mainstream" and will remain "eternally foreign" because of how race is constructed in the United States. Second, Japanese Americans try to maintain their cultural values, which stress social interdependence and maintaining family and community ties. A large-scale study of ethnic involvement among second- and third-generation Japanese Americans in California showed their continuous participation in ethnic communities.[37] In other words, despite a high degree of assimilation, Japanese Americans remain permanent foreigners in a strongly racialized America.

Korean Americans: In-Group Commitment, Church Centered, and Mission Focused

High Affiliation and Strong In-Group Commitment. Christianity plays a vital role in the daily lives of post-1965 Korean immigrants, especially in the following aspects: weekly worship service attendance, amount of time spent in church activities, and financial giving.[38] According to the 1997–99 Presbyterian Racial and Ethnic Panel Studies, 78 percent of Korean Presbyterians attend Sunday worship services every week, which is exceptionally high compared to Latinos (49 percent), African Americans (34 percent), and Caucasians (28 percent). In contrast to Korean immigrants, the 1997–98 Queens Survey revealed that 41 percent of Chinese immigrants go to church worship at least once a week, which is about half of Korean participation.[39] In terms of financial commitment, 62 percent of Koreans gave $2,000 or more in offerings to their church,[40] which is higher than among African Americans (35 percent), Hispanics (26 percent), and Caucasians (40 percent). Moreover, about 27 percent of Koreans contributed over $5,000 to the church.

Church-Centered Korean Community. Korean immigrant communities have been marked by church-centeredness from the beginning. Six reasons for the church-centeredness among Koreans in America are: First, American missionaries to Korea encouraged migration to the United States, and Christians have been more inclined to migrate from the beginning. Among the first group of immigrants, two church leaders led worship during the voyage to America. Second, not long after their initial settlement, Korean Christians held Christian worship services of their own, partially as a result of their experiencing discrimination from American Christians. Third, church members cared for other Koreans, helping overcome the hardships associated with migration. Fourth, Korean immigrants enthusiastically planted churches because churches provided for their spiritual needs and functioned as community centers.[41] Fifth, Korean churches began to provide a safe place for Koreans to fellowship with other Koreans, besides proving social status to its members who were struggling with an identity crisis. Lastly, Korean churches helped Koreans maintain their culture and pass their ethnic identity to later generations.

Mission-Oriented Korean Churches. Since 2000, South Korea has been the second-largest foreign missionary sending country in the world. In 2018, there were 21,378 Korean missionaries serving 154 mission agencies in 146 countries.[42] Korean American churches are rooted in missionary-initiated immigration and their close links to the churches in Korea have made the Korean immigrant churches very passionate about foreign missions.[43] They have created organizations such as KOSTA (Korean Students in America), Korean World Mission Conference (KWMC), Global Korean Young Adult Mission (GKYM), and so on. For example, a Korean Church in California takes part in mission by sending and supporting many missionaries: "At Grace Korean Church in Fullerton, one of the largest Korean churches in the United States, the entryway of the church serves as a photo gallery that highlights the work of 208 missionaries serving in 47 countries like Bangladesh, Vietnam, Sweden, and Italy. Inside the church's new 'Vision Center' with a 3,000 seat auditorium, there is a sign on a giant board that reads 'Mission is prayer. Mission is warfare. Mission is martyrdom.' Demonstrating their seriousness about missions, half of Grace Korean Church's budget is set aside to support mission work."[44]

In 2008, GKYM launched an initiative to mobilize the next generation of Korean immigrants for world mission. GKYM has two characteristics: "1) focusing on Korean young adults in North America, who have bi/multi-lingual skills and abilities to adapt to other cultures, 2) high rate of mission commitment among participants."[45] At the 2011

GKYM festival, 782 Korean young adults committed themselves to long- and short-term missions.[46]

Common Issues

While the experiences of Korean, Chinese, and Japanese immigrants are marked by their unique histories and traits, they share some common issues, such as an emphasis on children's education, a significant generation gap, a silent exodus, and a hybridized identity.

Emphasis on Education. The focus on education and higher educational attainment is an outstanding feature of Chinese Americans as well as other Asian Americans. According to the Pew Research Center,[47] the proportion of those possessing bachelor's degrees or higher among the Chinese population in the United States is 54 percent compared to 30 percent in the American population. Sixty-six percent of US-born Chinese have a bachelor's degree or higher.

Chinese and Korean after-school institutions demonstrate how much Chinese and Korean immigrant populations emphasize education. Korean and Chinese immigrants came to the United States for better economic and educational opportunities for children. Since the late 1980s, Chinese immigrants have developed private institutions and college-preparatory centers such as *buxiban* and *kumon*. As of 2004, some 135 academic after-school institutions existed among the suburban Chinese of Los Angeles alone. In the same way, for Korean immigrants, 209 *hagwons* (private educational institutions) offered SAT preparatory courses in the Greater Los Angeles area.[48] Not surprisingly, when the California Institute of Technology did not consider race for admission,

Asian American enrollment reached up to 43 percent of the student population in 2013.[49]

Identity Crisis and Hybridity. Even though most young Chinese Americans experience ethnic detachment, they long for a renewed sense of community and struggle with hybrid ethnic identity, particularly among American-born Chinese (ABCs). For example, according to one Chinese American, "I was born in the US 27 years ago. I grew up with other White Americans. . . . Now that I am out of school practicing as a physician, I definitely feel that people treat me like an ethnic and a member of another racial group. I am reminded that I am Chinese although my orientation and lifestyle are more American than Chinese. . . . I am a US citizen. Yet, I am treated as if I am not equal to other Americans."[50]

Identity crises among Asian immigrants are a common and ongoing problem in the United States. First-generation immigrants struggle with their geographical and cultural displacement, while the second or later generations struggle psychologically. According to Josephine Kim, Korean American students are in danger from issues related to this identity crisis, such as "suicidal tendencies, depression, anxiety, perfectionism, low self-esteem, body image issues, substance abuse, and identity confusion."[51]

The Generation Gap and the Silent Exodus. In Helen Lee's 1996 article in *Christianity Today*, "Silent Exodus," the author raises a critical question: "Can the East Asian church in America reverse the flight of its next-generation?"[52] Focusing on Korean American churches, Lee indicates three main problems of the second generation in a first-generation-dominant church: (1) language barriers, (2) hierarchical leadership, and (3) different cultural preferences. She emphasizes language barriers between first and second generations in worship as well as issues of church governance. Since the second generation grew up in America, they desire a democratic and horizontal style of leadership rather than a hierarchical and authoritative one. Many second-generation Koreans do not prefer or fit well in Caucasian churches either, while some are settling in pan-Asian churches that are led by second- or third-generation Asian American leaders.

Implications

Recognize Hybridity as a Blessing and Strategic Tool. A biblical and theological understanding of hybridity reveals that it is not a mark of inferiority but a blessing and a strategic tool for mission. Hybridity is characteristic of God's people, as shown with Abraham, Joseph, Moses, Daniel, Paul, and many others in the Bible. If we cannot understand the importance of hybrid identity, it will be difficult to leverage the fullest potential of immigrants for God's mission. Julius-Kei Kato claims there is a "more positive side to hybridity's vital role in the contemporary world. . . . We can religiously or theologically view and interpret human reality to transcend the typical binary division of the world into 'us' and 'them' (with 'us' often identified as the good guys and 'them' the not-so-good guys) and, thus, promote compassion, peace, harmony, respect, and justice among entities which could be very different from one another."[53] When we overcome this dichotomous approach and fully utilize our hybrid identities, we can promote not only peace and harmony but also the mission.

Raise Enough Pastors. We need to devote special efforts to raising enough Chinese and Japanese pastors for the people in America and their homelands. All three ethnic groups became more Christianized in America after immigration, but the number of Korean churches and the percentage of Korean Christians in America are relatively high. The number of Chinese and Japanese churches in America is 1,679 and 195, respectively, while the number of Korean American churches is 4,454. Korean American churches began at the onset of Korean immigration, which was initiated by American missionaries, and Korean immigrant churches have played an essential role in providing for both spiritual and social needs for all. As the Korean church grew, many Korean pastors came to the United States for theological studies, and many of them stayed to provide leadership for Korean American churches. In fact, "Korean Americans form the largest nonwhite group in American evangelical seminaries."[54]

In contrast, Chinese and Japanese populations are struggling to raise and provide enough pastors to fulfill the demands of churches both in America and in their homelands, where they desperately need transfusion from the outside. Without next-generation church leaders, there is no bright future in ethnic churches. Ethnic churches and seminaries should provide scholarships, especially for Japanese and Chinese seminarians.

Practice Horizontal Leadership. Younger Korean and Chinese immigrants have suffered from the generation gap and negative experiences with hierarchical culture at home and in the church. Because of this, many leave their ethnic churches and sometimes their faith as well. However, Japanese immigrants do not have the same complaints about leadership problems because the experience of internment camps led to the development of different structures of leadership within the Japanese American population. The new structures have minimized the generation gap to some extent. For example, "churches had different paradigms of leadership coexisting under one roof—one style led by the first generation, the *issei*, and [another] style led by the second."[55] Korean and Chinese American churches need intentional and systemic efforts to give leadership and autonomy to the younger generations.

Support Campus Ministries. East Asian college students are at a critical junction: they can leave the church and faith or they can meet their own Savior and become committed to kingdom work. On the one hand, Asian college students are in danger of a "silent exodus." On the other, Korean and Chinese students are active in gathering through ethnic or pan-ethnic Christian organizations such as InterVarsity Christian Fellowship and Asian American Christian Fellowship. College campus ministries are essential in various ways. For example, they can help second-generation Asian Americans maintain and strengthen their faith, evangelize unreached Asian students, and promote "reverse missions" through Asian international students. Leiton Chinn recognizes the value of campus ministries for diaspora missions and claims, "The opportunities for engaging in diaspora missions on North American campuses have never been as great as they are now. The question is, *will the church actually see them, and if so, how will the people of God respond?*"[56] Allen Yeh stresses the possibilities of evangelizing Chinese students from mainland China who come to prestigious universities in America.[57] They are essential not only for themselves but also for people in their homeland. Since the Chinese government has become more and more negative and exclusive regarding missionary activity, China needs indigenous kingdom workers. Japan has freedom of religion but needs active kingdom workers from the outside due to their dearth in Japan.

Move toward Pan-Asian and Multicultural Churches. In twenty-first-century multicultural America, Asian hybridity can be a powerful tool for reaching out to unreached people, especially other minorities. In this regard, second generations are the most potent source for this multicultural movement. Dave Gibbons insists, "They [second-generations] see the diversity everywhere else in society, but if they don't see it in the church, they think the church is superficial."[58] There are numerous Korean churches in every state of America, and almost all of them have English ministries that can easily become multiethnic or multicultural churches.

Conclusion

More than a century ago, God called Chinese, Japanese, and Koreans to the unknown land of America. As God brought Joseph to Egypt to save Israel, God has a plan for them and all nations. Both Japanese and Chinese immigrants need more missionaries for both those in the United States and those in their ancestral homelands. China needs more educated pastors who can teach theology without visa and language barriers. Japanese in both America and Japan desperately need Japanese pastors who have a vision for evangelizing their people. Due to the strong emphasis on education among Asians, college campus ministries are strategic. The campus ministry can evangelize or strengthen second-generation immigrants and help them understand how their hybrid identity can serve kingdom purposes. The exceptional growth of Korean immigrant churches in the United States and their mission focus can help them develop into multiethnic and multicultural churches. A more flattened leadership style must be practiced with hybridized second-generation Koreans. All in all, Korean, Chinese, and Japanese hybrids and their shared commonness present many opportunities for diaspora missions among Asian Americans and far beyond.

Notes

1 Jynnah Radford, "Key Findings about U.S. Immigrants," Pew Research Center, June 17, 2019, https://www.pewresearch.org/fact-tank/2019/06/17/key-findings-about-u-s-immigrants/.

2 Radford.

3 Abby Budiman, "Asian Americans Are the Fastest-Growing Racial or Ethnic Group in the U.S. Electorate," Pew Research Center, May 7, 2020, https://www.pewresearch.org/fact-tank/2020/05/07/asian-americans-are-the-fastest-growing-racial-or-ethnic-group-in-the-u-s-electorate/.

4 Gary Y. Okihiro, *American History Unbound: Asians and Pacific Islanders* (Oakland: University of California Press, 2015), 120.

5 Okihiro, 122.

6 C. N. Le, *Asian American Assimilation: Ethnicity, Immigration, and Socioeconomic Attainment* (New York: LFB Scholarly Publishing, 2007), 15.

7 Le, 16.

8 Winston Tseng, *Immigrant Community Services in Chinese and Vietnamese Enclaves* (New York: LFB Scholarly Publishing, 2007), 48.

9 Le, *Asian American Assimilation*, 17.

10 Won Moo Hurh, *The Korean Americans* (Westport, CT: Greenwood, 1998), 36.

11 Byoung Ok Koo, *Transitioning from an Ethnic to a Multicultural Church: A Transformational Model* (Eugene, OR: Wipf & Stock, 2019), 28.

12 Tongshik Ryu, *A History of Christ United Methodist Church, 1903–1988* (Seoul, South Korea: Christ United Methodist Church, 1988), 26.

13 Ho-Youn Kwon, Kwang Chung Kim, and R. Stephen Warner, eds., *Korean Americans and Their Religions: Pilgrims and Missionaries from a Different Shore* (University Park: Pennsylvania State University Press, 2001), 13.

14 Jung Ha Kim, *Bridge-Makers and Cross-Bearers: Korean-American Women and the Church* (Atlanta: Scholars, 1997), 4.

15 Daisuke Akiba, "Japanese Americans," in *Asian Americans: Contemporary Trends and Issues*, ed. Pyong Gap Min (Thousand Oaks, CA: Pine Forge, 2006), 151.

16 Ronald Takaki, *A Different Mirror: A History of Multicultural America* (Boston: Back Bay, 1993).

17 Le, *Asian American Assimilation*, 18; Laura Hamilton Waxman, *Japanese American Internment Camps* (Minneapolis: Lerner, 2018), 11.

18 Ruth H. Gim Chung, "Gender, Ethnicity, and Acculturation in Intergenerational Conflict of Asian American College Students," *Cultural Diversity and Ethnic Minority Psychology* 7, no. 4 (2001): 383.

19 Eui-Young Yu, "Korean Population in the United States as Reflected in the Year 2000 U.S. Census," presented in the Population Association of Korea Annual Meeting in Seoul, Korea, December 1, 2001, 3.

20 Tseng, *Chinese and Vietnamese Enclaves*, 45.

21 Gustavo Lopez, Neil G. Ruiz, and Eileen Patten, "Key Facts about Asian Americans, a Diverse and Growing Population," Pew Research Center, September 8, 2017, http://www.pewresearch.org/fact-tank/2017/09/08/key-facts-about-asian-americans.

22 Pew Research Center, "Chinese in the U.S. Fact Sheet," September 8, 2017, https://www.pewsocialtrends.org/fact-sheet/asian-americans -chinese-in-the-u-s/.

23 Fenggang Yang, "Chinese Conversion to Evangelical Christianity: The Importance of Social and Cultural Contexts," *Sociology of Religion* 59, no. 3 (1998): 240.

24 Pew Research Center, "Asian Americans: A Mosaic of Faiths," July 19, 2012, https://www.pewforum.org/2012/07/19/asian-americans-a-mosaic-of-faiths-overview/.

25 Meifen Wei, Tsun-Yao Ku, Hwei-Jane Chen, Nathaniel Wade, Kelly Yu-Hsin Liao, and Gwo-Jen Guo, "Chinese Christians in America: Attachment to God, Stress, and Well-Being," *Counselling and Values* 57 (October 2012): 163.

26 Brian Hall, "Social and Cultural Contexts in Conversion to Christianity among Chinese American College Students," *Sociology of Religion* 67, no. 2 (2006): 138.

27 Fenggang Yang, *Chinese Christians in America: Conversion, Assimilation, and Adhesive Identities* (University Park: Pennsylvania State University Press, 1999), 39.

28 Hall, "Social and Cultural Contexts," 141–42.

29 Pew Research Center, "Japanese in the U.S. Fact Sheet," September 8, 2017, https://www.pewsocialtrends.org/fact-sheet/asian-americans-japanese-in-the-u-s/.

30 Akiba, "Japanese Americans," 154.

31 Akiba, 158.

32 Akiba, 159.

33 Pew Research Center, "Japanese in the U.S. Fact Sheet."

34 Pew Research Center, "The Rise of Asian Americans," June 19, 2012, https://www.pewsocialtrends.org/2012/06/19/the-rise-of-asian-americans/.

35 Akiba, "Japanese Americans," 171.

36 Akiba, 172.

37 Akiba, 172. See S. S. Fugita and D. J. O'Brien, *Japanese American Ethnicity: The Persistence of Community* (Seattle: University of Washington Press, 1991). Fugita and O'Brien conducted this large-scale survey.

38 Koo, *Transitioning*, 28–29.

39 Pyong Gap Min, "Immigrants' Religion and Ethnicity," paper presented at the 2003 Annual Meeting of the American Sociological Association, Atlanta, GA, August 19, 2003.

40 Kwon, Kim, and Warner, *Korean Americans and Their Religions*, 82.

41 Won Moo Hurh and Kwang Chung Kim, "Religious Participation of Korean Immigrants in the United States," *Journal for the Scientific Study of Religion* 29, no. 1 (March 1990): 20; S. Steve Kang, *Unveiling the Socioculturally Constructed Multivoiced Self: Themes of Self Construction and Self Integration in the Narratives of Second-Generation Korean American Young Adults* (Lanham, MD: University Press of America, 2002), 1; Sharon Kim, *A Faith of Our Own: Second-Generation Spirituality in Korean American Churches* (New Brunswick, NJ: Rutgers University Press, 2010), 23.

42 Steve Sang-Cheol Moon, "Missions from Korea 2019: Support Raising," *International Bulletin of Mission Research* 43, no. 2 (2019): 188.

43 Koo, *Transitioning*, 39–43.

44 Rebecca Y. Kim and Sharon Kim, "Revival and Renewal: Korean American Protestants beyond Immigrant Enclaves," *Studies in World Christianity* 18, no. 3 (December 2012): 296.

45 Koo, *Transitioning*, 43.

46 Dae Won Kim, "Segye Hanin Chungnyun Sunkyochookje" [Global Korean Young Adults Mission Festival], *Christian Today*, March 20, 2012, https://www.christiantoday.co.kr/news/254468.

47 Pew Research Center used 2000 and 2010 population estimates of US Census Bureau and 2015 population estimates from 2015 American Community Survey.

48 Min Zhou and Susan S. Kim, "After-School Institutions in Chinese and Korean Immigrant Communities: A Model for Others?," Migration Policy Institute, May 3, 2007, https://www.migrationpolicy.org/article/after-school-institutions-chinese-and-korean-immigrant-communities-model-others.

49 Scott Jaschik, "The Numbers and the Arguments on Asian Admissions," Inside Higher ED, August 7, 2017, https://www.insidehighered.com/admissions/article/2017/08/07/look-data-and-arguments-about-asian-americans-and-admissions-elite.

50 Morrison G. Wong, "Chinese Americans," in Min, *Asian Americans*, 137–38.

51 Quoted in Deborah Blagg, "The Culture of Counseling," Harvard Graduate School of Education, October 20, 2010, https://www.gse.harvard.edu/news/10/10/culture-counseling.

52 Helen Lee, "Silent Exodus," *Christianity Today*, August 12, 1996, 50.

53 Julius-Kei Kato, *Religious Language and Asian American Hybridity* (New York: Palgrave Macmillan, 2016), 3.

54 Kim, *Faith of Our Own*, 5; Kim and Kim, "Revival and Renewal," 292.

55 Lee, "Silent Exodus," 52.

56 Leiton Edward Chinn, "Diaspora Missions on Campuses: John R. Mott and a Centennial Overview of the International Student Ministry Movement in North America," in *Global Diasporas and Mission*, ed. Chandler H. Im and Amos Yong (Oxford: Regnum, 2014), 243.

57 Allen Yeh, "The Chinese Diaspora," in *Global Diasporas and Mission*, 94. In 2019, there were 369,548 Chinese; 52,250 Korean; and 18,105 Japanese international students in the United States. See Erin Duffin, "Number of International Students Studying in the United States in 2018/19, by Country of Origin," Statista, November 19, 2019, https://www.statista.com/statistics/233880/international-students-in-the-us-by-country-of-origin/.

58 Quoted in Lee, "Silent Exodus," 53.

Bibliography

Blagg, Deborah. "The Culture of Counseling." Harvard Graduate School of Education, October 20, 2010. https://www.gse.harvard.edu/news/10/10/culture-counseling.

Budiman, Abby. "Asian Americans Are the Fastest-Growing Racial or Ethnic Group in the U.S. Electorate." Pew Research Center, May 7, 2020. https://www.pewresearch.org/fact-tank/2020/05/07/asian-americans-are-the-fastest-growing-racial-or-ethnic-group-in-the-u-s-electorate/.

Chinn, Leiton Edward. "Diaspora Missions on Campuses: John R. Mott and a Centennial Overview of the International Student Ministry Movement in North America." In *Global Diasporas and Mission*, edited by Amos Yong and Chandler Im, 236–243. Oxford: Regnum, 2014.

Chung, Ruth H. Gim. "Gender, Ethnicity, and Acculturation in Intergenerational Conflict of Asian American College Students." *Cultural Diversity and Ethnic Minority Psychology* 7, no. 4 (2001): 376–386.

Duffin, Erin. "Number of International Students Studying in the United States in 2018/19, by Country of Origin." Statista, November 19, 2019. https://www.statista.com/statistics/233880/international-students-in-the-us-by-country-of-origin/.

Fugita, S. S., and D. J. O'Brien. *Japanese American Ethnicity: The Persistence of Community*. Seattle: University of Washington Press, 1991.

Hall, Brian. "Social and Cultural Contexts in Conversion to Christianity among Chinese American College Students." *Sociology of Religion* 67, no. 2 (2006): 131–147.

Hurh, Won Moo. *The Korean Americans*. Westport, CT: Greenwood, 1998.

Hurh, Won Moo, and Kwang Chung Kim. "Religious Participation of Korean Immigrants in the United States." *Journal for the Scientific Study of Religion* 29, no. 1 (March 1990): 19–34.

Jaschik, Scott. "The Numbers and the Arguments on Asian Admissions." Inside Higher ED, August 7, 2017. https://www.insidehighered.com/admissions/article/2017/08/07/look-data-and-arguments-about-asian-americans-and-admissions-elite.

Kang, S. Steve. *Unveiling the Socioculturally Constructed Multivoiced Self: Themes of Self Construction and Self Integration in the Narratives of Second-Generation Korean American Young Adults.* Lanham, MD: University Press of America, 2002.

Kato, Julius-Kei. *Religious Language and Asian American Hybridity.* New York: Palgrave Macmillan, 2016.

Kim, Dae Won. "Segye Hanin Chungnyun Sunkyochookje" [Global Korean Young Adults Mission Festival]. *Christian Today,* March 20, 2012. https://www.christiantoday.co.kr/news/254468.

Kim, Jung Ha. *Bridge-Makers and Cross-Bearers: Korean-American Women and the Church.* Atlanta: Scholars, 1997.

Kim, Rebecca Y., and Sharon Kim. "Revival and Renewal: Korean American Protestants beyond Immigrant Enclaves." *Studies in World Christianity* 18, no. 3 (December 2012): 291–312.

Kim, Sharon. *A Faith of Our Own: Second-Generation Spirituality in Korean American Churches.* New Brunswick, NJ: Rutgers University Press, 2010.

Koo, Byoung Ok. *Transitioning from an Ethnic to a Multicultural Church: A Transformational Model.* Eugene, OR: Wipf & Stock, 2019.

Kwon, Ho-Youn, Kwang Chung Kim, and R. Stephen Warner, eds. *Korean Americans and Their Religions: Pilgrims and Missionaries from a Different Shore.* University Park: Pennsylvania State University Press, 2001.

Le, C. N. *Asian American Assimilation: Ethnicity, Immigration, and Socioeconomic Attainment.* New York: LFB Scholarly Publishing, 2007.

Lee, Helen. "Silent Exodus." *Christianity Today,* August 12, 1996. https://www.christianitytoday.com/ct/1996/august12/6t9050 .html.

Lopez, Gustavo, Neil G. Ruiz, and Eileen Patten. "Key Facts about Asian Americans, a Diverse and Growing Population." Pew

Research Center, September 8, 2017. https://www.pewresearch
.org/fact-tank/2021/04/29/key-facts-about-asian-americans.

Min, Pyong Gap, ed. *Asian Americans: Contemporary Trends and Issues*. Thousand Oaks, CA: Pine Forge, 2006.

Moon, Steve Sang-Cheol. "Missions from Korea 2019: Support Raising." *International Bulletin of Mission Research* 43, no. 2 (2019): 188–195.

Okihiro, Gary Y. *American History Unbound: Asians and Pacific Islanders*. Oakland: University of California Press, 2015.

Pew Research Center. "Asian Americans: A Mosaic of Faiths." July 19, 2012. https://www.pewforum.org/2012/07/19/asian-americans-a
-mosaic-of-faiths-overview/.

———. "Chinese in the U.S. Fact Sheet." September 8, 2017. https://
www.pewsocialtrends.org/fact-sheet/asian-americans-chinese-in
-the-u-s/.

———. "Japanese in the U.S. Fact Sheet." September 8, 2017.
https://www.pewsocialtrends.org/fact-sheet/asian-americans
-japanese-in-the-u-s/.

———. "The Rise of Asian Americans." June 19, 2012. https://www
.pewsocialtrends.org/2012/06/19/the-rise-of-asian-americans/.

Radford, Jynnah. "Key Findings about U.S. Immigrants." Pew Research Center, June 17, 2019. https://www.pewresearch.org/fact
-tank/2019/06/17/key-findings-about-u-s-immigrants/.

Ryu, Tongshik. *A History of Christ United Methodist Church, 1903–1988*. Seoul, South Korea: Christ United Methodist Church, 1988.

Takaki, Ronald. *A Different Mirror: A History of Multicultural America*. Boston: Back Bay, 1993.

Tseng, Winston. *Immigrant Community Services in Chinese and Vietnamese Enclaves*. New York: LFB Scholarly Publishing, 2007.

Waxman, Laura Hamilton. *Japanese American Internment Camps*. Minneapolis: Lerner, 2018.

Wei, Meifen, Tsun-Yao Ku, Hwei-Jane Chen, Nathaniel Wade, Kelly Yu-Hsin Liao, and Gwo-Jen Guo. "Chinese Christians in America: Attachment to God, Stress, and Well-Being." *Counselling and Values* 57 (October 2012): 162–180.

Yang, Fenggang. *Chinese Christians in America: Conversion, Assimilation, and Adhesive Identities*. University Park: Pennsylvania State University Press, 1999.

———. "Chinese Conversion to Evangelical Christianity: The Importance of Social and Cultural Contexts." *Sociology of Religion* 59, no. 3 (1998): 237–257.

Yeh, Allen. "The Chinese Diaspora." In *Global Diasporas and Mission*. Oxford: Regnum Books International, 2014.

Zhou, Min, and Susan S. Kim. "After-School Institutions in Chinese and Korean Immigrant Communities: A Model for Others?" Migration Policy Institute, May 3, 2007. https://www .migrationpolicy.org/article/after-school-institutions-chinese-and -korean-immigrant-communities-model-others.

12

Practicing Diasporic Habitus

Asian Americans in International Missions

Peter T. Lee

Introduction

Asian diaspora communities in North America are known for their strong Christian affiliation.[1] While Asian American Christianity has been well documented, stories of Asian Americans who serve in international missions are seldom told.[2] Little is known about their experiences and the implications for the Asian American church and international missions. Before serving as missionaries, these Asian American Christians had already experienced diasporic living as immigrants, whether as first, second, or 1.5 generation. Immigrants are known to go through turbulent experiences that result in hybridized social practices, blending various cultural forms from their old and new environments. The social and cultural processes experienced by these migrants are quite complex. While the experiences of each community and generation may be different, all generations of Asian immigrants tend to face some form of marginalization and discrimination as ethnic minorities in North America.

What happens when diasporic people move to a new geo-cultural setting as Christian missionaries? What do they experience when diasporic people join an international mission agency and work alongside a culturally diverse group that serves together in an entirely different culture? Answering these questions can shed new light and offer missiological insights on social, cultural, and religious processes taking place at the intersection of migration, diaspora, and international missions. A better understanding of this unique Asian American group would likely provide fresh insights for multicultural ministry, cultural and social processes of hybridization, and life in multiple diasporas.

Studying Asian Americans in Global Mission

In 2018, I conducted a field study in a North African country (NAC) with a large Muslim population and limited religious freedom.[3] I interviewed forty-seven Christian missionaries who were members of multicultural teams of international mission organizations. Among these interviewees were six Asian American missionaries. Three of them were Canadian citizens, while the other three were US citizens. They traced their roots to Korea, China, and a Southeast Asian country. Two were married couples and two single women, and their ages ranged from the midthirties through the early fifties. They lived in three different cities in the NAC. These six Christian workers were part of three large international mission organizations that started in the United States or the United Kingdom. While their backgrounds varied, they shared some common experiences, such as having lived in a large metropolitan area in North America, and had been active participants in the life and ministry of an ethnic immigrant congregation before they came to the NAC. Three of them were first generation; two were 1.5 generation; one was second generation born in North America.[4]

I probed their experiences in the NAC and their international mission teams, paying attention to relational tensions, conflicts, and personal changes. I sought to learn more about complex intercultural social processes at play. I looked for ways in which their social experiences in North Africa and their work with their multiethnic team mediated and influenced intercultural social processes happening at the individual level. Through my analysis of the data, several key findings emerged. I further explored ways to interpret the meanings of the data and synthesize themes that explained the phenomenon. Here, I will present three themes drawn from the study.

Practitioners of Diasporic Habitus

One of the outcomes of missionary life for these Asian American Christians was the change in their personal and social dispositions. When they initially arrived in North Africa, they had to adapt to different life structures and social norms, as we can see in the cases of my interlocutors. Michelle, who left behind a corporate career in Canada, found it challenging to live a much less structured life. Joseph, who valued punctuality, struggled with people not showing up on time for scheduled appointments. Nicole, a second-generation

Asian American from a large metropolitan city in the United States, initially had to deal with local male and female roles that were quite different from what she was used to.

Compared to their white colleagues, however, the Asian American missionaries generally seemed to have experienced less severe shocks or significant changes while living in North Africa. It is not that they did not experience any changes or were less aware of them. They also had to adapt and change, but they tended not to highlight these changes as much. These personal changes are generally the outcome of their intercultural social experiences over time. My research findings suggest that the more intense the social experiences, the greater the impact on personal dispositions. Both the local setting in North Africa and the multicultural environment within the team provided a complex and dynamic cultural context that influenced these changes in the Christian workers.[5] For these Asian American missionaries, however, the impact of these cultural forces—both local forces in the NAC and international forces within the multicultural team—seemed to be more muted than that of their other colleagues. One explanation for this muted impact is that perhaps as Asians, they found more similarities in values with the NAC local people than did their Western colleagues, and as immigrants in North America, they had already adjusted to Western social norms central to their multicultural teams.

These Asian Americans had already gone through some intense cultural adaptation experiences when they immigrated from their homeland in Asia or grew up as minorities in North America. When they arrived in North Africa and joined their multicultural teams, they adapted to the new setting, but many changes had already taken place in their previous immigrant experience in North America, and social norms in the NAC were not as shocking to them. These factors seemed to have functioned as their resources for facing challenges in this new environment. The changes in them would have happened during their migrant experiences and their missionary experiences in North Africa. These changes would have encompassed many domains, including personal, relational, social, linguistic, professional, and cultural.

French sociologist Pierre Bourdieu coined an intriguing notion, *habitus*, that helps explain the phenomenon under study. Habitus is "a system of acquired dispositions functioning on the practical level as . . . classificatory principles as well as being the organizing principles of action."[6] It represents "dispositions *acquired through experience*, thus variable from place to place and time to time."[7] Bourdieu emphasizes that habitus is obtained through and produced by practice.[8] In habitus, Bourdieu integrates structure and agency, creating a system of systems that seems to contradict itself and yet explains a complex social process that brings changes in individuals, communities, and societies. Habitus leads to individuals' everyday practices that generate structures that, in turn, govern those very practices.[9] Without invoking a language of culture or ethnicity, Bourdieu provides a robust means to explain complicated social processes that shape people's changing dispositions and behaviors.

What if this notion is applied to describe the experiences of people such as my Asian American interlocutors? Instead of calling the changes in their personal dispositions cultural changes or changing cultural identity, I propose to adopt Bourdieu's notion, combine it with the term *diasporic* to denote their immigrant experiences, and develop a concept of *diasporic habitus*. This is not a new term, although it has rarely been used. Both British sociologist David Parker and cultural studies scholar Ien Ang used it to describe immigrant life experiences.[10] I propose to use *diasporic habitus* to denote "a system of internalized dispositions and schemes acquired through repeated practices by those who live *meaningfully* in a country or culture different from their own."[11] I might also add that this acquired system of dispositions produces particular social practices generating that very system. This seemingly circular process evolves through intercultural social experiences.

We may say that our Asian American interlocutors *live in diasporic habitus* and *live out diasporic practice*. Through their diasporic living in North America, they inhabit *diasporic habitus* and also carry it with them into the new setting in North Africa. It generates a particular social practice markedly different from that of those who have never experienced a diasporic life. Nevertheless, as they interact with their new team members and new local environment in the NAC, their *practice* changes, and so does their *habitus*. Their diasporic habitus continues to evolve as it adds a new dimension of lived realities in North Africa. It is not possible to fully develop and unpack this notion here. It might suffice to say that this idea needs to be explored further among mission scholars, for it problematizes static notions of culture and identity. It entails individual changes through social interactions. When a critical mass of people in a community acquires a system of social dispositions and schemes, they can potentially affect change in the surrounding community and larger societal structures.

People accept, reject, adapt, adjust, or blend various social and cultural elements they experience, effectively creating new personal practices and social norms in the process. In this way, we can explain diasporic habitus by using the lens of cultural hybridization.[12] This process seems to get more complicated in the diaspora; for serial migrants such as these Asian American missionaries, it would be even more intensified, dynamic, and multilayered. The diasporic practice generated will rely on the kind of diasporic habitus created; the type of diasporic habitus acquired would vary greatly depending on one's circumstances and experiences.

Notions such as "cultural intelligence" or "dimensions of national culture" that tend to link certain human characteristics to particular geographical locations can be replaced by a notion of diasporic habitus that represents the whole ecosystem of the dynamic intercultural social processes that take place in the "Third Space" of cultural contact zones.[13] There is a world in the intercultural liminal spaces in-between that cannot adequately be described using the traditional static categories. This ecosystem, which I would like to call *diasporic habitus*, needs to be explored further. Perhaps this kind of thinking will help us depart from the mistakes of the former generations of mission scholars of reifying culture and making culture do too much.

Residents of Multiple Cultural Homes

Another notable change in my interlocutors was their sense of having multiple cultural homes. They grew more comfortable socially in the NAC while maintaining a connection with their past diasporic life in North America. They retained connections to all three of their past and current life settings—their Asian country of origin, their diasporic life in North America, and their current ministry context in the NAC.

Michelle is a good example. For her, traveling back and forth between Canada and the NAC seemed to be a natural thing. She had lived in the NAC for nearly two decades, and it had become her true "home." She did not maintain as strong a tie with her country of origin in Southeast Asia, but her current connections with both her life in Canada and her life in North Africa were quite strong; both Canada and North Africa were her home not only culturally but also literally. She would identify with the NAC, often using "we" or "us" as she was describing it and its people, but also explained that going back to Canada was easy, and there was little adjustment she had to make. It seemed that she had grown comfortable in both places to a level where she felt at ease in both, although both were her adopted homes. Her preferred social environment was, however, a setting with cultural diversity. She had many relationships with people from many different cultures. Her team members hailed from many nations, and there was a high degree of cultural diversity among her friends in Canada. In a sense, she had multiple cultural homes connected through a bond of multicultural relationships and communities. It seemed that one of her cultural homes could not exist without the others. What seemed to hold them together was her relationships with these diverse groups of people in multiple places.

Developing multiple cultural homes is, however, not unique to Asian American missionaries; other missionaries serving in intercultural contexts also develop a sense of multiple cultural homes. But how would Asian Americans differ from those without any immigrant experiences? It is helpful to remember that these Asian American missionaries had already experienced a degree of isolation, discrimination, and marginalization as immigrants in North

America. Some of these experiences continue in the NAC and even within their mission organizations. They are frequently asked the question "Where are you from?" by their colleagues in their mission agencies and local people in the NAC. Answering "Canada" or "the United States" frequently raises eyebrows and results in further interrogation. Even when their legal names were "Ben," "Katie," or "Nicole," they would sometimes be asked what their "real names" were.

Local people in the NAC often called them "Chinois" or "She-noo-y," which means the Chinese. When used with a gesture of making slanted eyes with their index fingers, it becomes a pejorative of mockery. The racial stereotypes and discrimination seemed to have followed them from North America to North Africa. The question of belonging often comes up in the minds of these Asian Americans. Where do I truly belong? Where do I feel at home and most comfortable? It is Asia for some; it is Canada or the United States for others. For many, home is everywhere or nowhere. They become increasingly unsure of where their "home" is. Although it varies from person to person, there is a certain level of "cultural homelessness" in these workers.[14] They had experienced social and cultural dislocation as immigrants in North America. Now they were further dislocated as they lived and worked in North Africa rather than North America.

There seemed to be two crucial outcomes of these experiences for Asian American Christian workers. First, the question of belonging could lead them to focus on the kingdom of God rather than an earthly kingdom. Second, multiple cultural homes could help them put greater value on relationships than geographical locations. These two are perhaps important components not only for international missionaries but also for followers of Christ in any cultural context. Having multiple cultural homes entails going beyond one's narrow confines of ethnicity, culture, nation, and even diaspora. While it risks personal loss and harm, this kind of dislocation may be necessary to develop a sense of "we as they" and "they as we," as Rudyard Kipling beautifully expresses in his poem.[15] We are reminded of the words of Jesus when he says, "Foxes have holes, and birds of the air have nests; but the Son of Man has nowhere to lay his head" (Matt 8:20). Jesus lacked a physical home. Though not a migrant in a strict sense, his life reflects a diasporic life that involves both having multiple homes and becoming culturally homeless. Diasporic life might be an essential feature for transcending human boundaries so that we may become, as the apostle Paul says, "all things to all people" (1 Cor 9:22).

Critics of Biased Multiculturalism

When asked about the team and organizational life within their mission agencies, several Asian American participants pointed out some of the biases, inequalities, and even hypocritical multicultural policies within their organizations. Joseph said that he tried to understand the perspective of his Western teammates. In a conflict situation within his team, he felt some major differences between Westerners and Asians when trying to resolve issues. Among Koreans, when there were conflicts, people tried to resolve them by a mutual apology between the parties in conflict with the recognition that both parties had some responsibilities; however, his organizational manual stated that one who offended another had to apologize, and when satisfied with the apology, the one who was offended was to accept that apology. It was frustrating for him, however, when he tried to follow the practices outlined in the manual. He said, "We don't do it like that." He explained that the peacemaking protocol was culturally lopsided. He thought that the organizational manual was too Eurocentric, with little room to accommodate relational norms practiced by Asians. Joseph pointed out, "When I look at it from a half-Korean and a half-Canadian point of view . . . if we practiced true multiculturalism, no single culture would be above or below another." But he thought that there was a cultural hierarchy within his mission agency, dominated by Westerners. If it were a truly multicultural organization, various cultural norms would be embraced and blended rather than one particular set of norms being forced upon everyone. He went as far as to say, "They [white members of the organization] have a hidden attitude of superiority in their DNA." He felt that discrimination was systemic within his organization's operations and structures.

Ben and Katie were a married couple from the United States who worked with another international mission organization. They mentioned that their organization had very few nonwhite members. They said that as ethnic minorities, they repeatedly experienced subtle racism. Ben said, "They [Western members] just don't know what to do with nonwhite workers." He said that he experienced three kinds of attitudes toward him from Western members of his organization—overreacting to him with superficial kindness, altogether avoiding him, or patronizing him. Ben felt that some Western members in his organization showed a sense of superiority. He said, "They will never admit to that, but this is the impression I get."

What these Asian American mission workers experienced in their respective mission agencies is concerning. They were members of three well-known and respected global mission organizations with more than a thousand staff workers from numerous countries serving around the world. Yet the experiences of these Asian American participants raise questions about the cultural biases that exist in their organizational practices. It makes one wonder whose multiculturalism they are practicing. Jonathan Y. Kim conducted a field study in 2012 on the perception of working relationships between members of multicultural mission teams in the Caucasus region. Kim concludes that these mission teams were multicultural in demographics only; they were mostly monocultural in their team operations.[16] The experiences of my participants in North Africa seem to agree with Kim's research findings from the Caucasus—multicultural practices of these international mission organizations tend to be partial at best.[17]

Western scholars have written mission literature that addresses issues of multicultural leadership and teamwork. While there are helpful discussions put forth by these authors, I find that their perspectives mostly reflect the kind of biased multiculturalism observed by Kim and my interlocutors. The views in the literature seem to be confined within a twentieth-century Western management framework. To be fair to these authors, they attempt to integrate biblical values, urging readers to practice them in missions. They criticize ethnocentric tendencies, show appreciation for cultural diversity, and emphasize an attitude of humility. Unfortunately, even with all their good intentions, they fail to address the elephant in the room—the Western-centric mindset from a bygone era still deeply ingrained in mission theory and practice. In a way, the writings of these scholars seem to perpetuate a Western-centric framework.

As Homi Bhabha warns us, today's multicultural practices tend to be fixated on "the scale of diversity" that only shows interest in counting the number of nationalities, cultures, or ethnic groups, whereas what we need is a renewed commitment to "the diversity of scale" that does not privilege any single cultural framework.[18] The Western mission leaders must wrestle with the question of whose multiculturalism they have been and are practicing. It is necessary to subvert Western cultural hegemony in Christian mission. Missiologists must make conscious efforts to remove the remnants of the Eurocentric mission framework embedded in contemporary mission theories, practices, and structures.

Conclusion: Asian Americans as Critics and Mediators in Global Mission

I have described three major themes arising out of the experiences of Asian American missionaries in international missions. Thinking about the implications of these experiences of Asian American missionaries, I have a couple of concluding thoughts regarding Asian Americans and their roles in international missions. First, Asian Americans in global missions can serve as critics of international mission communities and their diaspora communities. They can bring to the fore the hypocrisy of unequal multiculturalism in international missions and the ethnocentric ghettoization of diaspora communities in North America. Their diasporic, hybrid practice can be, to borrow Bhabha's language, "a form of incipient critique" that brings about change from within as insiders of these communities while maintaining a perpetual outsider view from the margin.[19] Second, their evolving *diasporic habitus* can enable them to be mediators in global Christian communities.[20] They may not only link between cultures but also connect the in-between spaces of cultures in diaspora communities and global mission movements.

Reveling in the potential contribution of diaspora Christians, Andrew F. Walls writes that the new Christian diaspora in North America may have "the capacity to advance Christian mission in both the Western and the non-Western worlds."[21] I do not think Walls's deliberate optimism is misplaced so long as diasporic Christian practices are allowed to reimagine international missions. These Asian American missionaries in North Africa, some of whose stories are told in this chapter, show a glimpse of how diasporic life beyond the diaspora might contribute toward the mission of the people of God. As practitioners of *diasporic habitus*, residents of multiple cultural homes simultaneously, these critics of Western (or whoever) hypocrisy in international missions may prove to be the kind of mediators and reconcilers much needed in the global Christian movement in the twenty-first century.

Notes

1 Paul Taylor et al., "The Rise of Asian Americans," Pew Research Center, April 4, 2013, 169, https://pewrsr.ch/36724zP.

2 Throughout this chapter, "Asian Americans" will refer to citizens and permanent residents of the United States and Canada who are of Asian descent.

3 The name of the North African country will not be disclosed to ensure the participants' privacy and safety. I will use the acronym NAC to refer to the country where this study was conducted.

4 Generally, first generation refers to those who immigrated as adults; 1.5 generation to ones who immigrated during their childhood or adolescent years; and second generation to children born to immigrant parents in the new land.

5 Peter T. Lee, "Hybridizing Mission: A Study of Intercultural Social Dynamics among Christian Workers of Multicultural Teams in North Africa" (PhD diss., Trinity Evangelical Divinity School, 2020), 265–80.

6 Pierre Bourdieu, *In Other Words: Essays toward a Reflexive Sociology*, trans. Matthew Adamson (Stanford, CA: Stanford University Press, 1990), 13.

7 Bourdieu, 10; Bourdieu's italics.

8 Pierre Bourdieu, *The Logic of Practice*, trans. Richard Nice (Stanford, CA: Stanford University Press, 1990), 53; Pierre Bourdieu, *Distinction: A Social Critique of the Judgement of Taste*, trans. Richard Nice (Cambridge, MA: Harvard University Press, 1984), 467; Pierre Bourdieu, *Outline of a Theory of Practice*, trans. Richard Nice (Cambridge: Cambridge University Press, 1977), 72.

9 Loïc J. D. Wacquant, "Toward a Social Praxeology: The Structure and Logic of Bourdieu's Sociology," in *An Invitation to Reflexive Sociology* (Chicago: University of Chicago Press, 1992), 19.

10 David Parker, "The Chinese Takeaway and the Diasporic Habitus: Space, Time, and Power Geometries," in *Un/Settled Multiculturalisms: Diasporas, Entanglements, Transruptions*, ed. Barnor Hesse (London: Zed, 2000), 73–95; Ien Ang, "Inhabiting the Diasporic Habitus: On Stuart Hall's Familiar Stranger: A Life between Two Islands," *Identities* 25, no. 1 (February 2018): 1–6.

11 Lee, "Hybridizing Mission," 281.

12 See Néstor García Canclini, "Introduction: Hybrid Cultures in Globalized Times," in *Hybrid Cultures: Strategies for Entering and Leaving*

Modernity, trans. Bruce Campbell (Minneapolis: University of Minnesota Press, 2005), xxiii–xlvi.

13 Homi K. Bhabha, *The Location of Culture*, Routledge Classics ed. (London: Routledge, 1994), 56; Jan Nederveen Pieterse, "Hybridity, So What? The Anti-hybridity Backlash and the Riddles of Recognition," *Theory, Culture and Society* 18, nos. 2/3 (April 2001): 239.

14 Cultural homelessness is a notion developed by some psychologists to denote a sense of loss and disorientation often experienced by international migrants. See Veronica Navarrete Vivero and Sharon Rae Jenkins, "Existential Hazards of the Multicultural Individual: Defining and Understanding 'Cultural Homelessness,'" *Cultural Diversity and Ethnic Minority Psychology* 5, no. 1 (February 1999): 6–26; Raquel C. Hoersting and Sharon Rae Jenkins, "No Place to Call Home: Cultural Homelessness, Self-Esteem and Cross-Cultural Identities," *International Journal of Intercultural Relations* 35, no. 1 (January 2011): 17–30; and Veronica Navarrete and Sharon Rae Jenkins, "Cultural Homelessness, Multiminority Status, Ethnic Identity Development, and Self Esteem," *International Journal of Intercultural Relations* 35, no. 6 (November 1, 2011): 791–804.

15 Rudyard Kipling, "We and They," in *Debits and Credits* (London: Macmillan, 1926), 277–78.

16 Jonathan Y. Kim, "Perceptions of Working Relationships among Multicultural Team Members in International Mission Agencies: A Languacultural Analysis" (PhD diss., Trinity International University, 2013).

17 It should be noted that some participants in my study and some in Kim's research were members of the same international mission organization.

18 Homi K. Bhabha, foreword to *Debating Cultural Hybridity: Multicultural Identities and the Politics of Anti-Racism*, ed. Pnina Werbner and Tariq Modood, 2nd ed. (London: Zed, 2015), xi.

19 Bhabha, ix.

20 Paul G. Hiebert has proposed the idea of "transcultural mediator."
   See Paul G. Hiebert, *The Gospel in Human Contexts: Anthropological
   Explorations for Contemporary Missions* (Grand Rapids, MI: Baker
   Academic, 2009), 187–99.

21 Andrew F. Walls, "Mission and Migration: The Diaspora Factor in
   Christian History," in *Global Diasporas and Mission*, ed. Chandler H.
   Im and Amos Yong (Eugene, OR: Wipf & Stock, 2014), 36.

Bibliography

Ang, Ien. "Inhabiting the Diasporic Habitus: On Stuart Hall's
   Familiar Stranger: A Life between Two Islands." *Identities* 25,
   no. 1 (February 2018): 1–6.

Bhabha, Homi K. Foreword to *Debating Cultural Hybridity: Multicultural Identities and the Politics of Anti-Racism*, edited by Pnina
   Werbner and Tariq Modood, ix–xiii, 2nd ed. London: Zed, 2015.

———. *The Location of Culture*. Routledge Classics ed. London:
   Routledge, 1994.

Bourdieu, Pierre. *Distinction: A Social Critique of the Judgement of
   Taste*. Translated by Richard Nice. Cambridge, MA: Harvard
   University Press, 1984.

———. *In Other Words: Essays toward a Reflexive Sociology*. Translated by
   Matthew Adamson. Stanford, CA: Stanford University Press, 1990.

———. *The Logic of Practice*. Translated by Richard Nice. Stanford,
   CA: Stanford University Press, 1990.

———. *Outline of a Theory of Practice*. Translated by Richard Nice.
   Cambridge: Cambridge University Press, 1977.

García Canclini, Néstor. "Introduction: Hybrid Cultures in
   Globalized Times." In *Hybrid Cultures: Strategies for Entering
   and Leaving Modernity*, translated by Bruce Campbell, xxiii–xlvi.
   Minneapolis: University of Minnesota Press, 2005.

Hiebert, Paul G. *The Gospel in Human Contexts: Anthropological Explorations for Contemporary Missions*. Grand Rapids, MI: Baker Academic, 2009.

Hoersting, Raquel C., and Sharon Rae Jenkins. "No Place to Call Home: Cultural Homelessness, Self-Esteem and Cross-Cultural Identities." *International Journal of Intercultural Relations* 35, no. 1 (January 2011): 17–30.

Kim, Jonathan Y. "Perceptions of Working Relationships among Multicultural Team Members in International Mission Agencies: A Languacultural Analysis." PhD diss., Trinity International University, 2013.

Kipling, Rudyard. "We and They." In *Debits and Credits*. London: Macmillan, 1926.

Lee, Peter T. "Hybridizing Mission: A Study of Intercultural Social Dynamics among Christian Workers of Multicultural Teams in North Africa." PhD diss., Trinity Evangelical Divinity School, 2020.

Navarrete, Veronica, and Sharon Rae Jenkins. "Cultural Homelessness, Multiminority Status, Ethnic Identity Development, and Self Esteem." *International Journal of Intercultural Relations* 35, no. 6 (November 1, 2011): 791–804.

Nederveen Pieterse, Jan. "Hybridity, So What? The Anti-hybridity Backlash and the Riddles of Recognition." *Theory, Culture and Society* 18, nos. 2/3 (April 2001): 219.

Parker, David. "The Chinese Takeaway and the Diasporic Habitus: Space, Time, and Power Geometries." In *Un/Settled Multiculturalisms: Diasporas, Entanglements, Transruptions*, edited by Barnor Hesse, 73–95. London: Zed, 2000.

Taylor, Paul, D'Vera Cohn, Wendy Wang, Kim Parker, Cary Fung, and Gretchen M. Livingston. "The Rise of Asian Americans." Pew Research Center, April 4, 2013. https://pewrsr.ch/36724zP.

Vivero, Veronica Navarrete, and Sharon Rae Jenkins. "Existential Hazards of the Multicultural Individual: Defining and

Understanding 'Cultural Homelessness.'" *Cultural Diversity and Ethnic Minority Psychology* 5, no. 1 (February 1999): 6–26.

Wacquant, Loïc J. D. "Toward a Social Praxeology: The Structure and Logic of Bourdieu's Sociology." In *An Invitation to Reflexive Sociology*, 1–59. Chicago: University of Chicago Press, 1992.

Walls, Andrew F. "Mission and Migration: The Diaspora Factor in Christian History." In *Global Diasporas and Mission*, edited by Chandler H. Im and Amos Yong, 19–37. Eugene, OR: Wipf & Stock, 2014.

Index

About the Authors

S_AM_ G_EORGE_, PhD, serves as a catalyst for diasporas of the Lausanne Movement and director of the Global Diaspora Institute at Wheaton College Billy Graham Centre (US). He holds a bachelor's in mechanical engineering and a master's in business management and  has worked in engineering and technology industries for nearly a decade. Later he studied practical theology and missiology in the United States and the United Kingdom. He lives with his wife and their two boys in the northern suburbs of Chicago, Illinois. His recent publications include *Refugee Diaspora* (William Carey), *Diaspora Christianities* (Fortress), and *Desi Diaspora* (SAIACS).

A_LEX_ G. S_MITH_, DMiss, has served under OMF for fifty-five years (twenty in Thailand) and is an international advocate in the Buddhist world and cofounder of SEANET, a network for Buddhist peoples. Born in Australia, he now lives in Oregon (US) with his wife.  He has three sons and four grandchildren. He is a speaker, trainer, mobilizer, and author of *Siamese Gold, A Christian's Pocket Guide to Buddhism*, and chapters in fifteen SEANET volumes on Buddhist ministry.

 John Arun Kumar, PhD, is a professor of Hinduism and head of the Department of Religion at the South Asia Institute of Advanced Christian Studies in Bengaluru, India. He also serves as a catalyst for Hinduism of the Lausanne Movement. He completed his PhD at the University of Leeds (UK). He serves as a contextual editor for the India Commentary on the New Testament series and has authored numerous articles and book chapters.

 Gerardo B. Lisbe Jr., DMin, serves as vice president of Baptist Theological College (BTC) and academic dean of Cebu Graduate School of Theology (CGST) located in Mandaue City, Philippines. He earned his doctor of ministry degree from International Theological Seminary in Los Angeles, California, and teaches courses in world missions and hermeneutics at both schools. He is also the president of a Cebu-based mission sending agency called Bethlehem Star of Peace (BSOP) that sends career missionaries to Southeast Asian countries and helps churches in Central Visayas start an Overseas Filipino Workers (OFWs) family ministry. He is married to Daryl, and they are blessed with two children.

Christy John Jacob, PhD, is a researcher in sociology who has studied nurses' migration from Kerala to North India. She has also worked among the Bhils, a tribal community in

India. She holds a PhD from Mohanlal Sukhadia University, Udaipur, Rajasthan, and is an alumnus of Delhi and Madras Universities. She is the spouse of a Liverpool, UK–based minister of an Indian immigrant congregation.

Prasad D R J Phillips, PhD, completed his doctorate at the University of Edinburgh and now serves as a faculty member at the Oxford Centre for Religion and Public Life in the United Kingdom and as a research associate in the Theology and Religion Department of the University of Pretoria. He coordinates the work of the Global Institute of Leadership Development, focusing on grassroots-level theological training. He currently lives in England and earlier lived in Abu Dhabi (UAE) and several states of North and South India.

Robbie B H Goh, PhD, is a professor in the Department of English Language and Literature and the dean of the Faculty of Arts and Social Sciences at the National University of Singapore. He obtained a bachelor of arts (honors) and a master of arts from the National University of Singapore and a PhD from the University of Chicago. His teaching and research interests are diaspora studies, Indian Anglophone literature, Christianity in Asia, late nineteenth-century English literature, and speculative fiction.

CHERIAN SAMUEL, PhD, is an economist by training and works as an evaluator for the World Bank in Washington, DC. He is of Asian Indian origin and lives with his wife and their two boys in northern Virginia. He serves with the Ecumenical Council of Kerala Christians in the Baltimore-Washington Metropolitan Area, which is focused on fostering a community with a common purpose and Christian heritage.

BILL TSANG, EdD, serves as the director of research at Youth Global Network (YGN), Hong Kong. He has been an honorary research associate at the Wah Ching Centre of Research on Education in China at the University of Hong Kong and a visiting professor at East China Normal University in Shanghai. He cofounded Lumina College in Hong Kong and earlier was an assistant professor in the Department of Social Work at the Chinese University of Hong Kong. He received a doctorate in human development and psychology from Harvard University, a master of arts in counseling psychology from Gordon-Conwell Theological Seminary, and a master of science in mechanical engineering from Virginia Tech. He specializes in social identities, migration, educational opportunities, and technology for underprivileged youth.

NAJI ABI-HASHEM, PhD, is an independent scholar and a clinical and cultural psychologist. He studied in Beirut and California, United States, and received a doctorate from Biola University. He is an ordained minister and an associate of Member Care International. He is involved with many professional organizations, presenting workshops at various academic institutes, and served on multiple boards of directors. He is a nonresident scholar at Baylor University Institute for Studies of Religion in Texas. He is based in Seattle with several months every year in Lebanon.

Byoung Ok Koo, PhD, serves as an assistant professor of practical theology at Reformed Graduate University and is the author of *Transitioning from an Ethnic to a Multicultural Church*. After working for Samsung Electronics for seven years, God led him to theological studies in South Korea and the United States, focusing on mission and evangelism. He lives with his wife and their daughter and son in Songdo, South Korea.

Peter T. Lee, PhD, serves as the chief coordinator of the Korean DMin program and an affiliate professor of intercultural studies at Trinity Evangelical Divinity School, Deerfield, Illinois. He also serves as a mission researcher with Operation Mobilization (OM) and worked in North Africa for ten years, where he led a multicultural ministry team and trained foreign business and development workers. He is a Korean American who grew up in Seoul and immigrated to the United States when he was fourteen years old. He is an ordained minister of the Presbyterian Church (USA).